THE COMPLETE CRITICAL C
ALEXANDER POPE

Was Alexander Pope the poet of reason, or a daring anti-establishment prophet?

What can a study of Pope tell us about the eighteenth century?

How did this outsider, subject to debilitating illness, become the leading poet of his generation?

So many questions surround the key figures in the English literary canon, but most books focus on one aspect of an author's life or work, or limit themselves to a single critical approach. *The Complete Critical Guide to Alexander Pope* is part of a unique series of comprehensive, user-friendly introductions which:

- offer basic information on an author's life, contexts and works
- outline the major critical issues surrounding the author's works, from the time they were written to the present
- leave judgements up to you, by explaining the full range of often very different critical views and interpretations
- offer guides to further reading in each area discussed.

This series has a broad focus but one very clear aim: to equip you with *all* the knowledge you need to make your own new readings of crucial literary texts.

Paul Baines is a Senior Lecturer in the Department of English Language and Literature at the University of Liverpool. He is the author of *The House of Forgery in Eighteenth-Century Britain* and co-editor of *Five Romantic Plays, 1768–1821.*

THE COMPLETE CRITICAL GUIDE TO
ENGLISH LITERATURE
Series Editors
RICHARD BRADFORD AND JAN JEDRZEJEWSKI

Also available in this series:

The Complete Critical Guide to Samuel Beckett
David Pattie
The Complete Critical Guide to Geoffrey Chaucer
Gillian Rudd
The Complete Critical Guide to John Milton
Richard Bradford

Forthcoming:

The Complete Critical Guide to Robert Browning
The Complete Critical Guide to Charles Dickens
The Complete Critical Guide to Ben Jonson
The Complete Critical Guide to D. H. Lawrence
The Complete Critical Guide to William Wordsworth

Visit the website of *The Complete Critical Guide to English Literature*
for further information and an updated list of titles
www.literature.routledge.com/criticalguides

THE COMPLETE CRITICAL GUIDE TO
ALEXANDER POPE

Paul Baines

London and New York

First published 2000
by Routledge
11 New Fetter Lane, London EC4P 4EE

Simultaneously published in the USA and Canada
by Routledge
29 West 35th Street, New York, NY 10001

Routledge is an imprint of the Taylor & Francis Group

Typeset in Schneidler by
HWA Text and Data Management, Tunbridge Wells
Printed and bound in Great Britain by
Biddles Ltd, Guildford and King's Lynn

British Library Cataloguing in Publication Data
A catalogue record for this book is available from the British Library

Library of Congress Cataloging in Publication Data
Baines, Paul, 1961–
The complete critical guide to Alexander Pope / Paul Baines
p. cm. – (The complete critical guide to English literature)
Includes bibliographical references and index.
1. Pope, Alexander, 1688–1744 – Criticism and interpretation.
2. Verse satire, English – History and criticism. I. Title. II. Series.
PR3634 .B25 2001
821'.5–dc21   00–056019

ISBN 0–415–20245–0 (hbk)
ISBN 0–415–20246–9 (pbk)

For Jenny and Gwen

CONTENTS

SERIES EDITORS' PREFACE

The Complete Critical Guide to English Literature is a ground-breaking collection of one-volume introductions to the work of the major writers in the English literary canon. Each volume in the series offers the reader a comprehensive account of the featured author's life, of his or her writing and of the ways in which his or her works have been interpreted by literary critics. The series is both explanatory and stimulating; it reflects the achievements of state-of-the-art literary-historical research and yet manages to be intellectually accessible for the reader who may be encountering a canonical author's work for the first time. It will be useful for students and teachers of literature at all level, as well as for the general reader, each book can be read through, or consulted in a companion-style fashion.

The aim of *The Complete Critical Guide to English Literature* is to adopt an approach that is as factual, objective and non-partisan as possible, in order to provide the 'full picture' for readers and allow them to form their own judgements. As the same time, however, the books engage the reader in a discussion of the most demanding questions involved in each author's life and work. Did Pope's physical condition affect his treatment of matters of gender and sexuality? Does a feminist reading of *Middlemarch* enlighten us regarding the book's presentation of nineteenth-century British society? Do we deconstruct Beckett's work, or does he do so himself? Contributors to this series address such crucial questions, offer potential solutions and recommend further reading for independent study. In doing so, they equip the reader for an informed and confident examination of the life and work of key canonical figures and of the critical controversies surrounding them.

The aims of the series are reflected in the structure of the books. Part I 'Life and contexts', offers a compact biography of the featured author against the background of his or her epoch. In Part II 'Work', the focus is on the author's most important works, discussed from a non-partisan, literary-historical perspective; the section provides an account of the works, reflecting a consensus of critical opinion on them, and indicating, where appropriate, areas of controversy. These and other issues are taken up again in Part III 'Criticism', which offers an account of the critical responses generated by the author's work. Contemporaneous reviews and debates are considered, along with opinions inspired by more recent theoretical approaches, such as New Criticism, feminism, Marxism, psychoanalytic criticism, deconstruction and New Historicism.

The volumes in this series will together constitute a comprehensive reference work offering an up-to-date, user-friendly and reliable account of the heritage of English literature form the Middle Ages to the twentieth century. We hope that *The Complete Critical Guide to English Literature* will become for its readers, academic and non-academic alike, an indispensable source of information and inspiration.

RICHARD BRADFORD
JAN JEDRZEJEWSKI

ACKNOWLEDGEMENTS

I am grateful to the Department of English Language and Literature, University of Liverpool, for a period of teaching remission which enabled me to complete this book. Several of my colleagues in the Department have generously shared their knowledge and enthusiasm with me: in particular, Julian Ferraro has given readily of his time, expertise, and books. I have learnt much from my conversations with students at Liverpool and at St John's College, Oxford. Katy Hooper has given, as always, steadfast support throughout. Finally, I would like to thank Richard Bradford and Jan Jedrzejewski, the series editors, and Liz Thompson, the development editor, for their help and encouragement throughout the making of this book.

ABBREVIATIONS AND REFERENCING

Throughout the text, references to Pope's poems are from *The Twicken-ham Edition of the Poems of Alexander Pope*, general editor John Butt, 11 volumes (London: Methuen, 1939–69), abbreviated as *TE*. Specific volumes are used as follows::

I	*Pastoral Poetry and an Essay on Criticism*, eds E. Audra and Aubrey Williams (1961)
II	*The Rape of the Lock and Other Poems*, ed. Geoffrey Tillotson, third edition (1962)
III.i	*An Essay on Man*, ed. Maynard Mack (1950)
III.ii	*Epistles to Several Persons (Moral Essays)*, ed. F.W. Bateson (1951)
IV	*Imitations of Horace, with An Epistle to Dr Arbuthnot and the Epilogue to the Satires*, ed. John Butt (1939)
V	*The Dunciad*, ed. James Sutherland, second edition (1953)
VI	*Minor Poems*, eds Norman Ault and John Butt (1964)

All references are to page numbers

Individual poems within these volumes are referenced as follows:

Arb	*An Epistle to Dr. Arbuthnot*
Bathurst	*Epistle to Bathurst*
Burl	*Epistle to Burlington*
Cob	*Epistle to Cobham*
D	*The Duncaid*
EA	*Eloisa to Abelard*
EC	*An Essay on Criticism*
EM	*An Essay on Man*
Ep. 2.i	*The First Epistle of the Second Book of Horace, Imitated*
Ep. 2.ii	*The Second Epistle of the Second Book of Horace, Imitated*
Epil. i	*Epilogue to the Satires, Dialogue I*
Epil. ii	*Epilogue to the Satires, Dialogue II*
Lady	*Epistle to a Lady*
RL	*The Rape of the Lock*
Sat. 2.i	*The First Satire of the Second Book of Horace, Imitated*
Sat. 2.ii	*The Second Satire of the Second Book of Horace Paraphrased*
WF	*Windsor-Forest*

Other abbreviations are:

Letters   *The Correspondence of Alexander Pope,* ed. George Sherburn, 5
        volumes (Oxford: Clarendon Press, 1956)
PW i   *The Prose Works of Alexander Pope: The Earlier Works 1711–1720,*
        ed. Norman Ault (Oxford: Basil Blackwell, 1938)
PW ii   *The Prose Works of Alexander Pope: Volume II: The Major Works
        1725–1744,* ed. Rosemary Cowler (Oxford: Basil Blackwell,
        1986)

For all other references, the Harvard system is used; full details of items cited can be found in the bibliography.

Cross-referencing between sections is one of the features of this series. Cross-references to relevant page numbers appear in bold type and square brackets **[28]**.

INTRODUCTION

This book examines the literary career of the poet Alexander Pope (1688–1744). The son of a merchant, Pope became the dominant poet of his generation despite considerable ill-health and deformity. As a Catholic, he was a politically suspect outsider, but turned his internal exile into a platform from which to comment on the social and political events of his time. Once regarded as too elegant, or too vicious, to be a true poet, Pope is now celebrated for the richness of his imaginative transfiguration of the world around him.

In Part I of this book, Life and Contexts, the main events of Pope's life are narrated in detail: his childhood in Windsor Forest, his early literary career, the success of his translation of Homer, his creation of a place of principled independence at his villa at Twickenham, his relations with women, the scandalous warfare of *The Dunciad,* the major satires of the 1730s, his political position, and the final darkening poetry. In Part II, Works, extensive readings of nine poems or sets of poems are given: *Essays on Criticism, Windsor-Forest, Rape of the Lock, Eloisa to Abelard, Essay on Man, Epistles to Several Persons, Epistle to Dr Arbuthnot, Imitations of Horace,* and *The Dunciad.* In Part III, Criticism, clear guidance to the main trends in criticism of Pope's work are given, with special attention to current areas of particular controversy: Pope and Politics; Pope, Gender and Body; Pope in Print and Manuscript.

The Complete Critical Guide to Alexander Pope presents a synthesis of the latest research on Pope while offering a fresh reading of the poems. Readers who need a clear account of Pope's life and background, or who need a reliable guide to particular poems, or who are interested in special aspects of the works, can begin in any section and follow the cross-references to other relevant sections; or the whole book can be read through as a handbook of Pope studies.

PART I

LIFE AND CONTEXTS

(a) A CATHOLIC CHILDHOOD

Because Pope was not primarily a lyric poet like Donne, or an explorer of private mental experience like Wordsworth, we tend to think of him as essentially a public voice, the satirist of civil follies rather than the analyst of personal emotions. Many of the vices Pope attacked are forms of egotism: avarice, power-seeking, narcissism. The lack of a real or implied partner to address poems to also suggests a reticence about private life which disappoints a voyeuristic age. Nonetheless personal character remained for Pope a fundamental element of poetic voice. Satire has to have a position from which to criticise the world; and since Pope could not acquire the kind of state position which validated the work of his closest model, John Dryden (1631–1700), he developed a position of moral authority derived from his own status as a private, right-thinking citizen, living in principled independence of state patronage, willing to implicate the personal experience on which his voice as a social critic was based. While one could read through the complete poems of Dryden without learning much about his life, Pope insistently manages a particular kind of self-involvement even in his most public, apocalyptic works. Much criticism of him – plenty of it more venomous and scurrilous than anything he produced himself in criticizing others – was based on his own life, character, and body. A competent artist, he controlled the dissemination of portraits and other images of himself, and bestowed extraordinary care on the presentation and publication of his work, mastering book trade processes as no writer had ever done before to produce a meticulous version of his 'corpus' in print [189–99]. In these ways, he seems a very modern figure. This first section will give an account of the main features of what we know of Pope's biography, and of how he turned his personal experience into public poetry.

Pope had, and has continued to have, several biographers. During his lifetime he befriended Joseph Spence, a minor poet and critic who compiled a large body of 'anecdotes' from Pope's conversation, indicating his views on various critical matters but also recording such facts as Pope could remember, or wished to be remembered, about his own life. 'Mr. Pope was born on the twenty-first of May, 1688', Spence ascertained (Spence 1966: 3); the time was 6: 45 p.m. and the place is thought to have been no. 2 Plough Court, just off Lombard Street, London, in what was fast becoming the financial centre of England. His father (also Alexander, 1646–1717) 'was an honest merchant and dealt in Hollands wholesale' (Spence 1966: 7): that is, he dealt in linens, exporting them as far afield as Virginia. The poet's mother, Edith (née

Turner, d.1733), was just short of forty-five when he was born; the poet was her only child, though there was a surviving half-sister, Magdalen, from his father's earlier marriage (a half-brother, Alexander again, had died in infancy).

Though Pope's father was the son of an Anglican vicar, he converted to Catholicism, perhaps during European travels; his mother was from a family which divided along Catholic and Protestant lines. Catholicism caused the family many problems. Though the Civil War itself ended with the restoration of Charles II in 1660, the issues which had caused it continued to divide the nation for another century. Rumours of a Catholic plot to assassinate Charles in 1679 (the 'Popish Plot') had been used to foment some bitter anti-Catholic sentiment during the first half of the 1680s, and the accession of the Catholic James II in 1685 brought the threat of a renewed Civil War much closer. Three weeks after Pope's birth, James II's wife gave birth to a son, providing a Catholic heir to the kingdom. Shortly afterwards James was forced to abandon the throne in favour of his daughter Mary and her Protestant husband William of Orange, a 'Glorious Revolution' as it was known to its supporters, which paved the way for the Protestant succession, though a number of attempts to restore the Catholic line would be made, the last and most serious occurring a year after Pope's death.

In London especially, heavily punitive measures against Catholics were enforced immediately on the arrival of William and Mary. Pope's father had amassed about £10,000 from his business, a fortune large enough to enable him to retire from business in the face of this on-slaught, thus greatly diminishing the effects of the legislation on Pope's boyhood: Pope's family vacated Plough Court for Hammersmith some time around 1692, and the main danger to his early life seems to have come from a wild cow which attacked him while he was, rather picturesquely, 'filling a little cart with stones' (Spence 1966: 3). He retained great affection for the women of his close and protective household: his nurse, Mary Beach, his aunt Elizabeth Turner, and especially his mother, who lived with him until her death in 1733. A priest who knew him told Spence that Pope 'was a child of a particularly sweet temper and had a great deal of sweetness in his look when he was a boy' (Spence 1966: 5–6). Johnson reports that 'His voice, when he was young, was so pleasing that he was called in fondness the "little Nightingale"' (Johnson 1905: 83).

As a Catholic Pope could not attend mainstream schools and could not attend university. He was taught to read by his aunt, and had developed a very precise calligraphy by imitating the typography of printed books, a talent which he often used in designing his books in later life (Spence 1966: 12). At the age of about eight Pope began to learn Latin and Greek from a priest. He subsequently attended clandestine Catholic schools, one in Twyford, from where he was removed after being punished for writing a satire on his master (his earliest satiric venture), and one near Hyde Park Corner, from which he is supposed to have on occasion visited the theatre; he also saw his hero, John Dryden, once (Spence 1966: 25). Pope was dismissive of his formal schooling: 'God knows, it extended a very little way' (Spence 1966: 8). Indeed, he seems to have valued his independent exploration of literature as a positive escape from the prison-house of grammar-based education, a formal trap which he would later denounce more publicly (Spence 1966: 21–2). At the age of eight he had 'discovered' Homer through translation (much as Keats was to do more than a century later): John Ogilby's *Iliad* (1660) and *Odyssey* (1665) were huge volumes 'Adorn'd with Sculptures' (engravings), and Pope always 'spoke of the pleasure it then gave him, with a sort of rapture only on reflecting on it' (Spence 1966: 14). With George Sandys's illustrated *Ovid's Metamorphosis Englished* (1626), and Statius's *Thebaid*, the Homer texts formed a rich repository of Greek and Latin mythology and narrative which stimulated Pope's imagination through his early career and beyond.

(b) FOREST RETREATS

In 1698 Pope's father bought a house at Binfield, Berkshire, from his son in law, Charles Rackett, who had married Pope's half-sister Magdalen. This residence on an estate of some nineteen acres of land, close to Windsor with the forest, castle and river Thames to explore, had a determining influence on Pope, turning enforced removal from the capital into the very model of principled retreat, an idyll never entirely besmirched by later events. Though Pope's early works such as the *Pastorals* (1709) and *Windsor-Forest* (1713) derive much from literary models, they derive something from an acute observation of the heraldic colouring within the castle and the exercise of agriculture and rural sports in the forest.

Here Pope was free to educate himself: his father's library was well-stocked, and he began to purchase books on his own account, acquiring early editions of Chaucer, Herbert and Milton. His half-sister told Spence that he 'did nothing but write and read', and his own image of himself spending whole days reading under trees, nicely suggests the twin influences of reading and nature: 'I followed everywhere as my fancy led me, and was like a boy gathering flowers in the woods and fields just as they fall in his way' (Spence 1966: 12, 13, 20). Having already developed a taste for English poets such as Waller, Spenser and Dryden, courtly and fantastic by turns, he described his years from the age of thirteen to twenty as 'all poetical', a voracious if sporadic 'ramble' through Greek, Latin, Italian and French poetry and criticism (Spence 1966: 19–20). At some point around 1703–04 he studied French and Italian in London, against the wishes of his family, concerned for his already insecure health (Spence 1966: 12–13).

The prelapsarian freedom which Pope remembered so fondly began to be eroded by two potent forces: illness, and a growing political sense [163–71]. About the time of the move to Binfield, Pope had the first major attack of the disease which was eventually to cripple him. Thought to be spinal tuberculosis, contracted through infected milk, 'Pott's disease' restricted his height to about four foot six, caused progressive curvature of the spine, and left him subject to severe headaches, fits, eye inflammations and respiratory problems. Though he surmounted these difficulties with exercise and fresh air, and experimented with various comic versions of his illness in private letters and in public poems, his sense of himself was deeply affected by his physical appearance. At the same time, the family's Catholicism (low-key and quietistic as it was) became a second marker of internal exile. His father's library contained much literature from the religious controversies of the seventeenth century, which Pope read, finding himself 'a Papist and a Protestant by turns, according to the last book I read' (Letters I: 453). The humanistic tolerance, self-knowledge and irony of Erasmus and Montaigne, both Catholics but men of principled independence of thought, offered an attractive route out of the morass of sectarian debate.

Pope's adolescence was also nurtured by a number of much older men with whom Pope became friendly and whom he impressed with his precocious reading and 'maddish way' (Spence 1966: 13). John Caryll, a local Catholic who was to play an important role in the genesis of The Rape of the Lock [65–77], had a wide circle of literary acquaintance and it was probably he who introduced Pope to the most brilliant actor of the Restoration stage, Thomas Betterton (1635–1710), as well as that stage's most uncompromising dramatist, William Wycherley (1640–1716). Pope resisted the blandishments of both to write for the stage, but assisted both men in 'correcting' their verses, a troublesome task but one which testifies to the closeness of the literary friendships and Pope's rapid rise to esteem. His earliest surviving correspondence is with Wycherley, in whose company he roamed London (he was mocked as 'Wycherley's Crutch' by unsympathetic observers: Spence 1966: 35). Pope also knew Dr Samuel Garth (1661–1719), patron of Dryden, physician, and wit, whose mock-heroic *The Dispensary* (1699) is one of the best models for comparison with Pope's own work in the genre, and Sir William Trumbull, a diplomat who had served with distinction under kings of violently different persuasions and who was now one of the twelve verderers of Windsor Forest. Benign, well-read and generous, Trumbull was an active nurturing force in Pope's development; they rode in the forest and talked literature 'almost every day' (Spence 1966: 31). William Walsh (1663–1708), similarly, showed Pope that it was possible to maintain a well-bred moderation in literature and politics, acting as a Whig M.P. under both William III and Anne, and being hailed by the Tory Dryden as the best critic of the age (Spence 1966: 32).

It was this circle of men to whom Pope submitted his early publishable literary efforts, for 'correction'; there is considerable surviving evidence of the close practical and technical attention Walsh in particular exercised over the *Pastorals*, the *Essay on Criticism* and *Sapho to Phaon*. Walsh had told Pope: 'that there was one way left of excelling, for though we had several great poets, we never had any one great poet that was correct – and he desired me to make that my study and aim' (Spence 1966: 32). Pope's one criticism of his master Dryden was that he wrote too quickly (Spence 1966: 24). Not that Pope spurned spontaneity: he claimed 'I began writing verses of my own invention farther back than I can remember'. But he had always been used to revising; his father set him verse exercises and was 'pretty difficult in being pleased and used often to send him back to new turn them' (Spence 1966: 7, 15). While still at school Pope wrote a play based on speeches from the *Iliad* for his schoolfellows to act, and completed another based on 'a very moving story in the legend of St Genevieve', as well as an epic poem, *Alcander*, in which, he smilingly recalled, he attempted 'to collect all the beauties of the great epic writers into one piece'. This four-book epic he later burned, 'not without some regret'; some lines were salvaged for other work (Spence 1966: 15–18).

Pope practised the craft of writing by imitating that which pleased him most in his reading. His earliest surviving poem is a verse paraphrase of a prayer from the Christian mystic Thomas a Kempis, not published in his lifetime and a rare indication of his religious background. Most of his early translations are from pre-Christian writers, notably Ovid, from whose *Metamorphoses* he produced some tales of monstrous or misdirected sexual activities when he was about fourteen (the most interesting of these, the story of the cyclops Polyphemus's love for

Galatea, remained unpublished in his lifetime). It was also from Ovid that he translated, about 1707, *Sapho to Phaon* **[172, 194]**, an intriguingly expressive poem in which the Lesbian poetess Sappho, abandoned by the youth Phaon with whom she has fallen in love, laments her confused sexual longings and reviews her languishing life as a poet. His version of Statius' *Thebaid*, book I, was written about 1703 (published 1712), and gave him confidence in the use of heroic couplets in 'high' style; the story itself, which deals with the internecine wars of succession after the resignation of the incestuous parricide Oedipus from the throne of Thebes, is a monstrous and gory exploration of politics, sex and death: there is nothing tame about Pope's interest in classical mythology. Pope also began translating sections of Homer, probably about 1707.

He also practised a form of 'imitation' or stylistic mimicking; around 1701 he was impersonating the polished amatory verses of Waller, the metaphysical conceits of Cowley, and the anti-feminist lyrics of the Earl of Dorset in particular. A short pastiche of Chaucer allowed him to tell a bawdy joke; 'The Alley', an imitation of Spenser, took the stanza form of *The Faerie Queene* and applied it mockingly to the filthy pathways of contemporary London. 'On Silence', a substantial imitation of Rochester's 'Upon Nothing', points forward to the sceptical social satire of his mature work. This work was all complete before 1709, but Pope later edited some of it as evidence of his poetic development, or simply as makeweights in anthologies.

(c) LITERARY LONDON

Pope was twenty when his first poems were published, in May 1709, significantly enough adjacent to the first full 'Copyright Act' which defined authorial property in ways which were to allow Pope to make more money from writing than any poet before him. The *Pastorals* appeared in *Poetical Miscellanies, The Sixth Part*, an anthology published by Jacob Tonson the elder, the most eminent publisher of the day: he had acquired the rights to Milton, Shakespeare, and Dryden, and ran a Whig club of authors known as the Kit-Cat Club. Pope contributed three works to the anthology (which also included work by Swift, later to become one of Pope's closest friends). Two of these emerged from Pope's self-imposed apprenticeship in translating and imitating: *January and May* was a rewriting in modern idiom of Chaucer's *Merchant's Tale*, written about 1704 and giving Pope the opportunity to be elegant and witty about sex and marriage; *The Episode of Sarpedon* was a translation from Homer's *Iliad*. The Chaucer imitation was to some degree also an imitation of Dryden, whose *Fables* (1700) had established the utility of 'polishing' the medieval poet into smoother and more moralistic form (though the story itself remains ribald enough, and Pope was later to add a version of the Wife of Bath's *Prologue*, also written about 1704, to his oeuvre). In the *Episode of Sarpedon*, comprising passages from *Iliad* XII and XVI, Pope explored a high heroic language in speeches of glory and death; again, the imitation is double, for one of the passages had been previously translated by John Denham, another of Pope's models. The two pieces are therefore both homage to earlier great poets, and the beginnings of a contest with them.

In the *Pastorals*, Pope announced his intention to challenge for such fame, since pastoral was the genre on which the epic poet cut his teeth (the examples of Virgil, Spenser and Milton were particularly in Pope's mind). 'First in these Fields I try the Sylvan Strains', the series opens, asserting originality and naturalism in the midst of imitation and the most 'artificial' literary genre around. Flaunting his allegiance to well-known pastorals such as Virgil's *Eclogues* and Theocritus's *Idylls*, Pope splices the allegorical and mythological song into English settings. Excising the comic rusticity which pervaded earlier English pastoral, Pope claims for England successorship to the enchanted ground of classical literature. Pope's virtuoso displays indeed are some of the last exercises in the genre, which had been hugely popular in the Renaissance but was beginning to run out of variations. In these painterly landscapes, shepherds pursue nymphs, vie with each other in poetical or musical skill, and invoke the aid of deities, with little or no attention to the actual business of rearing sheep.

Pope had been anticipating publication of *Poetical Miscellanies* for a few years and in his correspondence with Wycherley struck poses of aristocratic indifference to the squalid world of literary fame and of comic reluctance to appear in print. In London he made the acquaintance of Henry Cromwell, an idle dandy with a poetical turn with whom Pope exchanged some correspondence of flamboyant maleness: Pope felt able to play at being a rake-about-town, perhaps in compensation for his sense of being denied sexual enjoyment by his physical limitations. Never to be Alexander the Great in any heroic sense, he knew he was 'that little Alexander the women laugh at' (*Letters* I: 114). In 1707 he had met Martha and Teresa Blount, granddaughters of Anthony Englefield, one of Pope's Catholic neighbours; from 1711 the intimacy became more conspicuous. A few elegantly bawdy poems survive from this period, suggesting that the poet who had imitated the Cavalier mode of Waller, Denham and Cowley, was still exploring the erotic potential of verse. More seriously, Pope showed Cromwell, a solid Latinist in spite of his rakish pose, versions of Statius and Ovid for his revision. Pope kept busts of authors such as Dryden, Milton and Shakespeare in his chamber as perpetual reminders of literary greatness (*Letters* I: 120); he was also working on a poem called *The Temple of Fame*, based on a somewhat more austere poem of Chaucer's than those to which Pope had hitherto given attention, *The Hous of Fame*. Here Pope once again produced homage and challenge to the literature of the past, attempting to envision in what was becoming a favourite form of artistic expression, neoclassical architecture, some secure means of recording greatness for posterity.

Pope had been working on *An Essay on Criticism* **[49–57]** since about 1707, and it had passed through his usual revisers. It was published on 15 May 1711, the first of his works to appear independently. Full of quotation, allusion and example, it offers a mediation between extreme critical positions and points towards an accessible community of judgement. Homer is celebrated as the pre-critical fount of Western literature, with Virgil as a sort of post-critical example of how one might recapture 'nature' by observing the rules formulated by the classical critics. The fragmentary *Poetics* of the Greek philosopher Aristotle (384–322 BC) laid down guidelines for the successful 'imitation' of nature in poetry and drama. The Roman poet Horace (65–8 BC) had turned Aristotelian principles into a more conversational and personal form of advice in the 'Epistle to the Pisos', commonly known as the *Ars Poetica* or 'Art of Poetry'. These works had formed the basis for most critical theorizing of the seventeenth century; in drama especially, the guidelines had become fossilised into 'Rules' in which truth to nature could only be achieved by very close forms of imitation – limiting the action of plays to one plot, in one location, on one day. There was much debate about the applicability of these rules in an English tradition, and Pope's master Dryden adopted the 'Rules' with much misgiving. Some relief from the Rules came in the shape of the treatise known as *Peri Hypsous* or *On the Sublime*, ascribed to 'Longinus' (written probably in the first century AD, and translated into English in 1652 (more influentially, into French by Nicholas Boileau in 1674); this concentrated on 'poetic fire', flights of the imagination, inspirational visions of boundlessness.

Pope had absorbed these critics very thoroughly. He was deeply aware of the tensions between theory and practice, imagination and judgment, and the ongoing European debate about the relative claims of Ancient and Modern learning, which Swift had satirised in *The Battle of the Books* (1704). He had models for the genteel style of the poetic essay: Horace, notably, but also Boileau's *Art Poétique* (1674, translated partially by Dryden, 1683), the Earl of Roscommon's *Essay on Translated Verse* (1684, following his translation of Horace's *Ars Poetica* into blank verse, 1680), and the Duke of Buckinghamshire's *Essay upon Poetry* (1682). Nonetheless an essay on *criticism* done in verse was a new thing and highly significant. Though the poem prefers the collective pronouns 'we' and 'you' to 'I', an ambitious claim to authority is being made: the list of ideally-qualified critics given at the end of the poem leads from Aristotle to Walsh, and the final lines of the poem are, in a characteristic gesture of self-inscription, about Pope's relation to his critical mentor.

The poem also contains Pope's first touches of accusatory satire. Amid the examples of bad criticism he cites is one Appius, loud, blustering, and tyrannical. This was a hit at John Dennis, poet and dramatist, who had published two Aristotelian treatises on criticism. Pope shared many of his critical views, but Dennis's dogmatism, vanity and paranoia was too easy a target. A month after Pope's *Essay* was published, Dennis gave Pope his first taste of public controversy by issuing *Reflections Critical and Satyrical, upon a late Rhapsody, call'd, an Essay upon Criticism*. This was an angry demolition of Pope, characterising his balanced couplets as contradiction, his comprehensiveness as rhapsodic incoherence, his gestures towards authority as upstart arrogance. Moreover, Dennis mounted a vicious attack on Pope's character and physique, suggesting that his familial Catholicism was active Jacobitism **[165–9]** and that his deformity represented his personality **[184–5]**: 'As there is no Creature so venomous, there is nothing so stupid and impotent as a hunch-back'd Toad' (Guerinot 1969: 3). Pope, who had a lifetime of this stuff to face and who always professed his indifference to it, was pained by this attack, though he rightly pointed out that Dennis's 'passion' proved how correct the initial criticism of him had been (Spence 1966: 42).

But Pope's career was not to be derailed by such as Dennis. The *Essay* brought him to the attention of Joseph Addison and Richard Steele, Whig politicians and journalists who began their highly influential paper *The Spectator* two months before Pope's poem appeared. *The Spectator* consisted of moderately humorous essays on topics of current concern, literary, philosophical or moral, eschewing (ostensibly at least) party politics for a notion of well-bred tolerance. The *Essay* was praised by Addison as 'a Masterpiece in its kind' later that year (no. 253, 20 December 1711), though Pope was mildly censured for (as he put it in thanking Steele for Addison's praise and his criticism) 'speaking too freely of my Brother-Moderns'. In the next year one whole issue was given over to publication of Pope's *Messiah*, a 'sacred Eclogue' based on Isaiah and Virgil's *Pollio* (no. 378, 14 May

1712), which again showed Pope's inheritance of the classical mantle, here with irreproachable religious colouring. Addison praised a *Miscellany* which Pope edited at the behest of Bernard Lintot, a rival publisher of rather less salubrious character than Tonson, which contained 'many excellent Compositions of that ingenious Gentleman' (no. 523, 30 October 1712).

One of these 'Compositions' was the two-canto version of *The Rape of the Locke*, already a dizzying venture in the mock-heroic use of epic language and images to describe small-scale social world of London. John Caryll had asked Pope to write a poem to try to reconcile two Catholic families at war over an incident in which Lord Petre had snipped off a lock of Arabella Fermor's hair – a trivial enough incident, perhaps, and regarded by Johnson only as 'a frolick of gallantry, rather too familiar' (Johnson 1905: 101), but one which had taken on an altogether darker significance. Pope's poem, which uses the inversions and miniaturisations of the mock-heroic form in a brilliantly even-handed analysis of both the weight and the triviality of the offence, was handed about in manuscript and Pope took the opportunity of Lintot's *Miscellany* to forestall any attempt to bring out an unauthorised edition (Spence 1966: 43–4). Again, the poem is also partly about poetic fame and the power of verse to produce social effects and personal immortality.

(d) KINGS AND QUEENS

By now there were rather greater, quasi-heroic conflicts to consider. England, with her European allies, had been at war with France for most of Pope's lifetime, partly because of France's support for the Jacobite claimants to the English throne and partly because of the general imbalance of political and economic power in Louis XIV's favour. A partial peace was concluded in 1697, but on the death of William III in 1702, without issue, Anne, James II's protestant daughter, succeeded to the throne and war was recommenced, with the Whig Duke of Marlbrough as Captain-General winning some decisive victories. But in 1710 the Whig ministry collapsed and the Tories came to ascendancy; pressure to end the war increased. Some of Pope's mature friendships were formed against this background, one might say partly by it. He grew friendly with John Gay (1685–1732), a poet and dramatist in a congenial mode of mock-heroic. Friendship with William Fortescue, a staunch Whig and lawyer (both terms of abuse in Pope's later years) shows Pope still maintaining Whig contacts, as with Addison and Steele. But in the crucial state of European affairs, it was hardly possible not to take sides, and other new allegiances leaned increasingly towards the Tory camp. John Arbuthnot (1667–1735) came from a Jacobite background, was Queen Anne's physician, and author of a series of prose satires against the war known collectively as *The History of John Bull* (1712). Perhaps most importantly, Pope met Jonathan Swift (1667–1745), clergyman and satirist, recently author of some sophisticated partisan papers, pamphlets and verse satires decrying the profiteering of Marlbrough and urging the necessity of the Tory peace. Swift and Arbuthnot formulated the influential view that the 'landed interest', meaning those aristocrats who farmed large country estates in the traditional way, was being systematically undermined by the 'monied interest', meaning not so much merchants (like Pope's father) but bankers, stockbrokers, and anyone who dealt in money as an abstract entity. This view was to operate very powerfully on Pope and on politics generally during the period, though the reality of the situation was considerably more fluid than satire suggested.

The peace, known as the Treaty of Utrecht, was eventually signed on 31 March 1713. Pope had anticipated the actual signing by publishing *Windsor-Forest* on 7 March **[57–64, 166, 170]**. This was a more localised and personal a vision of rural England than the *Pastorals*, yet once again Pope has several literary models in mind, and the poem depends for some of its effects on a communal literary heritage which would include Virgil's *Georgics* (poems celebrating a more practical agricultural life than the *Eclogues*), English topographic poems such as Sir John Denham's *Cooper's Hill* (1642), and works of national mythology such as Michael Drayton's *Poly-Olbion* (1622) and William Camden's antiquarian *Britannia* (1586). In celebrating the Peace as the dawn of a new age of prosperity and empire Pope characterises Windsor Forest, and Windsor Castle, as zones of true sovereignty, celebrating Anne, the last of the Stuarts, as a talismanic sovereign. The poem is at once the last expression of a Tory kind of mythology of kingship and an elegy for it, written in the rather sombre knowledge that on the death of Anne, whose children all died in infancy, the Act of Succession of 1701 would ensure that Britain would be ruled by the House of Hanover, sympathetic to the Whig interest, antipathetic to Catholics and with a far more secular turn of mind.

(e) SCRIBLERUS

The quality of Pope's poem was immediately recognised by Swift, who instructed 'Stella' (his friend Esther Johnson): 'read it' (Mack 1985: 199). Addison was said to be upset by the poem, and is known to have promoted a 'rival' poem on the peace, *On the Prospect of Peace* (1712) by Thomas Tickell (1686–1740), which Pope admired. Pope was still close enough to the *Spectator* group to contribute some seven papers to its successor, Steele's *The Guardian*, including a couple of affectionately mocking squibs on 'the club of little men', the earliest of many attempts to defend his physical appearance through irony. There were signs of a split: Steele and Addison had praised the 'Englishness' of the pastorals of Ambrose Philips, published in the same *Miscellany* as Pope's *Pastorals*, and puffed them in a series of *Guardian* papers. Pope contributed an anonymous extra paper, superficially continuing the praise of Philips, but when read more closely, a devastating parodic exposure of his imbecile style against the classical elegance of Pope's work (a more straightfaced 'Discourse on Pastoral Poetry' was included in the *Works* of 1717).

More problematic was the case of Addison's *Cato*, a phenomenally successful tragedy which opened in London on 14 April 1713. Dramatizing the resistance of the republican Cato to the tyrant Caesar, and his eventual suicide, it was claimed by both Whig and Tory factions, with the 'tyranny' it decried being identified equally with the absolutist style of monarchy of the Pretender and with the overweening ambition of Marlbrough. In a rare foray into the theatre, Pope contributed the prologue, a paean to British self-confidence as the inheritors of Roman virtue; it was considered rather Whiggish in cast. When Dennis attacked the play in *Remarks upon Cato* (1713), Pope responded with a spoof pamphlet, the anonymous *Narrative of Dr. Robert Norris, Concerning the Strange and Deplorable Frenzy of Mr. John Denn–*, in which the quack physician Norris reports his attempts to treat the critic, driven mad by universal praise of the play. It is possible that Pope's pamphlet troubled Addison with its evidence of Pope's impulsive scurrility; Addison probably did not know of Pope's epigram 'On a Lady who P-st at the Tragedy of Cato', in which the poet exorcised whatever temptation to snigger underlay his genuine admiration of the play.

Through his Whig contacts Pope met Charles Jervas (1675–1739), an eminent portrait painter, from whom he took painting lessons in the years 1713–1714, and with whom he lived when in London. But it was to Swift's circle that Pope began to incline: though still in contact with Addison's 'little senate' at the Whig coffee house Button's, where he met figures such as the dramatist Nicholas Rowe and the poet Edward Young, by early 1714 he was frequenting meetings of the so-called Scriblerus Club, consisting of Swift, Gay, Parnell, Arbuthnot (in whose rooms in St James's Palace the club often met), and Robert Harley, the Tory minister. The purpose of the club was to kick about satirical ideas, loosely grouped around the figure of an invented learned fool, Martinus Scriblerus, a figure committed to all pedantic and ludicrous abuses (as the Scriblerians saw them) in science, medicine, law, philosophy, and religion. It was from this vigorous exchange of witty ideas that the three greatest satires of the Augustan age were eventually to emerge: Swift's *Gulliver's Travels* (1726), Pope's *The Dunciad* (1728), and Gay's *the Beggar's Opera* (1728). For much of 1714 the club enjoyed the last summer of Tory power with an exuberance set against the failing health of Anne. On 4 March 1714 Pope published a separate edition of *The Rape of the Lock*, enlarged to five cantos by the enriching addition of a mock-epic card game and some quasi-celestial 'machinery', miniaturised 'sylphs' derived from Rosicrucian lore **[65–76, 153, 155–6, 174–5, 177, 181–2]**. It sold 3,000 copies in four days, a wild success. Presciently aware of the kind of obsessive Jacobite-hunting about to haunt criticism of literature, Pope also issued a spoof *Key to the Lock* (1715), zealously exposing the poem as a treasonable political allegory **[166–8]**.

(f) EPIC INTENT

Pope also began work on the decidedly not mock-epic work of translating Homer's *Iliad*. The design of this work was based on Dryden, who after completing an impressive version of Virgil's *Aeneid* (1697) had translated the first book of *The Iliad*. On 23 March 1714 Pope signed an epoch-making contract with Bernard Lintot, the bookseller to whom he had defected. Pope, a merchant's son it should be remembered, realised that he could make better terms with Lintot, anxious to add some class to his list, than with Tonson, who had driven a much harder bargain with Dryden for the *Aeneid*. Like that translation, Pope's was to be a subscription venture: that is, a number of purchasers would subscribe in advance of publication and would be listed in the prefatory matter to the book. It was a kind of diffused patronage, replacing a nobleman's responsibility to fund publication of a book in return for a fawning dedication with a notion of belonging to a more widespread élite. It meant that the publication costs of especially lavish books, such as the Homer was to be, could be defrayed in advance, but equally it meant that subscribers were being asked to buy something on the grounds of reputation alone; it says something about the esteem in which Pope's relatively modest output to 1714 was held, that he was able to get the venture going at all.

Getting subscribers proved to be a laborious business, involving much canvassing on the part of Pope's friends, Whig and Tory, over the period from late 1713 to 6 June 1715, when the first volume, containing books I–IV of *The Iliad*, was released to subscribers. Though never exactly indigent, Pope's paternal fortune was always under threat of sequestration, and he needed money on his own account. He handled the administration of the scheme with a rare degree of business skill; his earnings from the Homer project enabled him to put some convincing substance into his pose of a disinterested aristocrat of poetry, with no need to pay court to any influential patron. He told Spence that the translation itself came very fluently: 'I wrote most of the *Iliad* fast – a great deal of it on journeys, from the little pocket Homer on that shelf there, and often forty or fifty verses on a morning in bed' (Spence 1966: 45); his letters of the period, however, indicate that speed notwithstanding the actual labour of translation of such a huge poem caused him a great deal of stress. Given his sporadic education, it is, as Johnson puts it with dry compassion 'not very likely that he overflowed with Greek' (Johnson 1905: 113), and his enemies were soon to make much of his lack of academic training for the task (he had help from the Scriblerian Thomas Parnell, a classicist with university training, on the commentaries that surrounded the Homeric text).

Addison was outwardly warm towards Pope's enterprise, and was thanked in the Preface alongside other friends of all parties; but he was secretly promoting, and 'correcting' a rival translation by Thomas Tickell (1686–1740), the first section of which was deliberately published two days after the first issue of Pope's. In the pamphlet war which surrounded these rival takes on the foundation of Western literature, Pope's religion, physique, and avarice were all attacked in turn (Guerinot 1969: 20–3, 35–40). It was however a short contest: Lintot wrote to Pope 'You have Mr Tickles Book to divert one Hour— It is allready condemn'd here and the malice & juggling at Buttons is the conversation of those who have spare moments from Politicks.' (*Letters* I: 294). Pope was however sufficiently angry at Addison's involvement in the conspiracy to derail his translation to send him a letter indicating his ability to retaliate in the form of a satiric sketch of Addison's undoubted strengths and fatal weaknesses, the passage now known as the 'Atticus' portrait, later incorporated in the *Epistle to Dr Arbuthnot*. A sort of reconciliation ensued, with compliments for Pope's translation in Addison's new journal *The Freeholder*, but the relationship never regained warmth.

This breach was exacerbated by the new political situation, as some of the attacks on Pope's *Iliad* showed. The Scriblerus Club was quickly aborted on the death of the Queen on 1 August 1714 and accession of the Elector of Hanover as George I: Arbuthnot lost his job as royal physician, and his rooms in St James's; Harley was imprisoned in the Tower on suspicion of treason by the new Whig ministry; Swift, defeated and disenchanted, returned to his Irish preferment; so did Parnell. A Jacobite rising in 1715 was swiftly defeated but made life even worse for Catholics like Pope, who were all liable to be thought disaffected if not actually treasonous. Perhaps under the threat of resuscitated anti-Catholic legislation, the Pope family decided to give up Binfield, depriving Pope of the 'few paternal acres' previously designed for his inheritance and celebrated in his 'Ode on Solitude'. In March 1716 Pope left Binfield, writing several elegiac letters comparing his loss to Adam's expulsion from Eden and various classical exiles (Mack 1985: 284–5). The family moved to Chiswick, to avail themselves of the protection of Richard Boyle, third Earl of Burlington (1694–1753), an unimpeachably Whig aristocrat, whom Pope had probably met through Jervas. The Earl was a notable patron of all the arts, returning from his grand tour laden with paintings, sculptures, and musical instruments. His house was built to his own eclectically neoclassical design, and his garden also deeply impressed Pope, who was later to dedicate an Epistle on the use of riches in architecture and gardening. Pope was on very easy terms with the Earl, despite the difference in social rank: in a brief, flirtatious note to Martha Blount, he boasted 'we are to walk, ride, ramble, dine, drink, & lye together. His gardens are delightful! his musick ravishing' (*Letters* I: 338).

(g) BOOKSELLERS AND LADIES

The loss of Binfield was partially compensated by this new access to aristocratic culture, which Pope for the most part frankly enjoyed. The nearness to London had more serious uses for Pope as he managed the subscription and printing of his *Iliad* translation. London had other attractions too, and in several light verses of the period he casts himself in mildly libertine character. He also became attracted to Lady Mary Wortley Montagu (1689–1762), the most talented woman writer of the period. When three of her manuscript satires on court life were published by the scavenging bookseller Edmund Curll, Pope, perhaps motivated by feelings of chivalry or perhaps by a more immediate sense of injury (Curll also ascribed them to Gay and to Pope himself), took immediate physical revenge. On 28 March 1716, two days after Curll's publication of *Court Poems*, Pope somehow managed to slip Curll an emetic, and then publicised the results in an imitation Grub-Street pamphlet: *A Full and True Account of a Horrid and Barbarous Revenge by Poison, On the Body of Mr. Edmund Curll, Bookseller* characterises Curll's bodily sufferings and confessions of literary crime with sadistic comedy of a kind which was to receive defter treatment in *The Dunciad.* Curll was already well known as a publisher of obscene or scurrilous books; he had a particular knack for tracking down personal papers and documents of famous authors, rushing cheap and scandalous biographies into print as soon as celebrities were dead (Pope's friend Arbuthnot claimed that Curll had thereby managed to add a new terror to death). He represented a new breed of completely shameless publisher, prizing commercial success above any notion of quality, and became the centrepiece of Pope's own antagonism to the book trade. Curll responded to the poison episode by publishing some of Pope's bawdier tavern pieces in an effort to discredit his 'classic' pose, and by sniping at the alleged Jacobitism of Pope's *Iliad* (of which the second instalment was published in March 1716) in the newspapers, alongside pamphlets such as John Oldmixon's *The Catholic Poet* (1716), in which Pope's bookseller is made to declare *'This Papish Dog ... has translated HOMER for the Use of the PRETENDER'* (Guerinot 1969: 40). Curll joined with Dennis in publishing *A True Character of Mr. Pope* (1716), a venomously abusive rant against the 'little monster': 'the deformity of this Libeller, is Visible, Present, Lasting, Unalterable, and Peculiar to himself. 'Tis the mark of God and Nature upon him, to give us warning that we should hold no Society with him, as a Creature not of our Original, nor of our Species' (Guerinot 1969: 44).

Against this public background Pope developed a kind of deliberately extravagant passion for Lady Mary, cultivated through the extreme epistolary gallantry of his correspondence with her while she was in Constantinople accompanying her husband's diplomatic mission between August 1716 and October 1718. Taking his cue from her situation in the Orient, imagined as a place of sexualised power and luxury, Pope wrote a series of letters of elaborately crafted amorous innuendo to Lady Mary, to which she responded with resolutely information-based travelogue, treating his overtures as mere raillery. At the same time, Pope was also writing flirtatious letters to the Blount sisters, who were perhaps rendered safe objects of affection not by aristocratic and geographical distance but simply by existing as a pair. From these experiences of the mind or body with women, Pope wrote two substantial poems casting his lot sympathetically with wronged women. His *Elegy to the Memory of an Unfortunate Lady* opens with a melodramatic apostrophe to the bleeding ghost of a young female suicide and continues to indict the familial politics which has forbidden a match with her desired lover and driven her to her death in exile. Alongside this we have *Eloisa to Abelard* **[77–82, 153, 177]**, an original take on the motif of the letter of an abandoned female lover popularised in Ovid's *Heroides*. Eloisa, a medieval heroine, laments the loss of her husband and lover Abelard to the castrating vengeance of her uncle. Both these poems conclude with vignettes of the sympathising poet, making a degree of personal investment part of the meaning of the poems.

(h) WORKS AND DAYS

Both these poems were published for the first time in *The Works of Alexander Pope*, which appeared on 3 June 1717, alongside the third volume of the *Iliad* translation, and available in the same large sizes, with the same attention to embellishments, paper quality and layout. Though not yet thirty, Pope felt able to align his own work with that of the greatest of classic poets, whom he was now translating. His main works (*Pastorals, Windsor-Forest, Essay on Criticism, Rape of the Lock* and *Temple of Fame*) offered monumental stature, with translations and miscellanies giving a sample of the juvenilia from which these achievements grew. It was a highly conscious act of self-presentation; the frontispiece depicting Pope was etched from a portrait executed by Jervas in 1714, and shows the poet from the waist up, showing no sign of the distinctive hunched back or diminished size, and giving Pope the air of a gallant young man. The Preface offered, in writing of 'great sprightliness and elegance' (Johnson 1905: 135) a similarly aristocratic poise: 'The life of a Wit is a warfare upon earth', Pope comments, speaking ruefully to his genteel audience as if they were somehow outside such mundane considerations. The process of careful self-editing, deleting and selection, to which Pope alludes, sought to raise the *Works* which were now offered with due deference to the public above the level of the Grub-Street antics of Curll and others. In claiming complete political independence, as an author who 'never made his talents subservient to the mean and unworthy ends of Party or self-interest' (*PW* I: 295) Pope began to develop the best role available to him in his politically excluded position.

Pope's father died suddenly on 23 October 1717, leaving him rather less than might have been expected (Johnson 1905: 85). At this point Francis Atterbury, Bishop of Rochester, tried to get Pope to turn protestant on prudential grounds, as Swift had before, resulting in a careful statement of Pope's position:

I am not a Papist, for I renounce the temporal invasions of Papal power, and detest their arrogated authority over Princes, and States. I am a Catholick, in the strictest sense of the word. If I was born under an absolute Prince, I would be a quiet subject; but I thank God I was not. I have a due sense of the excellence of the British constitution. In a word, the things I have always wished to see are not a Roman Catholick, or a French Catholick, or a Spanish Catholick, but a true Catholick: and not a King of Whigs, or a King of Tories, but a King of England. Which God of his mercy grant his present Majesty may be...

(Letters I: 454)

The statement is perhaps less loyal than it seems – the possibility of *not* being a quiet subject is implied, and the final sentence lacks the expected obsequiousness; not for the last time, Pope had to generate a political position between subservience and hostility.

The final two volumes of Pope's translation of *The Iliad* were released to subscribers on 12 May 1720. It was a massive success, dominating the reception of Homer into the Romantic period and creating a new polite readership for the foundational poet of Western culture. Though it was occasionally disliked for its ornamental or musical character against the supposed strength and simplicity of the original, in the main it was found to be 'the noblest version [translation] of poetry which the world has ever seen; and its publication must therefore be considered as one of the great events in the annals of learning' (Johnson 1905: 119). The Preface, a full-dress literary essay which deserves to be read alongside Pope's *Essay on Criticism*, displays a remarkable enthusiasm for the qualities which some found lacking in the translation, notably the 'Invention' (imagination) of the poet: 'It is to the Strength of this amazing Invention we are to attribute that unequal'd Fire and Rapture, which is so forcible in *Homer*, that no Man of a true Poetical Spirit is Master of himself while he reads him' (*PW* I: 224). The poem went to the heart of everything: destiny, power, sex, glory, death, the Gods. Everything which ennobles human beings and everything which degrades them was, for Pope's generation, here. Pope's response to this universal poetic master was almost visionary, an access of godlike power, a virtual experience of military and amatory excess. This unsettling but stimulating encounter was now very fully mastered, at least for the present.

(i) TWICKENHAM

With the funds earned from this monumental achievement, Pope set about creating for himself an equally visible monument to inhabit. After considering building himself a house on some of Burlington's land in London, inadvisable because of anti-Catholic legislation, he had settled down river at Twickenham in early 1719, leasing a five-acre estate from Thomas Vernon. This relatively modest estate in a semi-rural setting but with good river and road connections to the capital served Pope's needs well; it was the first house which he was master of, and was to remain his home, and a vital element in his conception of himself, until his death. He remodelled the existing house along newly-fashionable Palladian or neoclassical lines, with a main block on three floors flanked by two-storey wings. Balconies gave good views over the Thames, which ran by at the foot of a sloping lawn. A passage ran under the house, and under the road between London and Hampton Court, to the main garden, which measured about 250 by 100 yards. The whole plot was slightly larger than Pope estimated the gardens of Alcinous to be, in his translation of that section of Homer's *Odyssey* (*PW* I: 147).

Here Pope had an orchard, a small vineyard, an orangery, greenhouses, and a kitchen garden for vegetables; landscaping the rest was a matter of providing serpentine and criss-crossing paths through wooded areas and up mounts to provide viewpoints, seats for reflection, sudden surprises and encounters. Pope was like many of his generation dissatisfied with the rigid symmetrical formalism of seventeenth-century garden design, as practised in extreme form in France. Pope had opposed topiary and artificial gardens in an essay in *The Guardian* in 1713 and in his own experiments and theories aimed for a subtler control of nature, more green, fluid, curved, locally-sensitive and small-scale. It was, however, conspicuously human: there were seats, obelisks, temples, inscriptions: this was nature methodised, as literature was supposed to be. Pope's efforts at Twickenham were enthusiastically received by visitors and observers: Horace Walpole, son of the Prime Minister Sir Robert Walpole whom Pope opposed with such virulence, noted: 'It was a singular effort of art and taste to have impressed so much variety and scenery on a spot of five acres' (Mack 1985: 361).

Pope also gradually expanded and decorated the passage under his house into a Grotto: 'he extracted an ornament from an inconvenience, and vanity produced a grotto where necessity enforced a passage' (Johnson 1905: 135). In opposition to the neoclassical pieties of the house itself, with its symmetry and open vista, the Grotto celebrated obscurity, enclosure, shade, coolness. The Grotto allowed for unusual visual perspectives: you could see into the garden from the Thames, and vice versa; you could, thanks to carefully placed mirrors, see some unusual inversion of scene:

> When you shut the Doors of this Grotto, it becomes on the instant, from a luminous Room, a *Camera obscura*; on the Walls of which all the Objects of the River, Hills, Woods, and Boats, are forming a moving Picture in their visible Radiations: And when you have a mind to light it up, it affords you a very different Scene: it is finish'd with Shells interspersed with Pieces of Looking-glass in angular forms; and in the Cieling [*sic*] is a Star of the same Material, at which when a Lamp ... is hung in the Middle, a thousand pointed Rays glitter and are reflected over the Place.
>
> (*Letters* II: 296–7)

Pope never lost a fascination with the darker undercurrents of landscape as represented in caves and fissures in classical epic, though in his literary work caves usually represent some form of pathological interior, a psychic aberration: the Cave of Spleen in *The Rape of the Lock* **[65–76]**, for example.

Pope was able to offer comfortable hospitality to his friends, which in turn enabled him to go visiting each summer. Pope was almost the reverse of a recluse; despite his personal discomforts and the inconveniences of travel, he envisaged his network of friends as a sort of guarantee of proper social values and as a source of potential regeneration against the corruption he increasingly saw at national level. Among the most important of these friends was Allen Bathurst, first baron Bathurst, among those ennobled by Queen Anne in order to ratify the Treaty of Utrecht in the House of Lords, and a mild Stuart sympathiser. Robust, good-humoured and prodigiously given to eating and drinking, Bathurst offered Pope an uncompetitive and energetic friendship fostered by a mutual interest in landscape gardening. He and Pope planted woods and modelled new water features at his estate at Richings, in Buckinghamshire, and more spectacularly at Cirencester Park, Gloucestershire, where Bathurst owned something like 4,000 acres of land. Three quarters of this was eventually covered in woodland, in an attempt to recreate a sort of Windsor Forest, redesigned for perambulation, with vistas, seats, intersecting paths and summer houses. Pope also gave assistance to other noble gardeners, and these practical efforts helped develop his views on nature, the environment, and the sociopolitical significance of the landscape garden, expressed in major works of the 1730s.

To some extent this garden perspective offered Pope a retreat as well as a position from which to comment. The years immediately following the *Iliad* project had more than their share of vexations. In 1720 London experienced a bout of stock market speculation and catastrophic collapse known as the South Sea Bubble; Pope, along with a great many others, lost money, though he was not ruined. Nonetheless, given the expenditure on house and garden, Pope probably needed money and his second Homer venture, a translation of *The Odyssey* (eventually published 1725–26), may have been prompted by financial need. This second excursion into classical territory did not have quite the gloss of the first. The story of Odysseus's wanderings after the fall of Troy is itself less conspicuously noble, less concentrated, more given to monstrosity and magic, more gruesomely comic, than the *Iliad*, though the essential skill and wisdom of its protagonist survives all encounters. For the work of translation, however, Pope called on two acquaintances, the minor poets William Broome and Elijah Fenton, to translate half the poem between them in what was originally to have been a secret collaboration. Complex subscription arrangements were made whereby each of the translators took a share of the main subscription and also solicited subscriptions on their account; the publisher (Lintot again) also made arrangements on his own behalf, which signalled the beginning of the end of his association with Pope. Word that the translation was not wholly Pope's leaked out, giving his enemies grounds to carp at his sharp practice (and his alleged lack of Greek); though Pope undoubtedly masterminded the project, urging his fellow-workers on and meticulously correcting their work, his comments in print about the authorship of the translation always appeared somewhat evasive and his friendship with the two contributors did not survive unscathed. It was as commercially and aesthetically successful as the *Iliad*, even earning Pope a Civil List grant of £200; and the Postscript (*PW* II: 51–66) made as positive a case for the poem as the Preface to the *Iliad*, even comparing the excellence of the poem to the excellence of the British constitution. But even Pope's most sympathetic biographer cannot but call the financial aspect 'a shabby business all round' (Mack 1985: 414).

The Bubble had more far-reaching effects, however. There had been two ineffectual attempts since 1715 to restore the Stuart claimant to the Throne, and the widespread financial problems following the Bubble, in which the Court was implicated, promoted a certain amount of anti-Hanoverian agitation. A new Jacobite plot was hatching in

1721–22, closely monitored by Government spies. This brought to the fore Sir Robert Walpole, a Whig who had endeared himself to the regime by protecting so far as was possible those members of the court who had unclean fingers in the Bubble; he now sought to use the Jacobite scare to polarise Whig and Tory, penalise Catholics, and make himself the leading politician of the day. In August 1722, he had Pope's friend Francis Atterbury, Bishop of Rochester (1662–1732) and a somewhat unlikely leader of the Jacobite cause in England, imprisoned in the Tower while by a variety of not very scrupulous means he obtained evidence against him. As a Catholic and close friend of the bishop, Pope was implicated; he gave evidence at Atterbury's show trial (8 May 1723) in the Lords, nervously (and probably truthfully) declaring that he had seen nothing to support the accusation (Spence 1966: 102–3). The outcome of the trial, which was wholly political, was never in doubt, despite some words on his behalf by Tories like Bathurst (and even one or two Whigs); Atterbury was actually guilty of the main charge. Nonetheless his banishment, and perhaps more, the manner of the trial, deeply disturbed Pope, not only because of the loss of a close friend, but because of the rise to power of a very formidable politician.

Pope had edited the poems of his dead friend Parnell in 1720–21, adding a nostalgic poem in praise of Robert Harley, the Tory leader imprisoned for his supposed Jacobite sympathies in 1715. He edited the works of John Sheffield, husband of a natural daughter of James II; in January 1723 the impression was impounded for the supposedly treasonable content of the essays; Pope himself may have been arrested. Pope wrote to Lord Carteret a prudent and dignified statement of his own political quietude and independence (*Letters* II: 160). Just after the Atterbury trial Charles Rackett, husband of Pope's half-sister Magdalen, was arrested for deer stealing in Windsor Forest, an offence which at this particular point in history carried political overtones. The Black Act, named after gangs of masked poachers, laid down a whole series of capital offences against property and greatly strengthened the hand of the regime under the guise of a defence of property. The outcome of the Rackett case is unknown, but it cannot have helped Pope's own sense of security.

(j) SHAKESPEARE

Over the years of the *Odyssey* translation, Pope was also working on an edition of Shakespeare at the behest of the younger Jacob Tonson, who had now assumed command of his uncle's eminent publishing business. Pope was paid a flat fee of £100 to prepare a new edition of the text in six volumes. He was not an obvious candidate for editor, and indeed Shakespeare is conspicuously absent from his acknowledged early reading, though the influence of close attention to the text is palpable in his later work. The text of Shakespeare had always been a rather embattled thing, since the First Folio prepared posthumously in 1623 had complained about spurious printings of the plays. These 'bad' quartos, or printings of single plays, co-existed alongside 'good quartos' which appear to emerge from more authoritative sources. Many plays existed in good, bad, and Folio forms. Not much explicit critical notice was taken of these variants during the seventeenth century. In the early eighteenth century, however, a new interest in recovering 'authentic' Shakespeare began to emerge, at least at textual level. Nicholas Rowe, a friend of Pope's and man of the theatre, was commissioned to produce a new text for the elder Tonson in 1709, and did much to normalise conventions of presentation (speech prefixes, act and scene numbering, scene locations). He also provided the first biography of Shakespeare, an entertaining account based on some fairly unreliable stories which circulated in theatre circles; it was reprinted with many subsequent editions. But it was Pope who made the first substantial claim to colla-tion (or cross-checking) of the extant early texts. There was very little in the way of public facilities for scholars at this date and Tonson put out advertisements requesting the loan of rare quartos to help Pope's endeavours (the edition contained a prominent list of those editions consulted). With the aid of these early printings Pope managed to reverse some of the drift towards textual randomness that the folios at their worst represented.

Pope took it upon himself to mark passages of especial beauty with marginal commas (whole scenes of this class were signalised with a star). He also removed from the main text to the foot of the page over fifteen hundred lines which he considered too bad or 'low' in character to have been written by Shakespeare: anachronisms, bombast and bawdy which a later age would celebrate as part of Shakespeare's com-prehensiveness, seemed to Pope evidence only of the trivialising incur-sions of ad-libbing populist actors, and he ditched them accordingly. Shakespeare himself appears in god-like manifestation in Pope's Preface, a vigorous and influential defence of Shakespeare's genius which forms one of the foundational documents in what would later become 'bardolatry': 'The Poetry of *Shakespear* was Inspiration indeed: he is not so much an Imitator, as an Instrument, of Nature; and 'tis not so just to say that he speaks from her, as that she speaks thro' him'. Shakespeare stands with Homer as above all the poetic of astonishing human insight and emotional force (*PW* II: 13–26).

Pope proposed a new model of Shakespeare editing; unfortunately for him, there was at least one other writer who more nearly approached the modern model of professional scholar: Lewis Theobald (1688–1744), a lawyer turned writer, who in March 1726 published *Shakespeare Restored: Or, A Specimen of the Many Errors, as well Committed, as Unamended, by Mr Pope in his Late Edition of this Poet*. Using his greater familiarity with Elizabethan drama, orthography and grammar, and a somewhat more efficient collation of a rather greater number of early printings of Shakespeare, Theobald was able to show that Pope's boasted editorial labour was much more erratic and unreliable than it should have been: he had missed obvious errors, emended where no emendation was necessary, failed to understand the sense of his author, and exhibited a complete lack of historical and contextual knowledge. The book (which was issued in the same format as Pope's edition, as if to be bound up with it), was quite obviously designed to humiliate Pope: with gleeful malice and self-confidence Theobald 'restored' the sense and text of Shakespeare against Pope's supposed blunders. It was the first Shakespeare war, and Pope lost.

(k) EPIC OF FLEET STREET

Such onslaughts could be set against more moderate criticisms of Pope's work, such as the *Essay on the Odyssey* (1726–27) by Joseph Spence, in whom, as Johnson put it, 'Pope had the first experience of a critick without malevolence' (Johnson 1905: 143), and with whom he soon became friends. But when *Shakespeare Restored* was published, Pope was particularly fortunate to have an older friend at hand. Swift was in England for the first time for over a decade, and was in unusually positive spirits: he had become a national hero in Ireland for leading the popular campaign to resist the attempts of Walpole's administration to impose cheaply-produced copper coinage on the Irish economy for the benefit of the English industrialist who was to manufacture them. Swift sought interviews with Walpole to ascertain what his prospects were for ecclesiastical promotion to an English benefice; but he was also carrying the manuscript of what was to become the most explosive satire of its time: *Gulliver's Travels*, eventually delivered to the publisher in an extremely secret and anonymous manner (Pope may literally have had a hand in it). Swift based himself at Pope's Twickenham villa from April to July 1726, and for that time something of the Scriblerus project revived between Pope, Swift, Gay and Arbuthnot. Pope and Swift reviewed some of their early publications and ideas, eventually issuing a series of *Miscellanies*. Swift is also said to have rescued from the fire the first sketches of Pope's *Dunciad*, and it may have been he who suggested the concept of a literary anti-hero to be crowned King of the Dunces by the goddess Dulness. At any rate, Pope was not one to shy away from antagonistic literary encounters, and his public response to Theobald's onslaught was to instal him as the chief hack writer in the ironic epic of praise to hack writers which *The Dunciad* ostensibly is **[130–49, 157–9, 166–7, 185–8, 189–98]**. Theobald played further into Pope's hands by publicly ascribing a new play, *The Double Falsehood*, to Shakespeare, thus indicating what Pope could take to be a talent for forgery unbecoming in an editor. He further compounded his crimes by presiding as a lawyer over his old friend Wycherley's deathbed marriage settlement, and by editing a posthumous volume of works by the poet which Pope thought had been tampered with. All this confirmed him as a legitimate target.

The moment of *The Dunciad*, however, was opportune in more ways than that of personal pique. Its origins lie clearly with the 'works of the unlearned' spoofs of the Scriblerus club; its basic narrative idea is knowingly borrowed from Dryden's *Mack Flecknoe* (1681). *The Dunciad* was preceded by an important prose satire, *Peri Bathous: or, the art of sinking in poetry*, a deadpan parody of the treatise known as *Peri Hypsous* ('Concerning the Sublime'), ascribed to Longinus, on which Pope drew in the *Essay on Criticism*. Pope's spoof selects some of the most ludicrous bombast from Pope's contemporaries – he does include some of his own early work – as praiseworthy examples of the 'modern' mode of writing. At the same time, *The Dunciad* follows hard on the heels of Swift's scathingly anti-Walpole *Gulliver's Travels*, in which the unlovely lineaments of British governmental practice, as viewed by Tories such as Swift and Pope, are clearly visible, and Gay's *The Beggar's Opera*, an immensely successful parody of foreign opera which with the thinnest possible disguise portrayed the government as a band of highwaymen. George I died on 11 June 1727, and optimists in the opposition hoped that George II, who had been estranged from his father, would dismiss Walpole and regenerate the political system with new blood. It rapidly became obvious that this was a pipe dream.

The Dunciad was originally published as a sort of hoax, anonymously, in a format meant to imitate the lowlife kind of publication the poem itself satirised: the cheap mass printing which Pope posited as one of the signs of the decay of culture. Arguments about the corrupting effects of a press unregulated (except by libel laws) had been going on since the licensing acts, which had limited seventeenth century presses to those managed by the Stationers' Company, had been allowed to lapse in 1695: in *Tale of a Tub*, for example, Swift impersonates a mad scribbler or hack writer to exemplify what was alleged to be a newly rampant and unrestrained press as venal, corrupt, illiterate, treacherous, and overweeningly self-confident. Much the same mythology underlies *The Dunciad*. Lewis Theobald is installed as the most eminent of the hacks, elected by the goddess Dulness to lead the assorted hacks from their current shabby neighbourhood in the penumbra of the 'City', already a byword for philistinism and poor taste, towards the seats of the court and parliament in the West End. Many of Pope's old enemies are named: Curll the bookseller, Lintot, with whom Pope had now completely broken, Dennis the critic, and so on: proliferation and a kind of undifferentiated lack of entity are part of what Pope suggests typifies members of the book trade. Many names were left blank, or only hinted at.

The poem caused uproar, as Pope had intended. As Richard Savage, a friend of Pope's but rather closer to the scene of Grub Street than he would have cared to admit, describes it (perhaps with assistance from Pope):

> On the Day the Book was first vended, a Crowd of Authors besieg'd the Shop; Entreaties, Advices, Threats of Law, and Battery, nay Cries of Treason were all employ'd, to hinder the coming out of the *Dunciad*: On the other Side, the Booksellers and Hawkers made as great Efforts to procure it.
>
> (*TE* V: xxii)

Pope kept pistols in his pocket and his dog at his side whenever he left his house at this time – perhaps a gesture of genuine defiance, or fear, or part of his image as lone crusader. A torrent of publication began: since 1715 Pope had been a ready target for his bodily deformity, his Catholicism, his business acumen (seen as sharp practice) and (probably most of all) his literary skill. *The Dunciad* could just about be construed as a public dressing-down of those who had attacked him, but Pope must have known that the poem, with its scurrilous depictions of a goodly proportion of contemporary writers in filthy and idiotic situations, would exacerbate the situation enormously. Over the next two years at least three dozen pamphlets traduced Pope in a variety of libellous ways. Some of these attacks are fairly spirited: 'Dauntless Curll', as Pope aptly characterised him in the poem, took the view that any publicity was good publicity and published not only several 'keys' identifying characters in *The Dunciad*, but also *The Popiad*, *The Curliad* and probably *The Female Dunciad*, in which Pope's sexual misdemeanours, blasphemous tendencies, literary trickery and spiteful nature were all trumpeted forth. Pope's plagiarism, the deceit over the *Odyssey* translation, Jacobitism, avarice, mental and physical deformity, ingratitude, treachery, lower class background, taste for smut and filth, were all ceaselessly recycled and inflated in angry fantasies of retribution. Pope was nicknamed Pope Alexander for his self-declared 'supremacy and infallibility'; he was pictured as a monkey, sometimes topped with a papal tiara (Guerinot 1969: 110–98).

For Pope, it was possible to use the furore merely as proof of the original point: he was able to absorb the attacks into a new version of the poem, which must have been part of the project from the beginning. Theobald was a cheap writer, demeaning culture into pantomime; but his scholarship represented a different form of assault on classic literature, one which was not so much illiterate as hyperliterate, a form of 'verbal criticism' which seemed to Pope pedantic and deadening in its concentration on the minutiae of textual history, and self-promoting in the confidence with which texts of classic authors could be emended. In *Shakespeare Restored* Theobald explicitly aligned his work with that of the great classical scholar Richard Bentley, a critic of brilliance and arrogance who had confidently made on the authority of his own genius several thousand alterations to the received texts of mainstream canonical authors such as Horace and Terence, and who had proposed in the 1720s to perform the same office for the Greek New Testament. (In 1732 he 'edited' Milton's *Paradise Lost*.) In 1729, in response to the supposedly 'imperfect' or piratical state of the first *Dunciad*, Pope brought out *The Dunciad Variorum*, in imitation of Bentleian scholarship. It is a mock-edition: the poem text appears (after a pile of preliminary material and before a series of appendices) above a sea of notes by 'Martinus Scriblerus', the literal-minded and pedantic scholar in whose name the Scriblerus club sought to ridicule any form of learning they deemed incompatible with traditional humanistic and classical concerns. Scriblerus proceeds to propose a series of stupid alterations to the text, quite oblivious to the ludicrous dead-ends his pedantic learning brings him to; Appendix IV gives an ominous list of proposed 'restorations' to the text of Virgil's *Aeneid*. At the same time, however, the notes, indexes, and appendices do actually contain much straightforward information (and some mischievous misinformation) in order to defend Pope's satiric vision of literary history and contemporary culture: *The Dunciad Variorum* concludes with 'A List of All our Author's Genuine Works', reminding readers of the classic status of his achievement. Pope was taking control of his role as author: from here he began to use his own printers and booksellers, ensuring his control over layouts, typography, and financial rewards.

(1) SYSTEM AND SATIRE

It is firmly recorded, if somewhat astonishing, that on 12 March 1729 Sir Robert Walpole presented a copy of *The Dunciad Variorum* to George II, who pronounced its author 'a very honest man' (*TE* V: xxviii). Nonetheless, *The Dunciad* clearly marks the beginning of the end of any possible understanding between Pope and Walpole; the line 'Still Dunce the second reigns like Dunce the first' (Book 1, line 6) burns Pope's boats, as *Gulliver's Travels* burned Swift's, and *The Beggar's Opera* (with its sequel of 1729, *Polly*, which Walpole banned) Gay's. After this affray, a conspicuous setting of boundaries between Pope's circle and the rest of contemporary literature (a sort of cultural antithesis befitting the master of the couplet), Pope set out to construct a more positive vision of social roles. Pope's political position became more clearly defined by his increasing friendship with Bolingbroke, who had returned from political exile at exactly the moment Atterbury was going into it in.

Pope had known Bolingbroke a little during the last years of Queen Anne, though he was more intimate with Harley, Bolingbroke's rival. Harley died in 1724, soon after Bolingbroke was conditionally pardoned, despite having fled the country on the accession of George I, and having acted as the Pretender's Secretary of State during the disastrous Jacobite campaign of 1715. Bolingbroke settled at Dawley Manor near Uxbridge, four miles from Pope's villa. His property was restored, but not his aristocratic title, and he was thus unable to act in any effective political way. Instead he became the central theorist of the opposition to Walpole, drawing to him Tories and disaffected Whigs – and Pope, who told Spence he found Bolingbroke 'something superior to anything I have seen in human nature' (Spence 1966: 121). Severing all visible ties with the Stuarts, Bolingbroke set about producing a new political ideology (sometimes called 'Country' ideology, as opposed to 'Court' thinking), based on traditional English attachment to land ownership and management and attacking the newly-emerged financial institutions (the Bank of England, founded in 1694, the National Debt, the growth of insurance, paper money, the stock market) as so much 'corruption' (a key term of political opposition). Walpole was characterised as a master of financial manipulation, bribing for votes, managing slush funds and gifting jobs in order to shore up his own power. To Swift's existing myth of the displacement of (Tory) land by (Whig) money, Bolingbroke added a new and rather saintly version of the solid classical virtues of independence and civic pride. He changed the name of his property to Dawley Farm, indicating the practice of stewardship of the land rather than merely ownership of it, and did in fact farm the 400-acre estate. For a decade Bolingbroke studied and wrote on constitutional matters, publishing his views in the opposition periodical *The Craftsman* and in independent pamphlets.

It was under Bolingbroke's encouragement that Pope began work on what he later termed his *opus magnum* or 'great work': the four-part *Essay on Man* (1733–34), offering an analytic account of man's place in the universe, and four 'ethic epistles' (1731–35), analysing particular aspects of human experience. More was planned, but these represent the surviving essence of the project. The first portion to be published was a verse Epistle to his longstanding friend, Lord Burlington (14 December 1731), originally called 'Of Taste' but better known as the *Epistle to Burlington* **[105–9]**. Here Pope expounded views on architecture and landscape gardening, and the appropriate use of wealth (exemplified in the taste Burlington displays at his villa in Chiswick and elsewhere). Most of Pope's presentations of positive virtue are offered in contradistinction to some vicious negative example; here, sensibly naturalised landscapes which 'consult the genius of the place in all', and enhance the features which already exist, are contrasted with the atrocious tastelessness of Timon's villa, where lavish expense serves only to produce hideously aggrandised buildings and gardens which torture natural forms into dehumanised symmetries. The riotous catalogue of bad taste includes a showcase library of unread books, a chapel with erotic paintings and inappropriate music, and a comically awful dinner.

The praise of Burlington was explicit and passed without comment, but the identification of Timon was a matter of much contemporary curiosity; it was soon rumoured that Pope had based it on a house in Berkshire known as Cannons, belonging to the Whig Duke of Chandos. Pope seems to have been genuinely taken aback by the attacks on his supposed treachery; he issued a firm public disclaimer of 'such Fool Applications', pointing out obvious differences between Cannons and the estate described in the poem, and he and Chandos exchanged courtly letters assuring each other of mutual esteem and the falseness of the accusation (Mack 1985: 499). The rumour however continued to circulate amongst those anxious to damage Pope's reputation, and appears to have been partially orchestrated by the Court and the Ministry, perhaps manoeuvring against a nascent enemy.

The second element of Pope's planned ethical series was the *Epistle to Bathurst* (1733) **[101–5]**, again on the subject of riches, but this time concentrating on avarice more than expenditure. Propelling the reader through a series of examples of the *misuse* of riches, Pope takes a distinctly Bolingbrokian line on 'blest Paper Credit', ironically celebrated as lending 'Corruption lighter wings to fly' because of its secrecy. Emphasising the contrary forces unleashed by extreme parsimony or profligacy, and suggesting that divine providence sees a resulting balance in these antithetical extremes, Pope builds the poem towards two final contrasting examples. The Man of Ross, a private man with a small personal fortune, uses money for the sole purpose of benefiting his local community. On the other side, Sir Balaam, a Whiggish dissenting merchant, is shown as being tempted to reject his God not by being made poor, as in the Book of Job, but by being made rich, whereupon he becomes proud, self-sufficient, moves in high society, corrupts his family and eventually 'takes a bribe from France' – a deeply ironic twist in which the Whig type does what Tories like Bolingbroke were always accused of doing.

Ostensibly didactic as these poems were, however, Pope could not resist teasing the public over publication of the *Essay on Man* **[82–93]**. Having published, under his own name and through his normal bookseller, the *Epistle to Bathurst* in the middle of January 1733 (following this up with the first of his 'Horatian' imitations in February), he brought out in February, March and May the first three epistles of the *Essay on Man* anonymously and through an unfamiliar bookseller. The three epistles were tremendously successful, and ascribed to various high-minded clergymen; at least two of Pope's duncely enemies incautiously heaped tributes on the poem before the knowledge of Pope's authorship became public. Few outside Pope's immediate circle associated the doctrinal confidence and theological optimism of the *Essay on Man* with a politically-suspect Catholic. Ostentatiously plucking the mantle of poet of the universe from Milton, Pope constructs a defence of God for the scientific age. Taking a cue from Newton's many achievements in physics, Pope contended (as Newton himself did) that the discovery of the 'watchmaker universe', bounded by irrefragable laws, was not an opening for atheistic rationalism, but the sublimest possible proof of the existence of a creator and the immanence of hierarchy and regularity throughout the known universe. The hypothesis (known from classical times, and especially through a poem that Pope deliberately draws on, the *De Rerum Natura* of Lucretius) that random collisions of atoms produced everything in the universe, including human nature, was opposed by this poetic analysis of an authored, ordered system.

(m) HORACE

Pope's optimism about the role of providence in this poem was to some extent a necessary counter to the disasters of his personal life, which was marked by several deaths about this period. Atterbury died in March 1732 and was given a somewhat mean funeral in Westminster Abbey. An even worse loss was that of John Gay, carried off swiftly but painfully by some sort of fever at the age of 47 (4 December 1732): Pope told Swift, 'one of the nearest and longest tyes I have ever had, is broken all on a sudden' (*Letters* III: 334). Pope was one of the pallbearers at the funeral, again in the Abbey. Pope's mother died on 7 June 1733, at the age of ninety. Her death had been long expected, but Pope was evidently shaken. He asked his friend the artist Jonathan Richardson to sketch her 'expression of Tranquillity [sic]' in death, 'as the finest image of a Saint expir'd, that ever Painting drew' (*Letters* III: 374).

Literary warfare continued from a different angle. Early in 1733 Pope had begun what was to be a series of 'Imitations' of the Roman poet Horace, setting out some major satiric conceptions under the guise of updating the earlier poet for the current situation **[119–30]**. Though Horace was sometimes regarded as the servile flatterer of a tyrannical emperor, his civilised, ironic manner was generally more congenial to Pope's ethic of moderation than the alternative satirist, Juvenal, whose exiled ranting is more akin to the more extreme aspects of *Gulliver's Travels*. 'Imitation' in this mature context does not indicate servility, but a sort of respectful appropriation and rivalry. Pope adopts the conversational and 'insinuating' mode of the Roman poet, whose work is placed on the opposite page from Pope's modern version, to give himself a voice of classic authority from which to comment on social issues. But the adoption of a Horatian position, while it stakes a claim and invites comparison between ancient and modern skill, is also ironic, for Pope is an outsider where Horace was a court favourite, and Pope has no patron whereas Horace was indebted to the emperor and other noblemen. The Horatian model was neither simple nor pacificatory.

In *The First Satire of the Second Book of Horace Imitated* (15 February 1733), Pope mildly assaulted Lord Hervey under the name 'Lord Fanny', alluding to his well-known effeminacy, and took a somewhat more virulent pot-shot at Lady Mary Wortley Montagu under what became her codename in his work, Sappho (the early Lesbian poetess). In suggesting that one might receive 'From furious *Sappho* scarce a milder Fate,/Pox'd by her Love, or libell'd by her Hate', Pope neatly encompasses two of the charges to which he had been giving a certain currency since about 1728: that Lady Mary was sexually promiscuous, and given to promoting scandalous accounts of himself and his friends. Quite what had turned Pope's earlier devotion into this sort of rancour is not certainly known: her personal hygiene, jealousy of other male friends, rejection of an inappropriate declaration of love from Pope, her hand in the circulation at court of attacks on him and his friends, her Whig allegiances – all these have been canvassed with greater or lesser cogency (Mack 1985: 553–8).

At any rate, vengeance was hers, in collaboration with Lord Hervey, in *Verses Address'd to the Imitator Of the First Satire of the Second Book of Horace. By a Lady* (9 March 1733), followed in November Hervey's own rather weaker *An Epistle from a Nobleman to a Doctor of Divinity.* The *Verses* constituted probably the most skilful attack on Pope ever published, turning satiric shafts from Pope's own poems against their author, and dismissing his work with aristocratic loftiness as mere vulgar abuse, fit product of a 'wretched little carcase' (Barnard 1973: 273–7). These two attacks, coming not from the usual Grub-Street hacks but from aristocrats of unassailable social position, wounded Pope deeply enough for him to compose 'A Letter to a Noble Lord', which remained in manuscript probably because Pope realised that his tone of dignified humility would invite further ridicule (*PW* II: 442–56). In the event Pope bided his time and reserved a more efficient and authoritative revenge in the *Epistle to Dr Arbuthnot* (1735) **[110–119]**.

Pope continued with another 'ethick epistle', the *Epistle to Cobham* (16 January 1734) **[93–6]**. Sir Richard Temple (1675–1749) had been created Viscount Cobham for his exploits in the wars against France and Spain; he was also colonel of the king's own regiment of cavalry. Though a diehard Whig and supporter of Walpole's regime, he had become friendly with Pope around 1725; his garden at Stowe became perhaps the most celebrated landscape garden of its time. Moreover, Cobham fell out with the administration in 1733: along with many others he opposed Walpole's plan for what Pope terms 'a general excise', an institutionalised internal customs service which would seek to garner duties on all kinds of goods within the country rather than at ports alone. The measure (which Walpole withdrew in the face of huge protest) was seen as a sinister attempt to institute a system of surveillance against the prized 'liberties' of the British subject. In May 1733, Walpole quashed further government enquiries into the frauds and embezzlements of the directors of the South Sea Company , and Cobham was one of those Lords who signed a written protest at this brazen shielding of corruption. He was summarily dismissed from his regiment in a similarly unabashed display of sheer power. Pope visited

Stowe soon after these events and drafted the Epistle that autumn. The celebration of Cobham's independence of mind (he was from now on an Opposition Whig, and his garden became a shrine to Opposition principles) is combined with a psychology of male character, developed from its earlier manifestation in Epistle II of *An Essay on Man* **[82–93]**. Progress on the *Essay* had been interrupted by the death of Pope's mother, whom he paid a public compliment in the fourth Epistle, published in January 1734. The longest of the epistles by some distance, and more miscellaneous in theme and character, it deals with 'happiness' and its manifestations under a wise and benign providence. The poem as a whole scored a European success and did much to secure Pope's reputation as England's most eminent poet.

Pope continued the series of Horatian imitations with the second satire of book II, addressed to a friend in Yorkshire, Hugh Bethel (4 July 1734), and offering a playful but dignified translation of Pope's internal exile as a form of paradisal moderation.

In that summer Pope 'rambled' from Twickenham to Bolingbroke's Dawley farm, then on to Chiswick, London, Rousham, Stowe, Cirencester, and Bevis Mount, where he spent six creative weeks touring, picnicking and writing. In September he went to Bath with Bolingbroke to meet Martha Blount, now established as his main female friend and companion. In December he published, anonymously, a new Horatian imitation: *Sober Advice From Horace* (or the second satire of Horace's Book 1), 'imitated in the Manner of Mr Pope'. Using Bentley's offensively-edited text of the poet for his source (which was displayed, according to his usual practice, on the opposite page to the 'version'), Pope selected one of the bawdiest and least ostensibly moral of all Horace's poems, imitated in fact in Pope's own best sad-dog manner of comic ruefulness about sexual matters, and tricked out with spoof 'Bentley' notes designed to mock the great editor's talent for showy but wrongheaded emendations.

Less comically, Pope was also working on the *Epistle to Dr Arbuthnot*, designed as a testimony to a long-standing friendship (it was published on 2 January 1735, eight weeks before Arbuthnot's death) **[110–9, 156]**. The *Epistle* gave Pope the opportunity to cement together various ideas, scenes and sketches, under the general category of a poet's complaint to a friend about the corruption of the current poetic scene and his victimisation within it. It is perhaps Pope's most complex self-portrait, as well as his most calculated battle-plan: the 'Sporus' portrait, stigmatizing Hervey's effeminacy as an offence against the balances of poetry itself, indicated just how much better Pope was than Hervey at slinging mud. A month later Pope released the *Epistle to a Lady* **[96–**

101, 171–182]. The unnamed 'lady' in question was Martha Blount, who stands in the poem as a model of female character within a poem which displays with humour and occasionally with vehemence the various pitfalls into which female character could be seen by male commentators to fall at this date in history.

(n) LETTERS

In April 1735 Pope published 'Volume II' of his *Works*, matching in format the 1717 volume and the Homer translations. Smaller editions for the less well-off followed. The *'magnum opus'* poems (*Essay on Man* and *Epistles to Several Persons*) stood alongside the Horatian satires and *The Dunciad* in giant array, with the addition of line numbers (this was a text to refer to accurately). In the next month, there appeared from Curll's shop two volumes of Pope's correspondence with early friends such as Garth, Wycherley, Walsh, Congreve, Steele, Addison and Gay among others. The elegance and wit for which Pope's poetry was celebrated was very much evident in his prose also, but that was mostly in ironic vein; his letters, of which he was justly proud, exhibit the same talents in the more positive sphere of personal friendship. Though the personal (or 'familiar') letter had become by this period more or less a recognised genre, connoting spontaneity, warmth, unstudied intimacy, it was still unheard of for anyone to publish their own correspondence. Letters of poets such as Rochester were published, but only after death, feeding and stimulating a public appetite for supposedly private detail.

Pope, however, with his by now habitual love of stratagem, elected to kill two birds with one stone. He had the letters printed in great secrecy over a period of years from 1729, and with tortuous and teasing manoeuvres, like an angler reeling in a particular slippery fish, dangled the printed sheets before the nose of Edmund Curll, who had openly advertised his interest in private *Popeiana* in the newspapers. Curll, who had added to his crimes by becoming a stooge for Walpole, eventually took the bait that was offered by a series of anonymous correspondents, and advertised the volumes. Pope got some aristocratic friends to have the edition impounded on the grounds that it suggested unauthorised publication of letters by members of the House of Lords – a ruse which failed, in fact, as the House could find nothing of the sort in the sheets they were shown, and freed Curll, who went his dauntless way, selling the volumes with miscellaneous padding thrown in and turning 'Pope's Head' into his bookshop sign. Nonetheless, Pope had succeeded in reminding parliament, which was then considering renewal of the Copyright Act, of the shameless incursions into authorial property practised by Curll and his kind, and he had established his rights over the large corpus of his own letters. And he had succeeded in getting into the public arena letters which showed less of the embarrassing rakishness of the collection which Curll had got hold of from Henry Cromwell's mistress and issued in 1726, and more of the wise, tender, warm friend that Pope felt himself to be. As the public satirist of his age, Pope needed the platform of private virtue to legitimate his position; after all the controversies and allegations, the letters showed a more affectionate and sensible character than anything that Dennis or Curll would willingly have admitted.

It was a publishing coup for Curll, but a propaganda success for Pope. The letters ran through 18 editions in 1735 alone, with reprints and piracies swelling the currency for the next few years. 'Pope's private correspondence thus promulgated filled the nation with praises of his candour, tenderness, and benevolence, the purity of his purposes, and the fidelity of his friendship' (Johnson 1905: 157). Broome, from whom Pope had become estranged over the *Odyssey* translation, wrote spontaneously to renew the friendship on reading the letters, and Ralph Allen, an admirer of Pope's talent who had doubted the goodness of his heart because of the 'asperity of his satirical pieces' was converted by the letters and soon became a close friend of the author. The letters 'exhibit a perpetual and unclouded effulgence of general benevolence and particular fondness. There is nothing but liberality, gratitude, constancy, and tenderness', opines Johnson, who however was characteristically sceptical of the theoretical 'naturalness' of these or any other letters and considered that Pope 'may be said to write always with his reputation in his head' (Johnson 1905: 160).

In May 1737 Pope brought out a magisterial and luxurious 'authorised' version of the letters, again in formats matching his literary output, justifying it with a long and very partial complaint against Curll. Most of his works contain very visible dedications to friends; the *Essay on Man* celebrates Bolingbroke, *The Dunciad* Swift, the epistles Cobham, Arbuthnot, and so on. Pope endeavoured to make such public statements of virtuous friendship continuous with actual private content in the letters. What no-one in the period except Pope knew was that he had treated the letters, recalled from friends over many years (he had endless trouble getting the most dangerous ones back from Swift), with a certain licence, as if they were indeed poems. He had revised and polished them, edited them, and in some cases spliced separate letters together and readdressed them. Letters supposedly to Addison and Congreve, it was discovered by Pope's nineteenth-century editors, were originally written to Caryll. This was done partly to replace correspondence now lost (Pope could not retrieve letters to Addison, who had died in 1719, or Congreve, who had died in 1729); but the Addison letters were also calculated to prove Pope's account of their quarrel. The sin of this fabrication now looks somewhat less cardinal than it did when first discovered, and Pope's actions need to be understood in the context of the virulent biography with which he was lumbered by the Dunces. Pope was at the same period becoming master of his image in art. There are few pictorial images of Pope taken without his consent, and a great many which he evidently authorised: terra cotta busts, oil paintings, medals and engravings, mostly omitting Pope's deformed stature below the shoulders and concentrating instead on Pope's expressive features, deployed in serious, contemplative mood, often with an unofficial laureation about the temples or an allusion to earlier poetic models (Wimsatt 1965).

(o) LAUREATE IN OPPOSITION

In 1737, when his authorised *Letters* were published, Pope resumed his Horace series with *Horace his Ode to Venus* (9 March), a charmingly self-mocking (and covertly self-celebrating) adieu to sexual pleasures. *The Second Epistle of the Second Book of Horace* came out in April, offering a comic catalogue of reasons for not writing alongside a pointed account of Pope's upbringing; and *The First Epistle of the Second Book of Horace* appeared on 25 May **[124–7]**. This latter poem, originally addressed to the Emperor Augustus in his role as benign patron, was now, with flagrant irony, addressed to the philistine George II. The Court was beginning to take serious notice of Pope's poetry of opposition and the Privy Council considered taking him into custody. Tension increased after the death of Queen Caroline, Walpole's protector, in November 1737, and many of the ensuing Horatian poems offer the Opposition, itself fragmented and disorganised, some cultural platform from which to act; Pope was sometimes celebrated as the alternative laureate in Opposition literature, and was equally abused in the government press for his friendship with Bolingbroke.

On 16 May and 18 July 1738 appeared the two dialogues later known as *Epilogue to the Satires* but originally published under the Orwellian title *One Thousand Seven Hundred and Thirty-Eight* **[127–9]**. Opposition hopes were high: Walpole was under pressure to abandon his pacific foreign policy and respond to Spanish incursions on British merchant fleets. In Dialogue I, a 'Friend' urges caution and restraint, pointing out that Horace's 'sly, polite, insinuating stile/Could please at Court, and make Augustus smile', whereas Pope had unwisely turned Horace into a figure wholly of opposition and criticism. Pope's response is to defend the role of the poet as effective social critic, holding 'in disdain' the corrupt ways of worldly management. The second dialogue, published after Walpole appeared to have survived a vote on the Spanish question, is more politically outrageous in its contempt for men of rank, citing 'the strong Antipathy of Good to Bad' as Pope's reason for writing – as if everything in the end were a sort of extreme moral couplet. Bolingbroke was staying with Pope when the poem was published; it was probably at this juncture that Pope's windows were broken, presumably by government thugs, an event Pope refers to with calculated nonchalance (Mack 1985: 714).

Pope ceased to write for a while (it is just possible he was pressurised by Walpole into suppressing a meditated third 'Dialogue': the fragmentary *1740. A Poem* suggests an even more embittered political exile) **[169]**. But controversy flared up in another quarter when a Swiss theologian, Jean-Pierre de Crousaz, accused Pope of heterodoxy in *The Essay on Man*, hitherto Pope's most unimpeachable work. Crousaz's *Examen* (1737), based on inadequate French-language versions, found Pope both self-contradictory and fatalistic; others in England took up the charge and began accusing Pope of falling under the sway of Bolingbroke's supposed 'Deism', a sort of minimal, ethical Christianity which dispensed with the need for priests and Divine Revelation in favour of a knowledge of God which one could infer from one's own reason. For once Pope did not have to enter the lists himself, for William Warburton (1689–1779), a Lincolnshire clergyman, began a long *Vindication* of the poem (1738–39), defending its theology as wholly orthodox in essence. Pope did not know that Warburton had once been an ally of Theobald and had attacked Pope with the worst of them (Mack 1985: 744), and he adopted this new friend with customary zeal: 'I know I meant just what you explain, but I did not explain my own meaning so well as you. You understand me as well as I do myself, but you express me better than I could express myself' (*Letters* IV:171–2). Pope introduced him to the generous Ralph Allen, whose daughter Warburton went on to marry: his clerical career advanced rapidly. Heavy-handed and pugnacious, Warburton was extremely learned in biblical and literary scholarship, and Pope called him 'the greatest general critic I ever knew' (Spence 1966: 217). In 1741 Pope refused an honorary doctorate offered by Oxford, the only overt qualification or honour he could ever have received, because the University had withdrawn a similar offer to Warburton.

Pope continued to enjoy summer rambles and winter stays with the Allens at Bath, feasted his friends, enjoyed company, gardened, revised his own work and work by Swift and Gay for publication, and collected mineralogical specimens for his grotto. Political interests remained: George Lyttleton, a nephew of Cobham, tried hard to engender intimacy between Pope and the tentative Opposition hero Frederick Prince of Wales (1707–51); it was uphill work, though Pope did give the Prince one of his dog Bounce's puppies (with a beautifully barbed epigram for the collar: *TE* VI: 372). Two of Pope's friends, David Mallet and James Thomson, wrote plays which fell foul of Walpole's censorship measure, the Licensing Act (1737); Pope showed support by turning up for the opening night of Thomson's *Agamemnon*, and his appearance, it is said, was greeted with a burst of applause. Later Garrick put on an especially pumped-up version of Richard III for Pope (Mack 1985: 760). His celebrity was indisputable; the painter Sir Joshua Reynolds, later a close friend of Johnson, records an occasion in 1742:

> Pope came in. Immediately it was mentioned he was there, a lane was made for him to walk through. Everyone in the front rows by a kind of enthusiastic impulse shook hands with him. Reynolds did like the rest and was very happy in having the opportunity.
>
> (Mack 1985: 761)

He praised new work by younger writers such as Samuel Johnson's Juvenalian imitation, *London* (1738), published shortly before his own *One Thousand Seven Hundred and Thirty-Eight*, and not dissimilar in spirit. For himself, he experimented with versions of the Psalms and with some moral odes, and for a time projected a non-ironic epic on the theme of Brutus, of which only the first eight-line sentence (identifying Pope as 'My Country's Poet, to record her Fame') survives. According to the plan of the work, *Brutus* would have been an English *Aeneid*, bringing Aeneas's grandson to British shores to found a commonwealth based on civic virtue. No doubt it would have appealed to the group of young Patriots, of whom Pope was the literary figurehead.

(p) ONE MIGHTY DUNCIAD

The publication of *The Memoirs of the Extraordinary Life, Works, and Discoveries of Martinus Scriblerus* in April 1741 was a last testimony to the collective work of the Scriblerus Club. Evidently Pope's work in this final form, the ridiculous and wrong-headed adventures of the polymath who lacks all common sense takes some very surreal turns, indicating a vein of grotesque fantasy which was about to find more characteristic form. Pope's final work was to be a darker version of this wayward mental life. On 20 March 1742 he published *The New Dunciad*, a sometimes obscure and bitter assault on the final death of culture (intellectual, poetic, artistic) under George II. The fall of Walpole, who on 11 February that year at last threw in the towel after twenty years of dominating British politics, and the generalness of the satire, which works on categories rather than individuals, perhaps saved it from the controversies which beset the earlier incarnations of the poem, though there was, as Pope expected, the usual rousing chorus (Guerinot 1969: 286–319). But new problems were engendered by a slighting reference to Colley Cibber, the actor who had been made Poet Laureate in 1730 (thus obligingly fulfilling Pope's prophetic account of the decay of culture in the *Dunciad* of 1728–29). As a stage-manager of unrestrainable self-confidence and cheek Cibber was sometimes used as a 'screen' to talk about Walpole in the Opposition press; in 1740 he published some charmingly brazen memoirs, *An Apology for the Life of Colley Cibber*, which included amongst its complacent self-praise the usual litany of Pope's crimes.

In *The New Dunciad*, Pope pictured Cibber sleeping on the lap of Dulness, a cameo which reminded Cibber of an incident which he had strangely let lie for over twenty years. According to his *A Letter from Mr. Cibber to Mr. Pope* (1742), Cibber, Pope and a certain lord were once taking tea in a brothel when one of the prostitutes, primed by the lord, took Pope into an adjoining room; after a while Cibber burst into the room, 'where I found this little hasty Hero, like a terrible *Tom Tit*, pertly perching upon the Mount of Love! But such was my Surprise that I fairly laid hold of his Heels, and actually drew him down safe and sound from his Danger' (Guerinot 1969: 293–4). Cibber makes very merry on the occasion, claiming to have saved the 'English Homer' from death by venereal disease, and a number of unusually explicit illustrations of the story were published (Guerinot 1969: 289; Mack 1985: 781).

Pope claimed privately that such things were his 'diversion' but his friends commented that he writhed with anguish while reading them (Johnson 1905: 188). Grievous as the insult was, and no doubt much elaborated, if true at all, Pope took his usual revenge, not by denying the story, but by expunging Theobald from his role as King of the Dunces, and installing Cibber instead, in *The Dunciad In Four Books*, finally revised and published in October 1743 **[130–49, 157–9, 166–7, 182–8, 189–98]**. The change is not altogether happy (no-one could accuse Cibber of having read too much, as – to Pope's mind – Theobald had), but the change is in keeping with the wider sense of apocalypse which haunts the poem. As a Hanoverian stooge, adapter of Shakespeare for the stage, and promoter of cheap theatrical sensations, Cibber exactly catches the mix of meretricious, stagey glamour and complacent cack-handedness which Pope saw as bringing final demise to British civilisation. The completed poem as it stands is a fitting culmination of Pope's career, incorporating work which had existed in some form all his writing life.

(q) THE END

Pope spent his last years cultivating his garden and his friendships. A mysterious 'Amica' (female friend) appears to have laid siege to him between 1737 and 1742, to the annoyance of Martha Blount, after falling in love with his work (Mack 1985: 796–801) **[171]**. His health worsened: he had some form of extreme asthma, his kidneys were failing, his body now had to be encased in a sort of iron frame to enable him to sit up (he made studied but genuine fun of this predicament). He employed students to read to him. And he continued to make extensive visits to friends, on one occasion marring somewhat his friendship with Ralph Allen over an incident in which Martha Blount seems to have been slighted. He continued to adjust the minutiae of his works with Warburton as designated editor. He made his will in December 1743, leaving his books and copyrights to Warburton – a bequest which Johnson estimated to be worth £4000 (Johnson 1905: 170) – and his manuscripts to Bolingbroke, neither of them as it turned out very happy bequests despite their value. Martha Blount was to receive the bulk of his money (Mack 1985: 768). He ordered that his body should be carried to the church at Twickenham as his mother's had been, by poor men of the parish. In January 1744 he declared, 'I *must* make a perfect edition of my works, and then I shall have nothing to do but die' (Spence 1966: 258). The doctors disagreed, to Pope's no doubt hard-won cheer: 'Here I am, dying of a hundred good symptoms' (Spence 1966: 263). In early May he sent advance copies of the so-called 'deathbed' edition of the four *Epistles to Several Persons*, with commentary by Warburton, announcing wryly, 'Here am I, like Socrates, distributing my morality among my friends, just as I am dying' (Spence 1966: 261). His mind began to wander; he had visions, hallucinations, lapses (though he never suffered the terrible dementia of Swift, who survived him by a year). He recovered enough to sit at table with his friends a few days before his death, to greet friends like Martha Blount, Lyttleton and Mallet, who came to take their leave as Pope had done when Arbuthnot was dying. He was carried into his garden, and he drove into Bushy Park the day before he died. Spence, Bolingbroke, and a few others, attended all the time; Nathaniel Hooke, a fellow Catholic, called a priest so that Pope, who never seems to have bothered much about the outward observances of the religion for which he suffered, could receive the sacrament: 'I do not think it essential, but it will be very right', he commented (Spence 1966: 268). Pope died on 30 May 1744, in the evening; Spence noted that 'his departure was so easy that it was imperceptible even to the standers-by' (Spence 1966: 269).

Further Reading

The best early biography is by Samuel Johnson (Johnson 1905), an attentive, appreciative account, written by a poet and critic whose early work overlapped with Pope's late poems; despite scepticism about Pope's higher motives, Johnson defended Pope against the gradual erosion of his poetic reputation. Anecdotal material from Pope's conversation is archived in Spence (1966). Among modern biographies, Sherburn (1934) gives a lively account of the pre-*Dunciad* years; Rosslyn (1990) offers an accessible and entertaining 'literary life', from a position of deep sympathy with Pope's work; and Berry (1988) gives the nuts and bolts of the life in calendar segments, giving us a rawer and less structured account of Pope's daily life. Ultimately, Mack (1985) stands as the rock of all biographical studies of Pope; though it has been criticised for being partisan and elegiac, it offers a wealth of authenticated detail unlikely ever to be seriously challenged.

PART II

WORK

(a) *AN ESSAY ON CRITICISM* (1711)
[*TE* I: 195–326]

The *Essay on Criticism* was Pope's first independent work, published anonymously through an obscure bookseller **[12–13]**. Its implicit claim to authority is not based on a lifetime's creative work or a prestigious commission but, riskily, on the skill and argument of the poem alone. It offers a sort of master-class not only in doing criticism but in *being* a critic: addressed to those – it could be anyone – who would rise above scandal, envy, politics and pride to true judgement, it leads the reader through a qualifying course. At the end, one does not become a professional critic – the association with hired writing would have been a contaminating one for Pope – but an educated judge of important critical matters.

Much of the poem is delivered as a series of instructions, but the opening is tentative, presenting a problem to be solved: "'Tis hard to say, if greater Want of Skill/Appear in *Writing* or in *Judging* ill' (*EC*, 1–2). The next six lines ring the changes on the differences to be weighed in deciding the question:

> But, of the two, less dang'rous is th' Offence,
> To tire our *Patience*, than mis-lead our *Sense*:
> Some few in *that*, but Numbers err in *this*,
> Ten Censure wrong for one who Writes amiss;
> A *Fool* might once *himself* alone expose,
> Now *One* in *Verse* makes many more in *Prose*.
> (*EC*, 3–8)

The simple opposition we began with develops into a more complex suggestion that more unqualified people are likely to set up for critic than for poet, and that such a proliferation is serious. Pope's typographically-emphasised oppositions between poetry and criticism, verse and prose, patience and sense, develop through the passage into a wider account of the problem than first proposed: the even-handed balance of the couplets extends beyond a simple contrast. Nonetheless, though Pope's oppositions divide, they also keep within a single framework different categories of writing: Pope often seems to be addressing poets as much as critics. The critical function may well depend on a poetic function: this is after all an essay on criticism delivered in verse, and thus acting also as poetry and offering itself *for* criticism. Its blurring of categories which might otherwise be seen as fundamentally distinct, and its often slippery transitions from area to area, are part of the poem's comprehensive, educative character.

Addison, who considered the poem 'a Master-piece', declared that its tone was conversational and its lack of order was not problematic: 'The Observations follow one another like those in *Horace's Art of Poetry*, without that Methodical Regularity which would have been requisite in a Prose Author' (Barnard 1973: 78). Pope, however, decided during the revision of the work for the 1736 *Works* to divide the poem into three sections, with numbered sub-sections summarizing each segment of argument. This impluse towards order is itself illustrative of tensions between creative and critical faculties, an apparent casualness of expression being given rigour by a prose skeleton. The three sections are not equally balanced, but offer something like the thesis, antithesis, and synthesis of logical argumentation – something which exceeds the positive-negative opposition suggested by the couplet format. The first section (1–200) establishes the basic possibilities for critical judgement; the second (201–559) elaborates the factors which hinder such judgement; and the third (560–744) celebrates the elements which make up true critical behaviour.

Part One seems to begin by setting poetic genius and critical taste against each other, while at the same time limiting the operation of teaching to those 'who have *written well*' (*EC*, 11–18). The poem immediately stakes an implicit claim for the poet to be included in the category of those who can 'write well' by providing a flamboyant example of poetic skill in the increasingly satiric portrayal of the process by which failed writers become critics: 'Each burns alike, who can, or cannot write,/Or with a *Rival's*, or an *Eunuch's* spite' (*EC*, 29–30). At the bottom of the heap are 'half-learn'd Witlings, num'rous in our Isle', pictured as insects in an early example of Pope's favourite image of teeming, writerly promiscuity (36–45). Pope then turns his attention back to the reader, conspicuously differentiated from this satiric extreme: '*you* who seek to *give* and *merit* Fame' (the combination of giving and meriting reputation again links criticism with creativity). The would-be critic, thus selected, is advised to criticise himself first of all, examining his limits and talents and keeping to the bounds of what he knows (46-67); this leads him to the most major of Pope's abstract quantities within the poem (and within his thought in general): Nature.

> First follow NATURE, and your Judgment frame
> By her just Standard, which is still the same:
> *Unerring Nature*, still divinely bright,

One *clear, unchang'd*, and *Universal* Light,
Life, Force, and Beauty, must to all impart,
At once the *Source*, and *End*, and *Test* of *Art*.
                                        (*EC*, 68–73)

Dennis complained that Pope should have specified 'what he means by Nature, and what it is to write or to judge according to Nature' (*TE* I: 219), and modern analyses have the burden of Romantic deifications of Nature to discard: Pope's Nature is certainly not some pantheistic, powerful nurturer, located outside social settings, as it would be for Wordsworth, though like the later poets Pope always characterises Nature as female, something to be quested for by male poets **[172]**. Nature would include all aspects of the created world, including the non-human, physical world, but the advice on following Nature immediately follows the advice to study one's own internal 'Nature', and thus means something like an instinctively-recognised principle of ordering, derived from the original, timeless, cosmic ordering of God (the language of the lines implicitly aligns Nature with God; those that follow explicitly align it with the soul). Art should be derived from Nature, should seek to replicate Nature, and can be tested against the unaltering standard of Nature, which thus includes Reason and Truth as reflections of the mind of the original poet-creator, God.

In a fallen universe, however, apprehension of Nature requires assistance: internal gifts alone do not suffice.

Some, to whom Heav'n in Wit has been profuse,
Want as much more, to turn it to its use;
For *Wit* and *Judgment* often are at strife,
Tho' meant each other's Aid, like *Man* and *Wife*.
                                        (*EC*, 80–03)

Wit, the second of Pope's abstract qualities, is here seamlessly conjoined with the discussion of Nature: for Pope, Wit means not merely quick verbal humour but something almost as important as Nature – a power of invention and perception not very different from what we would mean by intelligence or imagination. Early critics again seized on the first version of these lines (which Pope eventually altered to the reading given here) as evidence of Pope's inability to make proper distinctions: he seems to suggest that a supply of Wit sometimes needs more Wit to manage it, and then goes on to replace this conundrum with a more familiar opposition between Wit (invention) and Judgment (correction). But Pope stood by the essential point that Wit itself could be a form of Judgment and insisted that though the marriage between these qualities might be strained, no divorce was possible.

Nonetheless, some external prop to Wit was necessary, and Pope finds this in those 'RULES' of criticism derived from Nature:

> Those RULES of old *discover'd*, not *devis'd*,
> Are *Nature* still, but *Nature Methodiz'd*;
> *Nature*, like *Liberty*, is but restrain'd
> By the same Laws which first *herself* ordain'd.
>
> (*EC*, 88–91)

Nature, as Godlike principle of order, is 'discover'd' to operate according to certain principles stated in critical treatises such as Aristotle's *Poetics* or Horace's *Ars Poetica* (or Pope's *Essay on Criticism*). In the golden age of Greece (92–103), Criticism identified these Rules of Nature in early poetry and taught their use to aspiring poets. Pope contrasts this with the activities of critics in the modern world, where often criticism is actively hostile to poetry, or has become an end in itself (114–17). Right judgement must separate itself out from such blind alleys by reading Homer: '*You* then whose Judgment the right Course would steer' (*EC*, 118) can see yourself in the fable of 'young *Maro*' (Virgil), who is pictured discovering to his amazement the perfect original equivalence between Homer, Nature, and the Rules (130–40). Virgil the poet becomes a sort of critical commentary on the original source poet of Western literature, Homer. With assurance bordering consciously on hyperbole, Pope can instruct us: 'Learn hence for Ancient *Rules* a just Esteem;/To copy *Nature* is to copy *Them*' (*EC*, 139–40).

Despite the potential for neat conclusion here, Pope has a rider to offer, and again it is one which could be addressed to poet or critic: 'Some Beauties yet, no Precepts can declare,/For there's a *Happiness* as well as *Care*' (*EC*, 141–2). As well as the prescriptions of Aristotelian poetics, Pope draws on the ancient treatise ascribed to Longinus and known as *On the Sublime* **[12]**. Celebrating imaginative 'flights' rather than representation of nature, Longinus figures in Pope's poem as a sort of paradox:

> Great Wits sometimes may *gloriously offend*,
> And *rise* to *Faults* true Criticks *dare not mend*;
> From *vulgar Bounds* with *brave Disorder* part,
> And *snatch a Grace* beyond the Reach of Art,
> Which, without passing thro' the *Judgment*, gains
> The *Heart*, and all its End *at once* attains.
>
> (*EC*, 152–7)

This occasional imaginative rapture, not predictable by rule, is an important concession, emphasised by careful typographic signalling of its paradoxical nature (*'gloriously offend'*, and so on); but it is itself countered by the caution that 'The Critick' may 'put his Laws in force' if such licence is unjustifiably used. Pope here seems to align the 'you' in the audience with poet rather than critic, and in the final lines of the first section it is the classical *'Bards Triumphant'* who remain unassailably immortal, leaving Pope to pray for 'some Spark of *your* Coelestial Fire' (*EC*, 195) to inspire his own efforts (as 'The last, the meanest of your Sons', *EC*, 196) to instruct criticism *through* poetry.

Following this ringing prayer for the possibility of reestablishing a critical art based on poetry, Part II (200-559) elaborates all the human psychological causes which inhibit such a project: pride, envy, sectarianism, a love of some favourite device at the expense of overall design. The ideal critic will reflect the creative mind, and will seek to understand the whole work rather than concentrate on minute infractions of critical laws:

> A perfect Judge will *read* each Work of Wit
> With the same Spirit that its Author *writ*,
> Survey the *Whole*, nor seek slight Faults to find,
> Where *Nature moves*, and *Rapture warms* the Mind;
> (*EC*, 233–6)

Most critics (and poets) err by having a fatal predisposition towards some partial aspect of poetry: ornament, conceit, style, or metre, which they use as an inflexible test of far more subtle creations. Pope aims for a kind of poetry which is recognisable and accessible in its entirety:

> *True Wit* is *Nature* to Advantage drest,
> What oft was *Thought*, but ne'er so well *Exprest*,
> *Something*, whose Truth convinc'd at Sight we find,
> That gives us back the Image of our Mind:
> (*EC*, 296–300)

This is not to say that style alone will do, as Pope immediately makes plain (305–6): the music of poetry, the ornament of its 'numbers' or rhythm, is only worth having because 'The *Sound* must seem an *Eccho* to the *Sense*' (*EC*, 365). Pope performs and illustrates a series of poetic clichés – the use of open vowels, monosyllabic lines, and cheap rhymes:

> Tho' oft the Ear the *open Vowels* tire ... (*EC*, 345)

And ten low Words oft creep in one dull Line ... (*EC*, 347)
Where-e'er you find *the cooling Western Breeze*,
In the next Line, it *whispers thro' the Trees*... (*EC*, 350–1)

These gaffes are contrasted with more positive kinds of imitative effect:

Soft is the Strain when *Zephyr* gently blows,
And the *smooth Stream* in *smoother Numbers* flows;
But when loud Surges lash the sounding Shore,
The *hoarse, rough Verse* shou'd like the *Torrent* roar.
(*EC*, 366–9)

Again, this functions both as poetic instance and as critical test, working examples for both classes of writer.

After a long series of satiric vignettes of false critics, who merely parrot the popular opinion, or change their minds all the time, or flatter aristocratic versifiers, or criticise poets rather than poetry (384-473), Pope again switches attention to educated readers, encouraging (or cajoling) them towards staunchly independent and generous judgment within what is described as an increasingly fraught cultural context, threatened with decay and critical warfare (474–525). But, acknowledging that even 'Noble minds' will have some 'Dregs ... of Spleen and sow'r Disdain' (*EC*, 526–7), Pope advises the critic to 'Discharge that Rage on more Provoking Crimes,/Nor fear a Dearth in these Flagitious Times' (*EC*, 528–9): obscenity and blasphemy are unpardonable and offer a kind of lightning conductor for critics to purify their own wit against some demonised object of scorn.

If the first parts of *An Essay on Criticism* outline a positive classical past and troubled modern present, Part III seeks some sort of resolved position whereby the virtues of one age can be maintained during the squabbles of the other. The opening seeks to instill the correct *behaviour* in the critic – not merely rules for written criticism, but, so to speak, for enacted criticism, a sort of '*Good Breeding*' (*EC*, 576) which politely enforces without seeming to enforce:

LEARN then what MORALS Criticks ought to show,
For 'tis but *half* a *Judge's Task*, to *Know*.
'Tis not enough, Taste, Judgment, Learning, join;
In all you speak, let Truth and Candor shine ...
Be *silent* always when you *doubt* your Sense;
And *speak*, tho' *sure*, with *seeming Diffidence* ...

Men must be *taught* as if you taught them *not*;
And Things *unknown* propos'd as Things *forgot*:
(*EC*, 560–3, 566–7, 574–5)

This ideally-poised man of social grace cannot be universally successful: some poets, as some critics, are incorrigible and it is part of Pope's
education of the poet-critic to leave them well alone. Synthesis, if that
is being offered in this final part, does not consist of gathering all writers
into one tidy fold but in a careful discrimination of true wit from
irredeemable 'dulness' (584–630).

Thereafter, Pope has two things to say. One is to set a challenge to
contemporary culture by asking 'where's the Man' who can unite all
necessary humane and intellectual qualifications for the critic (*EC*, 631–
42), and be a sort of walking oxymoron, 'Modestly bold, and humanly
severe' in his judgements. The other is to insinuate an answer. Pope
offers deft characterisations of critics from Aristotle to Pope who
achieve the necessary independence from extreme positions: Aristotle's
primary treatise is likened to an imaginative voyage into the land of
Homer which becomes the source of legislative power; Horace is the
poetic model for friendly conversational advice; Quintilian is a useful
store of 'the justest *Rules*, and clearest *Method* join'd'; Longinus is
inspired by the Muses, who 'bless *their Critick* with a *Poet's Fire*' (*EC*,
676). These pairs include and encapsulate all the precepts recommended
in the body of the poem. But the empire of good sense, Pope reminds
us, fell apart after the fall of Rome, leaving nothing but monkish superstition, until the scholar Erasmus, always Pope's model of an ecumenical
humanist, reformed continental scholarship (693-696). Renaissance
Italy shows a revival of arts, including criticism; France, 'a Nation born
to serve' (*EC*, 713) fossilised critical and poetic practice into unbending
rules; Britain, on the other hand, '*Foreign Laws* despis'd,/And kept
unconquer'd, and *unciviliz'd*' (*EC*, 715–16) – a deftly ironic modulation
of what appears to be a patriotic celebration into something more
muted. Pope does however cite two earlier verse essays (by John
Sheffield, Duke of Buckinghamshire, and Wentworth Dillon, Earl of
Roscommon) **[13]** before paying tribute to his own early critical
mentor, William Walsh, who had died in 1708 **[9]**. Sheffield and Dillon
were both poets who wrote criticism in verse, but Walsh was not a
poet; in becoming the nearest modern embodiment of the ideal critic,
his 'poetic' aspect becomes Pope himself, depicted as a mixture of
moderated qualities which reminds us of the earlier 'Where's the man'
passage: he is quite possibly here,

Careless of *Censure*, nor too fond of *Fame*,
Still pleas'd to *praise*, yet not afraid to *blame*,
Averse alike to *Flatter*, or *Offend*,
Not *free* from Faults, nor yet too vain to *mend*.
                                        (*EC*, 741–44)

It is a kind of leading from the front, or tuition by example, as recommended and practised by the poem. From an apparently secondary, even negative, position (writing on criticism, which the poem sees as secondary to poetry), the poem ends up founding criticism on poetry, and deriving poetry from the (ideal) critic.

Early criticism celebrated the way the poem seemed to master and exemplify its own stated ideals, just as Pope had said of Longinus that he '*Is himself* that great *Sublime* he draws' (*EC*, 680). It is a poem profuse with images, comparisons and similes. Johnson thought the longest example, that simile comparing student's progress in learning with a traveller's journey in Alps was 'perhaps the best that English poetry can shew': 'The simile of the Alps has no useless parts, yet affords a striking picture by itself: it makes the foregoing position better understood, and enables it to take faster hold on the attention; it assists the apprehension, and elevates the fancy' (Johnson 1905: 229–30). Many of the abstract precepts are made visible in this way: private judgment is like one's reliance on one's (slightly unreliable) watch (9–10); wit and judgment are like man and wife (82–3); critics are like pharmacists trying to be doctors (108–11). Much of the imagery is military or political, indicating something of the social role (as legislator in the universal empire of poetry) the critic is expected to adopt; we are also reminded of the decay of empires, and the potential decay of cultures (there is something of *The Dunciad* in the poem). Much of it is religious, as with the most famous phrases from the poem ('For Fools rush in where angels fear to tread'; 'To err is human, to forgive, divine'), indicating the level of seriousness which Pope accords the matter of poetry. Much of it is sexual: creativity is a kind of manliness, wooing Nature, or the Muse, to 'generate' poetic issue, and false criticism, like obscenity, derives from a kind of inner 'impotence'. Patterns of such imagery can be harnessed to 'organic' readings of the poem's wholeness. But part of the life of the poem, underlying its surface statements and metaphors, is its continual shifts of focus, its reminders of that which lies outside the tidying power of couplets, its continual reinvention of the 'you' opposed to the 'they' of false criticism, its progressive displacement of the opposition you thought you were looking at with another one which requires your attention.

Further Reading

Johnson thought the poem perhaps Pope's greatest work: 'it exhibits every mode of excellence that can embellish or dignify didactick composition, selection of matter, novelty of arrangement, justness of precept, splendour of illustration, and propriety of digression' (Johnson 1905: 228–9). It has been less popular in modern times, but Empson (1950) gives an exhilarating display of the ramifications of the word 'Wit' in the poem. For a reading of the poem's strategies of imagery and metaphor see Spacks (1971: 17–40). Morris (1984) champions the poem's serious and intelligent commitment to the practice of literary criticism. Savage (1988) delves deeply into the poem's mythological and classical roots to discuss the far-reaching significance of Pope's use of 'Nature'.

(b) *WINDSOR-FOREST* (1713)
[*TE* I:145–94]

The hyphenation of Pope's title reminds us that the poem unites two objects of attention: a town overlooked by an ancient royal castle, and a wooded area originally set out for royal use, but also available for solitary reflection on natural beauty: Pope will celebrate 'Thy Forests, *Windsor*! and thy green Retreats,/At once the Monarch's and the Muse's Seats' (*WF*, 1–2), explicitly linking poetry and politics. The poem was written over a long period, and does not propose a single location for its viewpoint; in this it is unlike Sir John Denham's *Cooper's Hill* (several versions between 1642 and 1668), the poem with which Pope's is most often compared. Denham's more limited topographic or 'prospect' poem uses its natural eminence as prompt for reflections on national issues, in a manner which Pope is certainly aware of; but Pope's is a more comprehensive and complex attempt to provide a vision of England, past, present and future, from the starting point of a well-known area. Thus the poem starts in Windsor Forest, but ends up voyaging down the Thames to London, and out to the world of commerce and empire; Denham's poem retreats in the opposite direction, moving from an aerial view of the City, which Denham (a Royalist) finds politically offensive, to the solitary views afforded by the hill of the title, overlooking the plain of Runnymede where Magna Carta was signed. Pope, writing at the other end of the civil upheaval which prompts Denham's reflections, has similar sympathies but (in 1713 at least) slightly more to celebrate **[14–15]**.

The poem cannot take the landscape for granted: it has work to do. 'The Groves of *Eden*, vanish'd now so long,/Live in Description, and look green in Song', Pope announces (*WF*, 7–8), and to rebuild a lost paradise is a very self-conscious poetic act of vision:

> Here Hills and Vales, the Woodland and the Plain,
> Here Earth and Water seem to strive again,
> Not *Chaos*-like together crush'd and bruis'd,
> But as the World, harmoniously confus'd:
> Where Order in Variety we see,
> And where, tho' all things differ, all agree.
>
> (*WF*, 11–16)

This aesthetic principle, known as *concordia discors* or 'concord in discord', by which the sum total of opposing elements produces a pleasing jigsaw-like harmony ('Order in Variety'), is a clear signal of the type of poem this is to be: the couplet, sometimes doubled into a quatrain, can be the perfect medium for the harmonious matching and balancing of discordant essences, and in this initial scene elements which might be 'together crush'd and bruis'd' are seamlessly paired off into appropriate couples: Hills, Vales; Woodland, Plain; Earth, Water. Using a pair of adverbs of direction ('Here ... There') to guide us round the 'chequer'd Scene' (*WF*, 17), Pope highlights those aspects which make up its balanced, static quality. It is something like conjuring, as if the landscape emerges into view as Pope points to it (as it does, of course, in the actual reading of the poem):

> There, interspers'd in Lawns and opening Glades,
> Thin Trees arise that shun each others Shades.
> Here in full Light the russet Plains extend;
> There wrapt in Clouds the blueish Hills ascend:
> Ev'n the wild Heath displays her Purple Dies,
> And 'midst the Desert fruitful Fields arise,
> That crown'd with tufted Trees and springing Corn,
> Like verdant Isles the sable Waste adorn.
>
> (*WF*, 21–8)

The landscape isn't just there, it is doing something: extending, ascending, displaying, arising, springing, adorning, all at the touch of the poet-observer. The magic extends into coloration: the vision is colourful, but not in any sense which might be described as natural. It is a form of extreme colour, purified, as if each element can only have one colour and that colour must be significant: not just green and black but 'verdant' and 'sable'.

The landscape is being made mythological: Pope celebrates this English landscape as a reclaimed version not only of Eden but of classical mythology: 'See *Pan* with Flocks, with Fruits *Pomona* crown'd,/Here blushing *Flora* paints th'enamel'd Ground' (*WF*, 37–8). All this means, literally, is that herds of sheep, orchards of fruit, and fields of flowers can be seen in the landscape. But Pope insists on the painted and ceremonial quality of his representation, enthroning the classical gods in Windsor Forest, enamelling the ground for Flora (goddess of vegetation) to 'paint'. It is a golden age, almost literally, and the reason is the transforming and magical presence of the last legally sanctioned member of the Stuart line, Queen Anne: 'Rich Industry sits smiling on the Plains,/ And Peace and Plenty tell, a STUART reigns' (*WF*, 41–2). The baroque orchestration of the scene has been leading up to this eulogy: to invest Windsor Forest with colours more usually associated with coats of arms in heraldry (as Pope does throughout the poem), and to discover in the landscape the presence of mythological figures, shows a momentary commitment to a mode of panegyric which Pope would abandon immediately at the Hanoverian accession. The reign of Anne is celebrated here as the flower of the Stuart line, that succession of monarchs whose magical and quasi-religious claims she resumed in her own reign.

Johnson, who celebrated Pope's 'variety and elegance, and the art of interchanging description, narrative, and morality', thought that the apparent 'want of plan' in the poem was natural: since 'the scenes, which they must exhibit successively, are all subsisting at the same time, the order in which they are shewn must by necessity be arbitrary' (Johnson 1905: 225). But the poem is not really driven by a succession of descriptive scenes: its contrasts are as much about time as space. After establishing an Edenic Windsor, Pope immediately plunges into extreme historical contrast: 'Not thus the Land appear'd in Ages past,/ A dreary Desart and a gloomy Waste', Pope writes (*WF*, 43–4), picking up his own earlier lines, "midst the Desart fruitfull Fields arise' and 'Like verdant Isles the sable Waste adorn' to enforce the catastrophic nature of the contrast. Lines 43–84 (numerically matching the paradisal opening, 1–42) detail the terrible 'appearance' of the landscape under invader kings, William the Conqueror and his son, William Rufus. These were kings who followed Nature only in the sense of hunting it to death (though in the New Forest, not Windsor, which escapes contamination). Pope makes the love of hunting take the form of a tyrannical abuse of human law whereby game animals were more valuable than human subjects – the New Forest was:

To Savage Beasts and Savage Laws a Prey,
And Kings more furious and severe than they:
Who claim'd the Skies, dispeopled Air and Floods,
The lonely Lords of empty Wilds and Woods.

(*WF*, 45–8)

Whereas Anne only figures, without being named, as the concealed
magical goddess who inspires fruitful labour, in this section the tyrants
who have created forest laws to protect their own realm of savage
play are everywhere, despoiling churches, ruinating cities, incriminating
subjects. Pope sees the deaths of William Rufus and another of William's
sons in hunting accidents as providential revenge for the tyrannic
oppression of indigneous subjects (*WF*, 79–84), though this also leaves
the passage open to being read as a criticism of William III, Anne's
predecessor in 'Ages past' and another foreign ruler of Britain whose
death was hastened by a fall while hunting **[166]**.

The section which follows sees a restoration of British political
liberties in concert with a restored fruitfulness of landscape, imprecisely
placed somewhere among 'Succeeding Monarchs' (*WF*, 85–92). When
these principles are agreed, it then becomes possible for hunting to
take its place among the proper uses of the forest landscape: Anne
herself was a notable hunter, and Pope, personally more sympathetic
to animals than most of his contemporaries, has to absorb the fact
that the Forest was a Royal hunting preserve by invoking a utility and
propriety to the scene: 'Vig'rous Swains' can hunt appropriately enough
(93–6), channelling the energy of youth into activities which might
have more aggressive implications – as is indicated by Pope's comparison
of the capture of partridges with the capture of a foreign town (107–
10). The pheasant which is shot in the immediately succeeding lines
reinforces this sense, for though the bird appears gloriously and richly
part of the stained-glass 'nature' of the first section, it is also vulnerable
to the violence of the second:

See! from the Brake the whirring Pheasant springs,
And mounts exulting on triumphant Wings;
Short is his Joy! he feels the fiery Wound,
Flutters in Blood, and panting beats the Ground.
Ah! what avail his glossie, varying Dyes,
His Purple Crest, and Scarlet-circled Eyes,
The vivid Green his shining Plumes unfold;
His painted Wings, and Breast that flames with Gold?

(*WF*, 111–18)

Still more given over to pathos are the Larks shot alongside lapwings and woodcocks: 'Oft, Oft as the mounting Larks their Notes prepare,/ They fall, and leave their little Lives in Air' (*WF*, 133–4). The best we have is the precarious power of the order of the seasons, which underlies and modulates the kinds of 'pleasing Toils' hunting affords (in Autumn, beagling, in Winter, shooting, in Spring, fishing, in Summer, hunting on horseback) against the possibility of excess, of return to Norman tyranny ('slaught'ring Guns', *WF*, 125, 'Leaden Death', *WF*, 132, 'Sylvan War', *WF*, 148). Pope's preference is clearly for a quieter kind of catch, that nature which offers itself to be 'painted' by art into unbroken surfaces:

Our plenteous Streams a various Race supply;
The bright-ey'd Perch with Fins of *Tyrian* Dye,
The silver Eel, in shining Volumes roll'd,
The yellow Carp, in Scales bedrop'd with Gold,
Swift Trouts, diversify'd with Crimson Stains,
And Pykes, the Tyrants of the watry Plains.
(*WF*, 141–6)

Like the pheasant, the fish are painted with an almost metallic sense of pure colour which submerges the emblematic catalogue of characteristics (political or natural) into a peaceful assemblage viewed through the tranquilizing mirror of water (or art).

The Lodona episode (171–218) alternatively transforms hunting through mythology. In the hunting section, summer energies of the 'Sylvan War' (hunt), with their faint sexual connotations are offset by the controlling presence of Anne, again unnamed, but likened to Diana, goddess of hunting *and* chastity. The story that follows describes the sexual pursuit of the chaste nymph Lodona by the savage god Pan (here quite removed from his pastoral and ceremonial role in line 37). At, or possibly before, the moment of rape, Lodona is metamorphosed in Ovidian manner into the River Loddon (a small river which flows into the Thames near Pope's then home, Binfield). Pope thus arranges a poetic exit for the pursued victim of sexual violence, not exactly into nature, but into that preserving, transforming gloss of surface which marks the visual colorations of the poem. What you see in the stream that Lodona has become is nature still, but nature surreally inverted into a chaste, emblematic picture:

Oft in her Glass the musing Shepherd spies
The headlong Mountains and the downward Skies,

The watry Landskip of the pendant Woods,
And absent Trees that tremble in the Floods;
In the clear azure Gleam the Flocks are seen,
And floating Forests paint the Waves with Green.

(WF, 211–16)

The poem (thus purified) 'flows' with Lodona/Loddon into praise of Father Thames, a Neptune-like figure beyond the reach of such passions (though Pope includes a vignette of the notoriously promiscuous Jove, 233–4). The poem retreats from passion and violence into an artistically-ordered inner world: we are at the centre of the poem when Pope chooses to celebrate rural retirement.

To retire from life at court is to 'follow Nature' (WF, 252), studying, exercising, watching the seasons, observing the cosmos. Such retirement is explicitly figured as poetic, designed for the man 'Whom Nature charms, and whom the Muse inspires' (WF, 238). Such a man, in fact, as Pope, who places his self-inscription in the poem at this point with an invocation of the Muses, female figures for whom desire may be safely expressed: 'Ye sacred Nine! that all my Soul possess,/Whose Raptures fire me, and whose Visions bless' (WF, 259–60). The landscape becomes a visionary home for 'God-like Poets' associated with Windsor such as Denham, Cowley, and Henry Howard, Earl of Surrey. Yet these poets cannot be simply associated with retreat, for Denham was active in the civil war and Surrey was a soldier: 'Matchless his Pen, victorious was his Lance' (WF, 293). And Pope does not claim for himself a line of succession from these poets: instead he claims this union of retirement and activity, poetry and politics, for George Granville, Lord Lansdowne, the dedicatee of the poem. The reason for ceding this task to Granville, who did combine the tasks of politician and poet, is that Pope is building up here to a celebration of the Treaty of Utrecht, which Granville had been involved in negotiating, and which was about to be signed, bringing an end to the War of Spanish Succession [14–15]. From 283 to 328 Pope artfully suggests, while partially executing it, the poem that Granville should write: a celebration of the martial conquests of Edward III, and a somewhat dense subsequent history, which would demonstrate Lansdowne's supposed ability to 'call the Muses to their ancient Seats' and 'Make *Windsor* Hills in lofty Numbers rise' (WF, 284, 287).

This would be a magical form of utterance. When Anne is actually named for the first time she acts as a sort of redemptive divinity, putting an end to a crisis which seems to be as much internal (the civil war giving rise to ongoing Whig-Tory strife) as external (the battle with

France): 'At length great *ANNA* said – Let Discord cease!/She said, the World obey'd, and all was *Peace!*' (*WF*, 327–8). The peace which the politician-poet Granville has been instrumental in negotiating is not just an end to the European war, in this mythology, but the composition of all strife everywhere. The celebration of the peace announced by Anna is voiced by another mythological figure, Father Thames. Highly coloured in the poem's baroque manner (azure, verdant, golden), Thames and his attendant tributaries look like an allegorical painting in a baroque palace. Pope fuses this heraldic throwback to the days of Stuart power with a more modern view of prosperity, commerce, and imperial power. Arriving from Windsor Forest, along the river, at the united cities of London and Westminster (375–80), where 'Kings shall sue, and suppliant States be seen/Once more to bend before a *British* QUEEN' (*WF*, 383–4), we find the power deriving from Windsor's monarchic source issuing from the port of London to control the world, with the trees of the forest, representing the British navy, launching out on voyages of commerce and exploration (385–92). *Pax Britannica* is seen to guarantee universal freedom, mutual commerce, an interesting interchange between primitive and civilised races, a world where 'Seas but join the Regions they divide' (*WF*, 400), indicated in the movements of the poem outward from Thames and inward to it ('Earth's distant Ends our Glory shall behold,/And the new World launch forth to seek the Old', *WF*, 401–2).

Pope seems however to have laced the celebratory mode of panegyric which he projects onto Landsdowne and Anne with points which inhibit full triumphalist assent. Thames tells us, for example, that 'The shady Empire shall retain no Trace/Of War or Blood, but in the Sylvan Chace' (*WF*, 371–2), that is, in hunting; but we have already seen how easily hunting shades into the excess of tyranny and rapacity. When Thames envisages the trade which will accrue to London from the Treaty, he uses a common enough figure whereby labour is completely removed from view, and nature itself seems to supply the goods (the trees which willingly 'rush' to become ships are doing the same thing, *WF*, 385–6):

> For me the Balm shall bleed, and Amber flow,
> The Coral redden, and the Ruby glow,
> The Pearly Shell its lucid Globe infold,
> And *Phoebus* warm the ripening Ore to Gold.
> (*WF*, 393–6)

In some ways, nature merely offers up its bright, warm, glamorous minerals; but a hint of violence left encoded in 'the Balm shall bleed', which has very nearly a sacrificial resonance ('The Corall redden' might have the same suggestion). Pope could have ended his vision of a glorious future with images of golden restoration: '*Peru* once more a Race of Kings behold,/And other *Mexico's* be roof'd with Gold' (*WF*, 411–12). Instead, Thames concludes his prophecy in 'deepest Hell', where various allegorical forces of disorder (*Discord, Pride, Terror*, and so on) have been exiled by 'Peace'. It is not quite comforting to have this array of tortured emotion displayed as the condition of universal peace: 'gasping Furies thirst for Blood in vain' (*WF*, 422).

As if to acknowledge this faint discrepancy, Pope turns his poem away from the celebration voiced by Thames, suggesting that Granville should be the poet to recite 'The Thoughts of Gods', while Pope himself should stay back in Windsor Forest, at the level of the *Pastorals* of 1709: 'Enough for me, that to the list'ning Swains,/First in these Fields I sung the Sylvan Strains' (*WF*, 433–4). This shying away from the role of public herald, with the continual deference to the man of public action, Granville, and the voicing of power through Thames and Anna, suggests that the poem is not quite so perfectly aligned with the Tory view of history as it is often thought to be.

Further Reading

Wasserman (1959), a complex reading of the poem in relation to Denham's *Cooper's Hill* and the concept of *concordia discors*, is the place to start. Rogers (1973a) analyses the poem's use of colour in heraldic and potentially political terms, while his later article (1979) explores the poem's alternating attentions to the dimensions of time and space. Caretta (1981) examines the poem's idea of history. Morris (1984) reads the poem in relation to Virgil and finds much ambiguity in Pope's description of military success, while Brown (1985) gives a more hostile account of the poem's political compromises; Brooks-Davies (1988) decodes the poem's magical political transformations to see it as a 'Jacobite Georgic ... that enshrines political failure at its heart' (142).

(c) *THE RAPE OF THE LOCK* (1712/1714/1717) [*TE* II: 79–212]

Pope's first 'heroi-comical poem' coupled together heroic language and contemporary life, producing a medium appropriate for a poet who was engaging in a massive epic translation but whose temperament was satiric. Originally designed as a palliative in a family quarrel **[14]**, it was itself expanded from the miniature squib of 1712 into a five-canto version complete with a race of mythological beings to act in parody of the epic 'machinery' of divine action **[17]**; in the later version (used here), contrasts of perspective, the conflation of big and little, high and low, animate and inanimate, offer Pope a fertile field both for imaginative play and for explorations of the strangeness of mental and emotional life. The poem poses explicit questions, but its answers are more diffuse.

> Say what strange Motive, Goddess! cou'd compel
> A well-bred *Lord* t'assault a gentle *Belle*?
> Oh say what stranger Cause, yet unexplor'd,
> Cou'd make a gentle *Belle* reject a *Lord*?
> In Tasks so bold, can Little Men engage,
> And in soft Bosoms dwells such mighty Rage?
> (*RL*, I: 7–12)

In his opening invocation, Pope has already identified 'am'rous Causes' as the stimulant to the Baron's 'dire Offence' (*RL*, I: 1); but the poem goes on to suggest more complicated manoeuvrings between 'mighty Contests' and 'trivial Things' (*RL*, I: 2).

Belinda is a little 'Belle', or fashionable beauty, celebrated in conventional language ('those Eyes that must eclipse the Day', *RL*, I: 14), but dozing her way through the morning, absolutely without responsibility or occupation. Her attempts at action are curious: we may take 'Thrice rung the Bell the Slipper knock'd the Ground,/And the press'd Watch return'd a silver Sound' (*RL*, I: 17–18) to indicate that she rings for her maid, knocks on the floor for attention, then checks the time, but her agency is nowhere specified and the objects appear to perform the actions themselves. Belinda is, in any case, put back to sleep again by her 'Guardian *Sylph*', Ariel, who puts into her head (in a parody of epic and biblical dreams) an attractive male figure to warn her of some impending disaster (I: 27–114). The long speech grafts onto Belinda's childhood imaginings ('Of airy Elves by Moonlight Shadows seen', *RL*, I: 31) a new mythology, which also serves to provide the reader with the necessary background: what Belinda takes to be her own autonomous activity in life is actually a contrivance of her miniature attendants, the 'light *Militia* of the lower Sky' (*RL*, I: 42). Female vanities, Ariel explains, continue after death, and the four main types of female characters return to elemental identities: Prudes become Gnomes, Termagants turn into Salamanders, 'Soft yielding Minds' become Nymphs, and Coquettes ('Whoever fair and chaste/Rejects Mankind', *RL*, I: 67–8) become Sylphs. Ariel has identified Belinda as a woman of this last kind, and seeks to protect her chastity against temptation: though '*Honour* is the Word with Men below' (*RL*, I: 78), all that really prevents the coquette from 'warm Desires' (*RL*, I: 75) is the guardian Sylph. Mental life is envisaged as a near-arbitrary play of forces; the Sylphs contrive to balance out desires so that no one male seems more attractive than another:

> With varying Vanities, from ev'ry Part,
> They shift the moving Toyshop of their Heart;
> Where Wigs with Wigs, with Sword-knots Sword-knots strive,
> Beaus banish Beaus, and Coaches Coaches drive.
> (*RL*, I: 99–102)

Men become a succession of metonymic objects, a series of external stimulants which substitute for desire in a heart which is itself no more than a catalogue of toys.

Exterior protection is forthcoming in the description of the 'Toilet' or dressing-table. A flamboyant parody both of epic scenes in which heroes are armed for battle, and descriptions of ritual sacrifice, the passage (I: 121–48) suggests how for Belinda, the entire world is turned into an available commodity, and how she turns herself (with the invisible aid of the Sylphs) into an object of desire.

> A heav'nly Image in the Glass appears,
> To that she bends, to that her Eyes she rears;
> Th'inferior Priestess, at her Altar's side,
> Trembling, begins the sacred Rites of Pride.
> Unnumber'd Treasures ope at once, and here
> The various Off'rings of the World appear;
> From each she nicely culls with curious Toil,
> And decks the Goddess with the glitt'ring Spoil.
> This Casket *India*'s glowing Gems unlocks,

And all *Arabia* breathes from yonder Box.
The Tortoise here and Elephant unite,
Transform'd to *Combs*, the speckled and the white.
Here Files of Pins extend their shining Rows,
Puffs, Powders, Patches, Bibles, Billet-doux.

(RL, I:125–38)

As 'awful Beauty puts on all its Arms' Belinda is close to blasphemy – through her self-devotion (with its reminiscences of Milton's Eve) and her casual arrangement of bibles among similarly plural objects of merely cosmetic or amatory importance (I: 138). But more significantly, Belinda can be accused of making herself up to look like the 'Image in the Glass', a material object for visual consumption. The epic powers of the 'cosmos' are reduced to '*Cosmetic* Powr's' (I: 124), or make-up; the world is distilled into miniatures on Belinda's dressing table: 'all *Arabia* breathes' from Belinda's perfume-box, the whole of India is apparently represented by what is in her jewellery box. Tortoise and elephant (mythological actors in a Hindu myth of creation) comically 'unite' into ivory and shell combs in what might appear an extreme perversion of the proportions of nature into the distortions of art.

Canto II launches the 'made-up' Belinda on the world in a similarly ambivalent guise. The desirable but untouchable female works to an unwritten code of coquettish behaviour (II: 9–18). But her transformation into object continues: 'On her white Breast a sparkling *Cross* she wore,/Which *Jews* might kiss, and Infidels adore' (*RL*, II: 7–8), suggesting that her commitment to religion is ornamental and attracts primarily sexual attention, itself displaced onto the ritual object rather than the human flesh. The 'painted Vessel' (*RL*, II: 47) might refer to the boat she is sailing in, or simply to her. Pope gives us the locks of hair as small but commanding engines of sexual power:

This Nymph, to the Destruction of Mankind,
Nourish'd two Locks, which graceful hung behind
In equal Curls, and well conspir'd to deck
With shining Ringlets the smooth Iv'ry Neck.
Love in these Labyrinths his Slaves detains,
And mighty Hearts are held in slender Chains.

(RL, II: 19–26)

After the lock is lost, Belinda's companion Thalestris asks a rhetorical question which indicates something of Belinda's labour in creating this metallic metonymy of herself:

Was it for this you took such constant Care
The *Bodkin, Comb,* and *Essence* to prepare;
For this your Locks in Paper-Durance bound,
For this with tort'ring Irons wreath'd around?
For this with Fillets strain'd your tender Head,
And bravely bore the double Loads of Lead?
                              (*RL*, IV: 97–102)

'Rape' comes from the Latin verb to 'seize' and does not etymologically imply sexual possession; but in terms of sexual politics, the Baron
clearly conceives that if Belinda has turned her sexuality into an object,
she can be possessed in the metonymic form of part for whole: 'Th'
Adventurous *Baron* the bright Locks admir'd,/He saw, he wish'd, and
to the Prize aspir'd' (*RL*, II: 29–30). For the Baron, like everyone in the
poem, is a creature of objects, and his parody sacrifice (II: 35–46), com-
plementing Belinda's ritual of self-worship, consigns 'the Trophies of
his former Loves' (women's garters and gloves) to the flames in order
to appeal for possession of the supreme 'Prize' (a prize is something
which is 'taken rather than given', often in war, etymologically not
very far removed from rape, and akin to the 'Spoil' with which Belinda
is equipped in *RL*, I: 132).

The Sylphs too regard Belinda's sexual purity as just another object
in her collection: Ariel warns them of some unknown 'dire Disaster'
in terms which appear (in the shifting balances and antitheses of the
couplet) to avoid making distinctions of moral scale:

Whether the Nymph shall break *Diana*'s Law,
Or some frail *China* Jar receive a Flaw,
Or stain her Honour, or her new Brocade,
Forget her Pray'rs, or miss a Masquerade,
Or lose her Heart, or Necklace, at a Ball;
Or whether Heav'n has doom'd that *Shock* must fall.
                              (*RL*, II: 105–10)

Inner and outer, costume and character, religion and entertainment,
are all the same to Ariel's Belinda: her chastity ('*Diana*'s Law') is as
breakable as a 'frail *China* Jar', and Ariel sets 'Fifty chosen *Sylphs*' to
guard Belinda's hoop-petticoat, a 'sev'nfold Fence' (by analogy with
Achilles's 'sev'n-fold Shield' in the *Iliad*) against sexual advances, as if
chastity was something you could preserve with whalebone **[174–7,
181–2]**.

Such delusive misapprehensions of value have a social cost, as the opening of Canto III indicates. The boat arrives at Hampton Court, one of Queen Anne's palaces and thus a site of political importance as well as social intercourse.

> Here *Britain*'s Statesmen oft the Fall foredoom
> Of Foreign Tyrants, and of Nymphs at home;
> Here Thou, Great *Anna*! whom three Realms obey,
> Dost sometimes Counsel take – and sometimes *Tea*.
> (*RL*, III: 5–8)

Politics and sex, politics and tea: Pope's mock-epic wonders if society estimates these activities at the correct points on the scale. Something very costly and problematic about social mores is glimpsed in an aside which is not the less chilling for mimicking the casualness it captures: Pope indicates the time of his epic event by reference to the kind of justice you are likely to get after a long day in a different sort of court: 'The hungry Judges soon the Sentence sign,/And Wretches hang that Jury-men may Dine' (*RL*, III: 19–22). It is only an aside, but it casts an especially ominous shadow across the ensuing card-game in which Belinda seeks to 'decide' the 'Doom' of two of her suitors.

Belinda becomes (in her own view) an epic or romance hero, her cards take on the aspect of martial forces, and her first words in the poem parody God's creative *fiat*: 'The skilful Nymph reviews her Force with Care;/*Let Spades be Trumps!* she said, and Trumps they were' (*RL*, III: 45–6). The pack of cards is transformed into a miniature version of the European war which had just come to an end:

> Now move to War her Sable *Matadores*,
> In Show like Leaders of the swarthy *Moors*.
> *Spadillio* first, unconquerable Lord!
> Led off two captive Trumps, and swept the Board.
> As many more *Manillio* forc'd to yield,
> And march'd a Victor from the verdant Field.
> (*RL*, III: 47–52)

They are only cards, as in *Alice in Wonderland*; yet as often in the poem the comic effect is not wholly controlling, and the conceit of warring armies enlivens the inanimate object in a surreal way (III: 47–100). When Belinda wins it is as if her instinct for sexual mastery, indeed her entire personal agency, has become transferred to and embodied in a playing card:

An *Ace* of Hearts steps forth: The *King* unseen
Lurk'd in her Hand, and mourn'd his captive *Queen*.
He springs to Vengeance with an eager pace,
And falls like Thunder on the prostrate *Ace*.
(RL, III: 95–8)

In this sexually overcharged atmosphere even the making of coffee takes on the aspect of something tremendous (the coffee-grinder has previously been likened to Ixion's wheel in hell, II: 133–6):

For lo! the Board with Cups and Spoons is crown'd,
The Berries crackle, and the Mill turns round.
On shining Altars of *Japan* they raise
The silver Lamp; the fiery Spirits blaze.
From silver Spouts the grateful Liquors glide,
And *China*'s Earth receives the smoking Tyde.
(RL, III: 105–110)

Nor is this comically excessive transformation of the social coffee ritual a mere digression, for when it comes to the actual 'rape' of the lock of hair, we learn that the Baron does not so much plan the act as get inspiration from coffee, which 'Sent up in Vapours to the *Baron*'s Brain/New Stratagems, the radiant Lock to gain' (*RL*, III: 119–20). Similarly, though the act is human, the description concentrates on those aspects which appear external to the conscious control of the Baron: the necessary scissors are a fascinating 'two-edg'd Weapon' from a 'shining Case', a 'little Engine', a 'glitt'ring *Forfex*' and a 'fatal Engine' (*RL*, III: 125–50). In the end, 'Fate urg'd the Sheers', Belinda's hair gives way to the force of steel as did 'th'Imperial Tow'rs of *Troy*' (*RL*, III: 174) and the Baron scarcely seems to exert more agency than Belinda had in summoning her maid in Canto I.

Belinda's initial reaction is heroic, but mocked: her 'Screams of Horror' (*RL*, III: 156) are undercut by the indication that such reactions are forthcoming in serious and trivial instances alike, 'When Husbands or when Lap-dogs breathe their last' (*RL*, III: 155–60). And yet Canto IV turns this perspective around again by suggesting that Belinda's reactions are also driven by forces beyond her conscious control. Umbriel, a Gnome (or ex-Prude), and 'a dusky melancholy Spright', representing the dark side of the poem, (*RL*, IV: 13) visits the 'Cave of *Spleen*' to garner more force for Belinda's hysteria. The canto is a sort of parody of underworld journeys in which heroes encounter the dead (*Aeneid*, book VI). But this underworld appears internal, for Pope is visiting the shady psychology of bodily-inspired melancholy. The 'Spleen' is an abdominal organ, thought in Pope's time to give rise to a range of conditions: migraine, depression, hysteria. Pope envisions a physical scene of bizarre psychological aberrations, again fusing the animate with the inanimate:

> Unnumber'd Throngs on ev'ry side are seen
> Of Bodies chang'd to various Forms by *Spleen*.
> Here living *Teapots* stand, one Arm held out,
> One bent; the Handle this, and that the Spout:
> A Pipkin there like *Homer's Tripod* walks;
> Here sighs a Jar, and there a Goose-pye talks;
> Men prove with Child, as pow'rful Fancy works,
> And Maids turn'd Bottels, call aloud for Corks.
> (*RL*, IV: 47–54)

Though 'Men prove with Child', the 'pow'rful Fancy' which transforms people into objects of surreal sexual suggestion is still in some ways a female domain: Umbriel addresses himself to the 'wayward Queen' who rules 'the Sex' (women) 'to Fifty from Fifteen' (in other words, from puberty to menopause). This turns Belinda's response to the loss of the lock into something which is driven by irrational bodily impulse, with undisclosed sexual significance. Umbriel gets 'Spleen' to gather up 'the Force of Female Lungs',/Sighs, Sobs, and Passions, and the War of Tongues' in 'a wondrous Bag' (mimicking Odysseus's bag of winds in *The Odyssey*, but also suggesting the womb); he also receives a 'Vial' filled with 'fainting Fears,/Soft Sorrows, melting Griefs, and flowing Tears' (*RL*, IV: 81–6). Emotion becomes something like a chemical experiment, and Umbriel returns to tear the 'swelling Bag', allowing 'all the Furies' to issue 'at the Vent' (*RL*, IV: 89–94), and breaks 'the Vial whence the Sorrows flow' (*RL*, IV: 142). The result is a 'raging' tirade from Thalestris, Belinda's Amazonian companion, against the triumphant male sex (IV: 93–122), and a weeping lament from Belinda (IV: 141–76). Emotions of this extent, the poem appears to suggest, cannot be authentic but must be artificially stimulated or produced by some element which would be better controlled.

It is in this spirit which Clarissa speaks at the opening of Canto V, a speech added by Pope in 1717, in order, as a (much later) note puts it, 'to open more clearly the MORAL of the Poem, in a parody of the speech of Sarpedon to Glaucus in Homer' (*RL*, V: 7–34; *TE* II: 199). Clarissa urges Belinda to value lasting 'good Sense' above the superficial and transient claims of Beauty and the social power it wields. This has been taken as the authorial view, imputed to a 'sensible' female character. Feminist critics especially have seen the poem as not merely poking fun at Belinda's over-reaction but as a wider attempt to socialise and domesticate a powerful young woman into mature self-possession, and acceptance of the state of marriage. The whole mock-epic framework can be taken as a comic inflation of an emotional situation which was already inflated (principally by the woman in the case) beyond its true value, though no critic would deny that such a satiric gesture has wider corrective and interrogative implications as well: if the behaviour of smart young people is so ridiculous when it takes itself so seriously, what (if it is not a cod-mythology of Sylphs and Gnomes) can possibly be responsible for it? The opening questions of the poem (I: 7–12) remain throughout. But the treatment of Belinda herself might easily suggest the necessary imposition of moral control; Ariel is forced to abandon her during the Baron's assault because, as he searches the 'close Recesses of the Virgin's thought' and watches 'th'Ideas rising in her Mind', he sees 'in spite of all her Art,/An Earthly Lover lurking at her Heart' (RL, III: 138–145). Pope seems to think it stranger that she should 'reject a Lord' than that the Lord should assault her (RL, I: 7–10), even though the Baron seems to want nothing from her but her hair (he has not proposed marriage or indeed made any explicit sexual advance). Ariel seems to sense Belinda's hidden sexuality; to gain her attention, the figure in the dream poses as an attractive young man 'That ev'n in Slumber caus'd her Cheek to glow' (RL, I: 24); Belinda is woken by her lapdog's tongue (I: 116), suggesting that she is receptive to sexual advances (the lapdog is a kind of substitute husband, as III: 158 indicates); and the vision vanishes because Belinda is more interested in the oversexed love-letter she finds on waking (I: 117–20). Even as the Baron advances she looks back three times, without defending herself (III: 138). She 'Burns to encounter two adventrous Knights' (RL, III: 26), declaring Spades (originally swords) to be trumps at the game of 'Ombre' (after Spanish hombre, Man), suggesting a kind of unconscious attempt to usurp phallic sexual power. Some of Pope's allusions in the poem remind us that the shearing of hair was in classical times a pre-marital ritual (Wasserman 1966). In other words, the Baron might simply have reminded her of her own sexual needs and the right way to initiate intercourse: perhaps Belinda herself is contrived to be one of the 'Maids turn'd Bottels', who 'call aloud for Corks' (RL, IV: 54).

This could not be a complete view of the poem's effects, however. Belinda's speech at the end of Canto IV appears to mock her as a hypocrite: 'Oh hadst thou, Cruel! been content to seize/Hairs less in sight, or any Hairs but these!' (RL, IV: 175–6). Rather the crime of actual rape (the 'Hairs less in sight' indicating pubic hair) than the theft of her own highly visible sexual weapon; she is going to have to tear the other lock off herself. But in another sense she has gauged the system in which she lives exactly right. It is a world of objects, rituals, gestures. Belinda's 'Honour' (her reputation for sexual chastity) has been evacuated into a mere word by Ariel (I: 78), then made into a hollow victory (III: 103), and finally turned into something which can be physically removed: the Baron swears by the 'sacred Lock' 'Which never more its Honours shall renew,/Clipt from the lovely Head where late it grew' (RL, IV: 135–6) to wear the lock forever: 'He spoke, and speaking, in proud Triumph spread/The long-contended Honours of her Head' (RL, IV: 139–40). It is not then merely Spleen which has made Thalestris complain:

> Gods! shall the Ravisher display your Hair,
> While the Fops envy, and the Ladies stare! ...
> Methinks already I your Tears survey,
> Already hear the horrid things they say,
> Already see you a degraded Toast,
> And all your Honour in a Whisper lost!
> (RL, IV: 103–4, 107–10)

This is a world in which appearance counts for more than reality, and possession of a symbol counts for more than the possession of what is symbolised.

Clarissa's speech, like Sarpedon's, is a reminder of transience and mortality; but in the *Iliad* it is also an incitement to battle. Pope places the speech at the start of Canto V, as a *possible* response, though astute readers will remember that Clarissa is the one who gave the Baron the scissors in the first place. But Belinda takes nothing of the advice except the concealed reminder of the incitement to warfare, which is what then takes place: Pope does not in the end put the lid on her anger and subjugate it to an easily available moral norm. Not only does Belinda resist, but she fights with a certain success through the rest of the Canto: Jove's scales (the most fully epic borrowing of the poem, from the *Iliad*, the *Aeneid*, and *Paradise Lost*) reckon the Lock more weighty than the combined 'Wits' of the Men. This does not mean that the battle is not comic, but it does suggest that Belinda is not necessarily wrong to reject Clarissa's advice.

The gender war (V: 35–102) is mock-epic in full cry: Homeric passions and mythological conflicts ('*Jove*'s Thunder roars, Heav'n trembles all around;/Blue *Neptune* storms, the bellowing Deeps resound', *RL*, V: 49–50) are superimposed on the aggressive rattle of female costume ('All side in Parties, and begin th'Attack;/Fans clap, Silks russle, and tough Whalebones crack', *RL*, V: 39–40). However, while the battle is taken seriously by the women as a struggle for power, it appears to be persistently regarded by the men as an especially titillating form of sexual game in which the 'killing' is all done by the conventions of lyric poetry:

> When bold Sir *Plume* had drawn *Clarissa* down,
> *Chloe* stept in, and kill'd him with a Frown;
> She smil'd to see the doughty Hero slain,
> But at her Smile, the Beau reviv'd again.
> (*RL*, V: 67–70)

Belinda's vengeful assault on the Baron has a sexual connotation ('die') for him which it doesn't have for her:

> See fierce *Belinda* on the *Baron* flies,
> With more than usual Lightning in her Eyes;
> Nor fear'd the Chief th'unequal Fight to try,
> Who sought no more than on his Foe to die.
> (*RL*, V: 75–8)

She subdues him with a mere pinch of snuff, comically, but then produces a 'deadly *Bodkin* from her Side' in a final appropriation, or reappropriation, of quasi-phallic power: the bodkin, we learn, has a history (*RL*, V: 87–96): 'Her great great Grandsire' wore it 'about his Neck/In three *Seal-Rings*', but these male insignia have subsequently been melted down through matrilinear successions of power into such an object as Belinda uses in her hair (IV.98). The threatened Baron, nonetheless, construes the assault sexually: 'ah let me still survive,/ And burn in *Cupid*'s Flames, – but burn alive' (*RL*, V: 101–2).

This is an impasse of understanding, heroic against comic, power against sex, and as usual in Pope the only way out is by poetry itself. Belinda gains the right to have the lock (her reputation, her chastity) restored, but what she actually receives is the poem itself (reputation of an arguably greater kind). The lock is not to be found; not that it has gone (as rumoured) to 'the Lunar Sphere' where the worthless junk which symbolises human love affairs fetches up (*RL*, V: 113–22). Instead:

> But trust the Muse – she saw it upward rise,
> Tho' mark'd by none but quick Poetic Eyes: ...
> A sudden Star, it shot thro' liquid Air,
> And drew behind a radiant *Trail of Hair*.
>
> (*RL*, V: 123–4, 127–8)

Belinda's hair becomes comet-like ('comet' is from the Greek for 'hair', because of its hair-like tail); its visibility becomes intangible, inviolable. Pope is offering his own poem as the compensatory vehicle of a stellar transformation: Belinda loses the lock but wins the poem, Pope claims, in adopting a male perspective on her redeemed 'fame':

> For, after all the Murders of your Eye,
> When, after Millions slain, your self shall die ...
> *This Lock*, the Muse shall consecrate to Fame,
> And mid'st the Stars inscribe *Belinda*'s Name!
>
> (*RL*, V: 145–6, 149–50)

'*This Lock*' is of course the poem, *The Rape of the Lock*, which serves to replace the missing lock (with all that it signifies).

While it is certainly possible to read the mock-epic form as a moral comment on a society which has confused its own best interests, its confidence as art seems to exceed its burden as satire. In the 'Toilet' passage in Canto I, for example, mock-epic can certainly point to an inversion of values in that it can make the serious appear trivial and the trivial important. But in miniaturising the world onto Belinda's dressing table Pope gives the objects a compressed life, and there is a kind of poetic thrill about presenting the world in this way: the 'various Off'rings of the World' are not dissimilar to those in the contemporary *Windsor-Forest*, 393–396, which no-one would accuse of being mock-heroic. There is an evident imaginative as well as satiric pleasure in confining emotions within things in the 'Lunar Sphere': 'There Heroes' Wits are kept in pondrous Vases,/And Beaus' in *Snuff-boxes* and *Tweezer-Cases*' (*RL*, V: 115–16). The sylphs have a satiric part to play in making human emotions look vacuous and contrived, and thus querying our sense of perspective and moral values; but they are also the light of pure imagination, representing the pleasures of freedom: 'Transparent Forms, too fine for mortal Sight,/Their fluid Bodies half dissolv'd in Light' (*RL*, II:161–2). Pope takes no less pleasure in making this insubstantiality visible than he does in the more strictly mock-heroic picture of possible punishments for neglectful sylphs stuck forever in cosmetics

(II: 123–36), or for that matter in the wierd but psychologically impressive pathologies of the Cave of Spleen and the malign gnomes in Canto IV, which resound far beyond their ostensible satiric function. While the miniature 'machinery' of the sylphs and gnomes brings an ethical scheme into sharp focus (we are forced to scrutinize because Belinda is viewed through a microscope, but we need to keep things in proportion), the focus also makes the ordinary world something strange and exciting. And attention to the play of light on objects (for such a painterly poet as Pope) is finally a self-conscious reflection on the poetic act itself.

Further Reading

Pope's early readers (even moralists such as Johnson) responded primarily to the poem's sometimes dark charm, though Dennis took the poem apart with customary literal-minded moralism (Barnard 1973: 97–106). Modern debate has to an extent recapitulated the divide between moral and poetic readings; Wasserman (1966) uses the allusions to classical epic submerged in the poem to produce a sustained moral critique of the heroine's behaviour, visible to the classically educated but not to Belinda. Brooks (1949) studies the poem as an elaborate sexual game, proceeding under known rules and conventions, with particular emphasis on the exposure of Belinda's moral character; the game of cards which is at the centre of the war is studied in detail in Wimsatt (1973). On the other hand, Rogers (1974a) sees the poem in the light of what Addison calls the 'fairy way of writing', its links to Shakespearian and Spenserian mythologies, and stresses its psychodramatic and hallucinatory 'quality of deliberate freakishness, wild prodigies, sudden transformations' (77). The appeal of this aspect of the poem to illustrators (the poem appeared with engravings from 1714 onwards) is richly presented in Halsband (1980). Martindale (1983) highlights the elements of play within the poem, which sometimes extend to a tongue-in-cheek take on the epic form itself (particularly in his miniaturisation of the sylphs from Milton's devils) by which we delight in incongruity as much as in satiric recognition. Fowler (1988) suggests a whole range of ways in which the imaginative 'machinery' of the poem extends and complicates our response to Belinda. Landa (1971) views the poem's notable obsession with objects as part of a contemporary fascination with England's suddenly and rapidly expanding commercial dominion over the world. The manner in which individuals become constructed out of the commodities they invest in has been studied in Nicholson (1979), and given an altogether more malign cast in Brown (1985), which is itself critiqued in Crehan (1997). Feminist criticism has been particularly active on the poem **[174–82]**. Readers interested in accessing some of the contemporary material (social, economic, critical, political) with which the poem engages, and on which modern 'political' criticism is based, should consult not only the *TE* volume (edited by Geoffrey Tillotson) but also editions of the poem with contemporary documents, by Tracy (1974), Kinsley (1979), and Wall (1998). Useful compilations of criticism can be found in Hunt (1968) and Bloom (1988).

(d) *ELOISA TO ABELARD* (1717) [*TE* II: 291–349]

Though voiced in the person of an eleventh-century French nun, *Eloisa to Abelard* has the reputation of being one of Pope's more intimately personal poems, partly because the emotional conflict of the speaker finds solace and release in the closing image of a sympathetic 'future bard' (the Pope who writes the poem), and partly because Pope used the poem privately to indicate something of his hapless sexual feelings towards the Blount sisters and (especially) Lady Mary Wortley Montagu **[19–20]**. It was this poem above all which proved to Pope's contemporaries that he had the capacity for feeling, tenderness, and imagination: 'how does my very soul melt away, at the soft Complaints of the languishing *Eloisa*?, an American reader wrote to Pope in 1727; it was 'the warmest, the most affecting, and admirable amorous Poem in the world', as a later critic put it (Barnard 1973: 154, 470).

In her confinement and pathos, Eloisa casts an interesting backward light on the miserable Belinda in *Rape of the Lock*. Nonetheless, as with that earlier poem, *Eloisa to Abelard* does in some ways embody and describe a complex interface between private and public, for it is as public a document as anything else Pope wrote, converting a private emotional situation into a literary form instantly recognisable as the 'Heroic Epistle', deriving chiefly from the *Heroides* of Ovid, a collection of verse epistles in florid style from (mainly) women to the lovers who have left them trapped at home (Penelope to Ulysses, Dido to Aeneas and so on). Pope translated Ovid's *Sapho to Phaon*, an example worth reading alongside *Eloisa to Abelard* **[10]**. But in producing a medieval version, Pope added a significant new element: while the form gives ample space to the expression of erotic disappointment, by transferring the situation to a convent Pope turns the mere absence of the lover into a conflict between desire and religious faith, flesh and spirit, commitment to God and love for a man. Indeed, the conflict is worse still, because Abelard, a theologian who had historically been Eloisa's teacher and husband, is not only absent but has been castrated on the orders of Eloisa's uncle for seducing her; so Eloisa's desire is not only unfulfilled but, confessedly, unfulfillable.

The *Letters* of Abelard and Eloisa (available to Pope in an English version of 1713) give (as Pope puts it in the 'The Argument' which heads the poem) a lively 'picture of the struggles of grace and nature, virtue and passion'. Pope's poem is only from Eloisa to Abelard, as if no reply existed. Historically there were replies, and visits, and eventually the burial together which Eloisa sadly celebrates as her one future prospect of communing with Abelard; but Pope's poem condenses that history into a solitary, conflicted longing, making the letter the site of opposed forces. Sometimes this interaction is very clearly focused within the symmetries offered by the couplet:

> I view my crime, but kindle at the view,
> Repent old pleasures, and sollicit new:
> Now turn'd to heav'n, I weep my past offence,
> Now think of thee, and curse my innocence.
>
> (*EA*, 185–8)

Sometimes it is a matter of contrasting the outer identity, as professed nun, with the inner sense of being Abelard's wife: 'Ah wretch! believ'd the spouse of God in vain,/Confess'd within the slave of love and man' (*EA*, 177–8). The poem as a whole is constructed as a series of mood swings, paragraph by paragraph or couplet by couplet, punctuated by alternative injunctions to Abelard to 'Come' or 'Come not', alternating between frustrated desire for Abelard and the virtuous promptings of the Church towards holy meditation, penitence for sexual 'crimes' and resignation. Eloisa's situation is one in which discernible choice becomes increasingly hard to identify, no matter how precisely the couplet disposes itself:

> How shall I lose the sin, yet keep the sense,
> And love th' offender, yet detest the offence?
> How the dear object from the crime remove,
> Or how distinguish penitence from love?
>
> (*EA*, 191–4)

The apparently watertight categories of the couplet become contaminated by those elements they might be used to insulate Eloisa from. Abelard's image is inextricably 'mix'd with God's' (*EA*, 12). Even in the onset of their tutor-pupil relationship, when Abelard schools her in theology, doctrine is blasphemously melded with the physique of the instructor:

> Guiltless I gaz'd; heav'n listen'd while you sung;
> And truths divine came mended from that tongue.
> From lips like those what precept fail'd to move?
> Too soon they taught me 'twas no sin to love.
> (EA, 65–8)

This infiltration of the divine by the sexual is thorough: when devoting herself to God, Eloisa recalls, her eyes were fixed on Abelard, not the cross. At her religious devotions, church music takes on an unmistakably sexual tone ('swelling organs lift the rising soul', *EA*, 272); Eloisa even eroticizes her death-scene, with Abelard performing 'the last sad office' as her priest: 'See my lips tremble, and my eye-balls roll,/Suck my last breath, and catch my flying soul! (*EA*, 323–4). Even after trying to expunge this semi-necrophiliac fantasy, Eloisa replaces it with another, that of Abelard's death, which also does not quite manage vestal purity, since she hopes that on arrival in heaven 'Saints embrace thee with a love like mine' (*EA*, 342).

Eloisa's letter is full of imperatives, the most frequent of which is 'come'. Abelard is asked to write, to visit the convent which he founded, to fill the 'craving Void' in whatever way still remains possible in his castrated state. Fundamentally, this is fantasy, as Eloisa knows.

> Still on that breast enamour'd let me lie,
> Still drink delicious poison from thy eye,
> Pant on thy lip, and to thy heart be prest;
> Give all thou canst – and let me dream the rest.
> (EA, 121–4)

But the battle between God and Abelard is not one that God can win, for in the end, Eloisa's capacity for 'dream', imagination, fantasy, acts as a substitute which will actively attempt to fill the space left by Abelard's castration. In her vision of the attack on Abelard she envisages her own ability to preserve him:

Alas how chang'd! what sudden horrors rise!
A naked Lover bound and bleeding lies!
Where, where was *Eloise*? her voice, her hand,
Her ponyard, had oppos'd the dire command.

(*EA*, 99–102)

Though the vision breaks off with its own form of castrated retreat into femininity ('I can no more; by shame, by rage supprest,/Let tears, and burning blushes speak the rest', *EA*, 105–6), her confidence in her ability to rescue the bound and bleeding lover with her voice, or hand, or dagger, is striking. Her imagination suggests a kind of mastery.

In the engraving which fronted the 1719 printing of the poem, Eloisa is depicted clutching an outsize quill pen, poised over a circular inkpot in a gesture which now seems transparently sexual: not only does writing in some way compensate for an imprisoned sexuality, it is Eloisa who masters the male art of writing. Eloisa herself comes close to equating writing with intercourse in asking for a letter from Abelard: 'Yet write, oh write me all, that I may join/Griefs to thy griefs, and eccho sighs to thine' (*EA*, 41–2). Letters themselves are a form of sexual expression available to women: 'They live, they speak, they breathe what love inspires', they 'Speed the soft intercourse from soul to soul' (*EA*, 51–8). The worst that Pope's enemies could find to say about the poem was that it was lubricious, or prurient (Guerinot 1969: 70, 150, 262); in modern times it has been described, not unsympathetically, as masturbatory (see Jackson 1983). It is merely Abelard's letter which causes sexual tumult, it is the written name 'Abelard' which Eloisa kisses at the start of the poem (8), which she seeks to hide in the close disguise of her heart (11–12), to retain with the holy enclosure of her lips (10), which her heart nonetheless inscribes on paper at the dictates of her heart (16). This ability to transform writing into sexual mastery, the word into the thing, can be likened to Eloisa's talent for filling the available space with imagination.

It may have a malign function as well. *Eloisa to Abelard* is, though set inside a convent, markedly given to depictions of landscape. Though Eloisa is 'In' (the first word of the poem) 'deep solitudes and awful cells', her thoughts 'rove ... beyond this last retreat' (*EA*, 5) and populate a world which is evidently internal in a different way, more like the cave of spleen which is Belinda's inside-out mental landscape in *The Rape of the Lock*. Abelard's foundation of the Paraclete is seen as a replenishing Eden in the mist of deserts ('And Paradise was open'd in the Wild', *EA*, 134), now lacking Abelard's fulfilling presence so that Black Melancholy, clearly an emanation from Eloisa, has filled and transformed it instead (155–70). Eloisa can fill her mental space with

'Fancy' (indicating dream or imagination): 'Fancy restores what vengeance snatch'd away', but her landscape remains marked by castration: in her dreams she and Abelard commune 'Where round some mould'ring tow'r pale ivy creeps,/And low-brow'd rocks hand nodding o'er the deeps' (*EA*, 244–5). She sets her own scene as a contrast between her emotional life ('I have not yet forgot myself to stone') and the deadness of the 'darksom round' which she inhabits:

> Relentless walls! whose darksom round contains
> Repentant sighs, and voluntary pains:
> Ye rugged rocks! which holy knees have worn;
> Ye grots and caverns shagg'd with horrid thorn!
> (EA, 17–20)

But this visionary encompassing is itself part of an imaginative projection of which the natural end is the space of the tomb. After several repetitions of the plea 'Come' to Abelard, Eloisa finally hears the instruction 'Come, sister, come' from a shrine (*EA*, 309), and promises 'I come, I come' (*EA*, 317), as if fulfilling the desire for union in the only way now possible.

In the end imaginative triumph is ceded to a greater poet, in the deft fast-forward by which Pope arrives at himself in the last 24 lines of the poem (343-366): finally 'some future Bard', joined 'In sad similitude of griefs to mine' (*EA*, 360), purifies the scene with his sympathetic writing:

> Such if there be, who loves so long, so well;
> Let him our sad, our tender story tell;
> The well-sung woes will sooth my pensive ghost;
> He best can paint 'em, who shall feel 'em most.
> (EA, 363–6)

We should sense in these lines something other than the 'sad similitude' by which Pope identifies himself with the wife of a castrated lover, for it is also a replacement of a fantasy which has failed (Eloisa's) with one which has not (Pope's).

Further Reading

Eighteenth-century critiques of the poem were unusually positive about it, despite its blasphemous suggestions and the immorality of Eloisa's longings (the poem was rumoured to be popular amongst kept mistresses (Barnard 1973: 11)); even twentieth-century criticism has largely approved its claims to a 'female' sensibility, often by contrast with Pope's more problematic versions of womanhood in *The Rape of the Lock* **[181]**. In an important article Gillian Beer argues that some genuine power emerges for female roles in this and other poems of its tradition because of its 'appeal to the authority of women, who were assumed to be naturally learned in the realms of erotic knowledge and suffering' (Beer 1982: 140). Though the form is based on disempowerment and martyrdom, it nonetheless encodes a constant protest against it. Other critics have approved of Eloisa's imaginative resolution, the genuineness of the Christian repentance, and Pope's psychological analysis of or identification with his heroine (Kalmey 1980; Jack 1988; Manning 1993; Williams 1995). Others remind us that Eloisa's voice is always ventriloqual, mediated and dramatized, and can be read as a sort of study in self-deception (Jackson 1983; Bygrave 1990). For these critics, Eloisa is displayed, as it were, as continually self-dramatizing, made to write of herself in the third person (*'Eloisa* yet must kiss the name', *EA*, 8), and invite voyeuristic interest ('See in her Cell sad *Eloisa* spread', *EA*, 303); her final retreat is to abandon the quill to the later male poet (who has of course been constructing this spectacle).

(e) *ESSAY ON MAN* (1733–34) [*TE* III: I]

In the opening lines of the *Essay on Man* **[34, 37]**, Pope proposes to 'vindicate the ways of God to Man' in a sweeping survey of God's 'mighty maze', and thus conspicuously picks up the mantle of poetic and theological authority from Milton, whose *Paradise Lost* sought to 'justify the ways of God to Man' (references to 'A Wild, where weeds and flow'rs promiscuous shoot,/Or Garden, tempting with forbidden fruit', *EM*, I: 7–8, make the 'target' poem still more obvious); but the context has changed from Milton's apocalyptic and fundamentalist account of the archetypal human Fall to a far more diagrammatic view of the universe, in which all forms of life, from flies to humans to angels, have an allotted, correct place. Pope's cosmos functions as an expression of complementary forces; Milton's dynamic narrative of war in heaven is replaced by a system of balances; catastrophe and redemption become stasis and resignation. No doubt Milton's poem derives some of its energies from the conflicts of the Civil War, while Pope's was written in an era of greater political stability, at least nominally. Nonetheless, despite the monumental (and sometimes couplet-like) symmetry of Pope's four-part 'Essay', the poem is perhaps not best read as a systematic treatise, but as a looser, more flexible treatment of the world in relation to some constant concerns. The 'Epistles' which make up the poem were published separately and take the form of a serious quasi-letter to a friend: 'Essay' in the sense of 'A loose sally of the mind; an irregular indigested piece; not a regular and orderly composition' (Samuel Johnson's definition).

Pope describes his *Essay* as 'steering betwixt the extremes of doctrines seemingly opposite ... forming a *temperate* yet not *inconsistent*, and a *short* yet not *imperfect* system of Ethics' (*TE* III.i: 7). The main gravamen of the *Essay* is thus an assault on pride, on the aspiration of mankind to get above its station, scan the mysteries of heaven, promote itself to the central place in the universe. Pope's manner is not bardic or prophetic like Milton's, but it does cast itself as having authority: 'Know then thyself, presume not God to scan...', an attitude borrowed from Milton's Raphael, who counsels Adam not to seek higher knowledge than is appropriate. But there is something disturbing about this assumption of authority. Milton's angel warns Adam against seeking heavenly knowledge in a voice scripted for him by the earthbound poet Milton in a poem whose vision of the cosmos from Hell, through Chaos, Eden and on up to Heaven is one of its main readerly pleasures. Similarly, Pope counsels concentration on the human scale in what is, nonetheless, his cosmological testament. Milton aspires to be the poet of God, and so indeed does Pope; if the latter is seeking to stifle adventurous mental journeys, he can only do so by giving them a certain amount of weight and interest.

The vision which is offered the reader after the opening invocation to the philosopher-friend to 'Awake!' is not however either simply satirical or straightforwardly didactic. Despite the continual use of imperative verbs such as See, Look, Mark, Note, which make it evident that it is part of the poem's didactic design to make visible the plan of the maze, the theological defence of God's providence depends on the assertion that we cannot know more than our own very limited place in the pattern. Pope seeks a way out of this paradox by contrasting visions: human vision is limited to its own state, but can reason and infer other states from that position.

> Thro' worlds unnumber'd tho' the God be known,
> 'Tis ours to trace him only in our own.
> He, who thro' vast immensity can pierce,
> See worlds on worlds compose one universe,
> Observe how system into system runs,

What other planets circle other suns,
What vary'd being peoples ev'ry star,
May tell why Heav'n has made us as we are.
(EM, I: 21–8)

Pope instantly oversteps the limits he places on human knowledge ("Tis ours to trace him only in our own'), by imagining an infinity of parallel universes, the knowledge of which is only available to the unidentified 'He' who is the subject of the long-delayed main verb 'May' at line 28; the 'He' ought to be God, but he seems oddly separated from his agency as Creator. But the delay between subject and object here actually makes the passage read the other way, and gives us for the duration of the sentence the sensation that we are in the position of the nameless 'He', envisaging other systems running into each other, watching other planets circling round other suns, imagining lives in other worlds.

Pope draws on Renaissance images of a 'great chain' (EM, I: 33) by which all creatures from microscopic organisms to angels are like links in a graded series which cannot be broken without destroying the hierarchical pattern; thus aspiration to see higher up the chain is conflated with aspiration to be higher up it. Again the proposition is that our limited vision cannot see only the limitations of our place in the chain, and not its active dynamism:

So Man, who here seems principal alone,
Perhaps acts second to some sphere unknown,
Touches some wheel, or verges to some goal;
'Tis but a part we see, and not a whole.
(EM, I: 57–60)

Our cosmological position is also limited temporally by our blindness to the future, and Pope reminds us of our superiority of knowledge over other creatures on earth, to indicate our own inferiority to creatures we cannot (but again, do) imagine (I: 81–6). We might imagine, for example, a Heaven

Who sees with equal eye, as God of all,
A hero perish, or a sparrow fall,
Atoms or systems into ruin hurl'd,
And now a bubble burst, and now a world.
(EM, I: 87–90)

But in doing so Pope has once again opened a syntactic window for the reader limited to seeing only a part, to imagine what it would be like to see the whole, to be the person 'Who sees ... as God of all' the role of all disasters from miniscule to cosmic in some functionally perfect arrangement. In some ways, Pope is giving room to that restless desire for advancement and knowledge which the poem's overall task is to stifle.

Pope discovers this intellectual pride to operate at more or less every level of human experience, including the bodily senses.

> Why has not Man a microscopic eye?
> For this plain reason, Man is not a Fly.
> Say what the use, were finer optics giv'n,
> T' inspect a mite, not comprehend the heav'n?
> Or touch, if tremblingly alive all o'er,
> To smart and agonize at ev'ry pore?
> Or quick effluvia darting thro' the brain,
> Die of a rose in aromatic pain?
>
> (*EM*, I: 193–200)

Pope is resisting the imaginative world opened up by improved microscopic technology, just as his cosmic vision ambivalently absorbs the epochal discoveries in physics made by Newton; his moral point is that Man has the right amount of perception for his state and position in the system, no more and no less. And yet the intensification of experience offered by shifting one's sense of one's senses (so to speak), has attracted him into one of the most memorable pieces of imagining in the entire poem. These lines on human senses open a new vista of creation in which the differences in perception ('The mole's dim curtain, and the lynx's beam', deaf fish against hyper-alert birds, stupid pig against thoughtful elephant) are seen as fascinatingly complementary. If we renounce inappropriate intensities of sensual experience, as Pope says we must, we can nonetheless celebrate them vicariously in other, notionally lesser creatures: 'The spider's touch, how exquisitely fine!/ Feels at each thread, and lives along the line' (*EM*, I: 217–8). Pope's 'line' becomes the line for this feeling to live along, an exquisite model of his theory of connection between self and exterior, creature and creature.

It is tempting (for Pope tempts us) to imagine what it would be like to dissolve the boundaries between reason and sensation, between the mind of the 'half-reas'ning elephant' and human reason – 'For ever sep'rate, yet for ever near!' (*EM*, I: 224). The reason we cannot, and should not seek to, break this bound or alter our place on the ladder, is correspondingly huge in its theological overtones. Since the system which Pope has imagined is cosmological, if anything steps out of line the entire cosmos is ruined:

> Let Earth unbalanc'd from her orbit fly,
> Planets and Suns runs lawless thro' the sky,
> Let ruling Angels from their spheres be hurl'd,
> Being on being wreck'd, and world on world,
> Heav'n's whole foundations to their centre nod,
> And Nature tremble to the throne of God:
>
> (EM, I: 251–6)

This is the over-reaching imagination turned Satanic, with the verb 'Let' ambiguously placed between a sort of ironic command to those who would aspire beyond their station, and a more internalised third person imperative, suggesting the poet as God-substitute could actually conjure such an impiety. As if to suppress that suggestion, poetry is then turned to the service of discovering the immanence of God not at the top of the scale, but in every part of 'one stupendous whole', as the soul of that body which is nature (EM, I: 267–80). This is a kind of sleight of hand whereby the scale becomes nullified as a system of differences and hierarchies, because God is in fact present in equal measure everywhere: 'As full, as perfect, in a hair as heart' (EM, I: 276). No point, then, but to 'Submit – In this, or any other sphere' (EM, I: 285), since all the angles are covered by God:

> All Nature is but Art, unknown to thee;
> All Chance, Direction, which thou canst not see;
> All Discord, Harmony, not understood;
> All partial Evil, universal Good:
> And, spite of Pride, in erring Reason's spite,
> One truth is clear, 'Whatever IS, is RIGHT.'
>
> (EM, I: 289–94)

Pope works up this dominating, pacifying rhetoric partly out of a sense of his own poetic audacity and its closeness to the aspirations of reason and pride. The final crowning hyperbole, 'Whatever IS, is RIGHT', is based on an assumed power of poetic imitation of God and a suppressed identification with that voice which might find much of what IS, to be WRONG.

The second Epistle sets about redeploying those energies of enquiry into the microcosmos of the human mind. Man is situated amid warring conceptions of his own nature: 'A being darkly wise, and rudely great', 'In doubt to deem himself a God, or Beast', 'Created half to rise, and half to fall' (*EM*, II: 3–18). Using his favourite device of the telling oxymoron, Man becomes a miniature cosmology which has internalised that war which Milton turns into narrative: he is both Adam and Satan, top and bottom of the scale. But the solution to the 'riddle' cannot be Newtonian science, which (Pope implies) insensibly slides from describing the universe to imagining that it controls it (*EM*, II: 19–30). Pope acknowledges Newton's genius as a scientist but limitations as a philosopher:

> Could he, whose rules the rapid Comet bind,
> Describe or fix one movement of his Mind?
> Who saw its fires here rise, and there descend,
> Explain his own beginning, or his end?
> (*EM*, II: 35–8)

The real mystery is the human mind, Pope declares, and after a further lofty dismissal of the new learning (II: 43–52), he offers a theory which does appear to attempt to fix 'the Mercury of Man', under the direction of 'Eternal Art' (*EM*, II: 175–7) – a kind of thermodynamics of the self: 'Two Principles in human nature reign;/Self-love, to urge, and Reason, to restrain' (*EM*, II: 53–4). This opposition is dynamic, functional – it is not that reason is good and self-love bad, but that both function according to 'their proper operation' within the human system.

Self-love is a kind of id, appetitive, desiring, urging, instigating action; reason is an ego which judges, guides, advises, makes purposeful the energies of self-love. Without these complementary forces human nature would be either ineffectual or destructive (this is the true cosmic drama):

> Man, but for that, no action could attend,
> And, but for this, were active to no end;
> Fix'd like a plant on his peculiar spot,
> To draw nutrition, propagate, and rot;
> Or, meteor-like, flame lawless thro' the void,
> Destroying others, by himself destroy'd.
> (*EM*, II: 61–6)

Pope is clearly fascinated by the energies of this self-love, which might 'flame lawless thro' the void', and is considerably less moralistic about it than one might expect. In his subsequent discussion, self-love is a strong, active 'moving principle', and reason appears rather tame and distant. Pope wants to strengthen reason's claim gradually; by the end of the passage we find 'Attention, habit and experience gains,/ Each strengthen Reason, and Self-love restrain' (*EM*, II: 79–80), allying each element with its opposite quality in a characteristic pattern. Pope gives weight to what moralists often shun: contending that 'strength of mind is Exercise, not Rest' (*EM*, II: 104), Pope wants to enjoy the tempestuous nature of this internal cosmos: 'Nor God alone in the still calm we find,/He mounts the storm, and walks upon the wind' (*EM*, II: 109–10).

Pope must find something resulting from this elemental strife, however, which explains differences in human characters, and he does this with the theory of the 'ruling passion', a kind of debased, dark version of self-love which Pope initially characterises as the 'Mind's disease' which is inherent from birth in the way death is (*EM*, II: 133–60). 'Passions, like Elements, tho' born to fight,/Yet, mix'd and soften'd, in his work unite' (*EM*, II: 111–12), Pope contends, to some extent converting an innate psychomachia into a dynamic 'well accorded strife' which 'Gives all the strength and colour of our life' (*EM*, II: 121–22). The middle section of the epistle actually posits a far more negative theory of the mind, in which a baneful 'ruling passion', aligned from birth with a kind of death instinct, dominates the individual in an almost toxic way (II: 141–4); a kind of internal fall, in which the mind's energies are all poisoned by some dominant characteristic (envy, hatred, greed). Reason can negotiate with this force (II: 162–4), but only 'Th' Eternal Art' (of God), can reclaim the disastrous energy of the ruling passion by grafting onto it some matching virtue: ''Tis thus the Mercury of Man is fix'd,/Strong grows the Virtue with his nature mix'd' (*EM*, II: 177–8). We are on a knife-edge between lust and love, avarice and prudence, anger and fortitude, with only 'The God within the mind' (*EM*, II: 204) to distinguish and prioritise the contrary energies.

Thus committed to a view of the psyche as functioning according to some 'mysterious use' which combines moral opposites in an aesthetic process determined by God, Pope can open the case for a social patterning required by inherent weaknesses in mental life: 'Each individual seeks a sev'ral goal;/But HEAV'N's great view is One, and that the Whole' (*EM*, II: 237–8). Aware of the multiplicity of shades of character between the tidy oppositions of Virtue and Vice (*EM*, II: 210), Pope offers in the last fifty lines of the epistle vignettes which refuse to show lives, however clearly defined individually, operating in isolation; each condition has its unexpected compensations ('See some strange comfort ev'ry state attend', *EM*, II: 271); but only in social interaction is the plan of God really being enacted. Across the structure of the epistle, Heaven has replaced science as the artist of the mind, with society as the place in which psychomachic forces operate to a benign ratio.

Epistle III opens with a bravura display of the 'chain of love', finding even in the most basic matter the tendency to unite:

> See plastic Nature working to this end,
> The single atoms to each other tend,
> Attract, attracted to, the next in place
> Form'd and impell'd its neighbour to embrace.
>
> (*EM*, III: 9–12)

Sociality is the basic pattern of all nature; life-cycles provide a chronological sequencing of the same principle, one which should remind us of our own place in the scheme, a mutual dependency of created things (III: 21–6).

In Pope's imagination, everything works by analogy with something else; relations between wild animals and human beings are transformed into visions of power relations between animals and other animals, wild and tame, domestic and feral (III: 49–70). The psychology which in Epistle II contrasted self-love and reason inside the human mind now contrasts animal instinct with human reason, providing a different set of conflicts and analogies. Again, 'honest Instinct' is valued surprisingly highly – 'Sure never to o'er-shoot, but just to hit,/While still too wide or short is human Wit' (*EM*, III: 89–90). Pope finds art in the spider's web, 'Columbus-like' courage to explore in the stork (*EM*, III: 103–6); he contends that instinct is God's direction, reason merely man's. Wresting the garden of Eden from Milton's narrative of Adam led astray by inferior Eve, Pope posits a 'state of nature' of undivided unity between human and animal, in which human Reason is instructed to learn from animal Instinct to find food, medicine, the arts of building, ploughing and sailing; even politics. Animals show the arts of society *before* mankind has them (III: 183–8).

Pope is in somewhat dangerous water here, and deliberately maintains absolute balance between two types of political system: a communitarian republic (the Ants), and a property-owning monarchy (the Bees). In discovering these 'subterranean works and cities' (*EM*, III: 181) to the eye, Pope is privileging the function of naturally-ordered society, of whichever kind, over any sort of individualism. How Pope gets from here to modern political systems is a good deal more vexed, though it has been plausibly suggested that in playing off 'patriarchal' theories of the origins of government (based on the authority of the father) against 'contractual' ones (based on mutual agreement), Pope finally has 'something for the contractualists, and something more for the patriarchalists' (Erskine-Hill 1988, 79–93). By secularising and naturalising the mythic origins of government, Pope adapts patriarchalism for civil society. From a state of nature in which gender divisions play no part at all except in providing the object of mutual desire, Patriarchs suddenly appear, 'by Nature crown'd ... King, priest, and parent of his growing state' (*EM*, III: 215–16). The patriarch becomes a type of God, and it is by analogy with such a god, Pope suggests, that people discover 'One great first father, and that first ador'd' (*EM*, III: 226). Thus hierarchical monarchy, and the belief system which underpins it, emerge along patriarchal lines. But Pope draws on both sides to celebrate a modern system which reconciles competing energies:

> 'Till jarring int'rests of themselves create
> Th'according music of a well-mix'd State.
> Such is the World's great harmony, that springs
> From Order, Union, full Consent of things!
> (*EM*, III: 293–6)

The 'mixed monarchy' for which Britain deemed itself famous is registered in the movement of Pope's verse as a series of checks and balances in which no one element predominates, just as the commons, the lords and the monarch were supposed to make up a political system which avoided the extremes of anarchy and tyranny (III: 297–302). In the end, Pope argues, the social nature of human interaction can be viewed by analogy with wider cosmology:

> On their own Axis as the Planets run,
> Yet make at once their circle round the Sun:
> So two consistent motions act the Soul;
> And one regards Itself, and one the Whole.
> (*EM*, III: 313–16)

'Regarding the whole' then became Pope's chief poetic problem.

Epistle IV was published somewhat apart from the earlier epistles, in 1734 **[37]**, and in many ways it is the least in keeping with the others, showing a pronounced tendency to dissolve its polished sense of order into a more stridently satirical account of human folly. Order is still 'Heav'n's first law' in Pope's scheme (*EM*, IV: 49), and human disparities still work in harmonious formation: 'All Nature's diff'rence keeps all Nature's peace' (*EM*, IV: 56). But the epistle shows Pope searching for a means of addressing the multivalence of human experience, and social inequalities in particular, without entirely being able to rely on the format of the vertical chain of being or the horizontal analogy from physics; in what is largely a catalogue of human errors on the subject of happiness, and a teaching of contempt for material good, Pope begins to quote some of his own earlier formulations in newly problematic contexts. So 'All partial Evil, universal Good' (*EM*, I: 292) is rephrased at IV: 114 as one of a range of possibilities for explaining the presence of 'Ill' in the world; 'Whatever IS, is RIGHT', the triumphantly confident punchline of Epistle I (*EM*, I: 294), appears now to need further qualification (IV: 145). Pope's answer to these problems – the presence of evil, inequalities of fortune, potential for happiness not being realised – is in the end located in a retreat from the world into personal Virtue. The public world is presented as increasingly corrupt and unstable, with fame intangible and misleading (IV: 217–58); the only universally available and reliable happiness is an inner conviction of virtuous life. There is path and pattern attached to the life of Virtue, for he who is 'Slave to no sect, who takes no private road' (*EM*, IV: 331) can perceive 'that Chain which links th'immense design' (*EM*, IV: 333), and acts his part in it. Pope's privileging of virtue is not however an isolating condition but a sort of precondition for outward-directed action. Inner virtue leads to civic virtue, charity, benevolence, but it must be that way round:

> God loves from Whole to Parts: but human soul .
> Must rise from Individual to the Whole.
> Self-love but serves the virtuous mind to wake,
> As the small pebble stirs the peaceful lake;
> The centre mov'd, a circle strait succeeds,
> Another still, and still another spreads,
> Friend, parent, neighbour, first it will embrace,
> His country next, and next all human race,
> Wide and more wide, th'o'erflowings of the mind
> Take ev'ry creature in, of ev'ry kind;
> Earth smiles around, with boundless bounty blest,
> And Heav'n beholds its image in his breast.
>
> (*EM*, IV: 361–72)

The physical metaphor of the mind rippling and overflowing into wider contexts itself oversteps its ostensible purpose here and reminds us of several of the physics-derived images in earlier epistles; this is the ecological system of mind, world and universe as it is supposed to work at the end of the argument.

But the actual end of the work is curious. Pope onece more addresses Bolingbroke, his 'guide, philosopher, and friend' (*EM*, IV: 390), according him as an exile from worldly political success the sort of inner virtue already established as God's true template and suggesting that Boling-broke's future fame might preserve Pope's as well. So much is placed in the form of a question (IV: 383–90). However, as Pope comments on the truth-value of his work, and moves finally into recalling the summaries of each earlier epistles so as to provide argumentative closure (IV: 391–8), the question mark, though grammatically required because the statement depends on the question to Bolingbroke, is lost, and the apparent certainties of Pope's own commentary on what he has achieved in his fearsomely disciplined attempt to systematise chaos are haunted by a ghostly sense of query.

Further Reading

The poem has been the subject of several full-length expositions which grant it varying degrees of philosophical coherence (Kallich 1967; White 1970; Nuttall 1984; Solomon 1993). For some critics, the pedagogic project of the poem is lucid and coherent; Varey (1979) sees the poem's instructive manner as an attempt to prompt the reader to a higher level of vision. But critics have also responded to the unsettling ways in which the poem seems to embody paradox and contradiction. For Jackson (1983, 67–86), the poem dramatises a series of complex psycho-logical falls, divisions, subversions, and conflicts, which probe and question the sources of the self's identity and stability. For Hammond (1986: 38–67), the poem's promotion of a supposedly neutral order of civic virtue conceals the partisan political nature of Pope's position, aligned with Bolingbroke and the opposition to Walpole **[163–71]**. For Brown (1985: 68–93), the poem is caught between an appropriation of early capitalist, self-help ideals and a commitment to an older Christ-ian ethic of self-abnegation. Copley and Fairer (1990) translate these divisions into an effect on the reader of the poem, continually addressed as if s/he were being offered 'polite' and accessible discourse, and as continually disabled by a shifting scale of perception which suggests that most readers are not in fact competent to comprehend the totality of the system available to the poet: the poem's 'expository formulations insist on the unknowability of the design it asserts' (220).

(f) *EPISTLES TO SEVERAL PERSONS* (1731–35) [*TE* III: ii]

Alongside the *Essay on Man* came four 'epistles' addressed to friends, three eminent men, and one obscure (and unnamed) woman. As with the *Essay on Man* itself, the skewing of the potential symmetry is significant, for Pope never quite resolved how much system, and how much satire, the poems were supposed to contain. In the second volume of his *Works* (1735), they were revised and grouped in their now conventional order (*Cobham, Lady, Bathurst, Burlington*), as *Ethick Epistles*, book II, where the *Essay on Man* supplied book I; clearly they constitute an attempt to bring the abstract ideas of the *Essay on Man* into the world of actual human experience. Other epistles to other people (Addison, Bolingbroke, Arbuthnot) were in some editions grouped with the four, which were sometimes called collectively 'Moral Essays', but in the edition of the poems which Pope had printed shortly before his death he called them *Epistles to Several Persons*, which seems more accurately to reflect their original separateness and tonal flexibility. However, it would be odd not to read the poems as in some ways a collective entity. There is much thematic overlap between them: Cobham, the addressee of the first epistle, is also one of the heroes of the last (*To Burlington*). The *Epistle to Cobham*, notionally about character, ends with sketches about riches, which is the theme of *To Bathurst* and *To Burlington*.

The *Epistle to Cobham* [36–7] is designed to act as the pivotal site for the continuing change of focus between the cosmic framework of *Essay on Man* and the micro-history which that poem begins to move towards, and which the epistles complete. In structure, *Cobham* is a question with an answer: how can we know the truths about human motivation and personality when so many obstacles and opacities lie between us and other minds, which are themselves extremely variable? Pope's answer is to 'Search the RULING PASSION', where character will always be constant, in the manner already described in Epistle II of *Essay on Man*. *Cobham* also shares with the *Essay* an obsession with optics and perception, and a challenging pedagogic technique whereby doctrine rescues us from chaotic paths into which the poetry deliberately leads us.

Quickly demolishing the satiric certainties which men who live only in their studies can lay claim to (1–22), Pope moves rapidly through a series of expanding vistas of human difference under which the unity of character begins to crack:

> Yet more; the diff'rence is as great between
> The optics seeing, as the objects seen.
> All Manners take a tincture from our own,
> Or come discolour'd thro' our Passions shown.
> Or Fancy's beam enlarges, multiplies,
> Contracts, inverts, and gives ten thousand dyes.
>
> (*Cob*, 23–8)

'Optics' was the title of one of Newton's best-known treatises, the one which fathomed the prismatic nature of white light; but here the triumph of empirical science is turned into the potential disaster of a subjectivism which can see nothing without its own contaminations. Such visual interference would normally be thought of as one of Pope's nightmares (it is characteristic of Dulness in the *Dunciad*). But there is evidently something not unattractive in this vein to Pope, for he uses it as a springboard to another imagining of the unimaginable, a physical landscape invisible to physics, an anatomy of the mind inaccessible to empirical science:

> Our depths who fathoms, or our shallows finds,
> Quick whirls, and shifting eddies, or our minds? ...
> Like following life thro' creatures you dissect,
> You lose it in the moment you detect.
>
> (*Cob*, 29–30, 39–40)

Offering what seems to be a metaphor for mental life ('Quick whirls, and shifting eddies') Pope then produces the mind itself ('or our minds') as if it were somehow even more unimaginable than metaphor; and he appears to enjoy the sleight of hand. Man, and Life, exceed attempts to explain them, which effect a kind of death ('dissect'). Self-knowledge, the great hope of *Essay on Man*, appears to be no refuge either, since 'Oft in the Passions' wild rotation tost,/Our spring of action to ourselves is lost' (*Cob*, 41–2); our 'internal view' (*Cob*, 49) is as fallible as our external sight, partly because our motivation is not even fully conscious. 'Not always Actions shew the man' (*Cob*, 61), for exemplary actions may stem from accidental motives; actions are often comically contradictory (71–86), and our judgement of them too often influenced by social position (87–100). Piling 'turns of mind' upon 'puzzling Contraries' (*Cob*, 133–4), Pope produces deliberately opposite snapshot contexts for facets of character to dazzle in:

> See the same man, in vigour, in the gout;
> Alone, in company; in place, or out;
> Early at Bus'ness, and at Hazard late;
> Mad at a Fox-chace, wise at a Debate;
> Drunk at a Borough, civil at a Ball;
> Friendly at Hackney, faithless at Whitehall.
>
> (Cob, 130–5)

Forms of social and political activity, no less than internal and private situations, produce opposite signs of 'character', as Pope goes on to illustrate in a series of satiric vignettes where the poet is apparently granted quasi-novelistic omniscience to determine true motivations beneath uninterpretable actions (136–65).

It is perhaps such poetic omniscience as this which allows Pope to propose an answer to the problem formerly elaborated in his own *Essay on Man*: 'Search then the Ruling Passion: There, alone,/The Wild are constant, and the Cunning known' (*Cob*, 174–5). Pope's key example is Philip, Duke of Wharton (1698–1731), a useful model of instability in that he came of Whig stock but became a Jacobite and Roman Catholic, eventually dying in a monastery in Catalonia after being outlawed for taking up arms against England in 1727. The Ruling Passion in this case is 'Lust of Praise' (*Cob*, 181), a 'clue once found' which 'unravels all the rest' (*Cob*, 178) precisely because it converts inner desire into outward appearance, thus dissolving the problematic boundary entirely. Wharton's identity actually *depends* on being assessed by others in a variety of contexts (parliament, club, literary scene, church, brothel, and so on, 180–91). Pope is enabled by this eva- cuation of content, this turning-inside-out of selfhood, to fix the oppositions of 'character' in couplets which unify in a single individual seemingly contrary qualities (198–203). 'Comets', those astronomical terrors which Pope had likened to destructive human energies in *Essay on Man*, become in this poetic system 'regular', as Wharton's character becomes 'plain' (*Cob*, 208–9).

The critic Walter Benjamin contends that 'Death is the sanction of everything the story can tell'; death confers meaning on the narratives of our lives and gives retrospective shape to them as the full stop defines the meaning of the sentence (Benjamin 1969: 94). Pope's final examples indicate character at the moment of death precisely to fix their characters at the moment when everything is real. Death shows you life, in a way opposite to the method of dissection, which destroys life (39–40). With the exception of the closing tribute to Cobham's patriotism [36–7], a very different sort of emanation of the private into the public from Wharton's self-promotion, the examples are all comic, indicating an intellectual problem overcome. The crone who dies blowing out a candle to save money, the lady who asks her maid to see that her make-up is not neglected in death, the 'Courtier smooth' who goes on promising to serve his clients in the afterlife, are all 'characters' whose personality is accessible and intelligible at this end of life, and the poem; all too concerned with appearances to notice their own motivations, they display their inner compulsions for us instead.

Though the poem is subtitled 'Of the Knowledge and Characters of MEN', it casually identifies women as the gender especially given over to dissembling (*Cob*, 177). In the *Epistle to a Lady, On the Characters of Women* [37–8, 173–81], Pope explores the problem of character in what appears to be a more extreme form. His main metaphor in the poem derives from painting: 'How many Pictures of one Nymph we view,/ All how unlike each other, all how true!' (5–6). Drawing on the common enough social practice whereby noble women had their portraits painted in various guises, classical, pastoral, and so on, Pope envisages women as engaged in a ceaseless self-presentation in comically incompatible roles, the uniforms of rank alongside fancy dress, domesticity merging with eroticism:

> Arcadia's Countess, here, in ermin'd pride,
> Is there, Pastora by a fountain side.
> Here Fannia, leering on her own good man,
> And there, a naked Leda with a Swan.
> (*Lady*, 7–10)

If the characters of men are opaque, the problem with women is that they strike attitudes, pose, display themselves in charade with no reference to content at all.

Nonetheless, in listing further examples of women's ability to frame themselves in random identities, Pope acknowledges: 'Whether the Charmer sinner it, or saint it,/If Folly grows romantic, I must paint it' (*Lady*, 15–16). Pope responds to the painted or performed nature of the gender by painting back, and claiming it is a challenge:

> Come then, the colours and the ground prepare!
> Dip in the Rainbow, trick her off in Air,

> Chuse a firm Cloud, before it fall, and in it
> Catch, ere she change, the Cynthia of this minute.
> *(Lady, 17–20)*

The character sketches that follow (21–150) are not merely satiric identifications of an essential instability in female character (though they are that), but a self-reflexive exercise in painterly skill, as if Pope has become the painter that women offer themselves to. As such, the instability curiously aligns itself with, and feeds, imaginative skill.

While the epistle might be drastically summarised in the Virgilian tag *varium et mutabile semper femina*, 'woman is always fickle and changeable', this is also a source of artistic, and sexual, desire: 'Ladies, like variegated Tulips, show,/'Tis to their Changes half their charms we owe' *(Lady, 41–2)*. Calypso (named after one of Odysseus's beguiling nymphs) was attractive in a way which the poet can barely define:

> Strange graces still, and stranger flights she had,
> Was just not ugly, and was just not mad;
> Yet ne'er so sure our passion to create,
> As when she touch'd the brink of all we hate.
> *(Lady, 49–62)*

She challenges any accepted formulation of beauty and skates perilously along the edge of something unnamed, but also incurs a kind of confession from the poet. Other portraits assess oppositions and extremes more confidently; Narcissa might be taken as a concentrated version of Eloisa, or Eloisa without sympathetic narrative perspective:

> Now Conscience chills her, and now Passion burns:
> And Atheism and Religion take their turns;
> A very Heathen in the carnal part,
> Yet still a sad, good Christian at her heart.
> *(Lady, 65–8)*

Philomedé so manages her oppositional qualities as to reverse the positive and negative connotations of different forms of sexual behaviour (69–72), while Flavia's performances and roles manage to confound even the oppositions of pleasure and pain, and life and death: 'You purchase Pain with all that Joy can give,/And die of nothing but a Rage to live' *(Lady, 99–100)*. In all these examples Pope is on sure ground, efficiently turning what might have been a sort of harmonious pattern into chaotic oxymoron.

The Atossa portrait, however, represents a greater challenge, for Atossa's energies cannot be tidily arranged in the contrary snapshots of Pope's couplets. She is 'Scarce once herself, by turns all Womankind!' (*Lady*, 116), insanely proud, storming, passionate, unpredictable. Nothing matches, she cannot even sin successfully: 'So much the Fury still out-ran the Wit,/The Pleasure miss'd her, and the Scandal hit' (*Lady*, 127–8). All the couplets can do (Pope proposes) is show the uniform direction of otherwise incompatible emotions: 'Who breaks with her, provokes Revenge from Hell,/But he's a bolder man who dares be well' (*Lady*, 129–30). Yet Atossa too is a creature of Pope's imagination, as he goes on to remind us:

> Pictures like these, dear Madam, to design,
> Asks no firm hand, and no unerring line;
> Some wand'ring touches, some reflected light,
> Some flying stroke alone can hit 'em right:
> For how should equal Colours do the knack?
> Chameleons who can paint in white and black?
>
> (*Lady*, 151–6)

Pope clearly can, if 'white and black' be taken as the basic antithesis of the couplet – and perhaps of the printed page, Pope's actual medium. It is interesting that to 'hit' these characters the painter/poet must become like them – abandoning 'firm hand' and 'unerring line' to wander, reflect, fly, 'do the knack' (a vulgarism). If Atossa can be likened to a self-involving satirist who 'Shines, in exposing Knaves, and painting Fools,/Yet is, whate'er she hates and ridicules' (*Lady*, 119–20), there must be some implications for Pope's role as satirical portraitist: he creates what he claims to describe.

The implications are gendered ones. Atossa's 'Eddy brain' (*Lady*, 121) might remind us of the 'shifting eddies' by which Pope characterised *all* male minds (*Cob*, 30), and the storming, passionate Atossa might be comforted to remember another Popean view of maleness: 'Oft in the Passions' wild rotation tost,/Our spring of action to ourselves is lost' (*Cob*, 41–2). If her life appears to be a warfare upon earth, we might recall that this was exactly Pope's characterisation of his own life as a 'Wit' in the Preface to the 1717 *Works* **[21]**. The gender separation on which Pope appears to base the pair of poems is not as absolute as it looks, since men's presence in *To a Lady* is usually a guilty one: blame is actually being apportioned to the various husbands and partners who populate the poem in ghostly, inept fashion, including the 'we' who love Calypso against better judgement (*Lady*, 50).

But just where gender oppositions might be undermined, Pope shifts the argument to realign public with male, and private with female 'character', as boundaries are reinscribed with apparent ruthlessness.

But grant, in Public Men sometimes are shown,
A Woman's seen in Private life alone:
Our bolder Talents in full light display'd;
Your Virtues open fairest in the shade.
(*Lady*, 199–202)

We are still in the world of portraiture here (shown, seen, light, display'd, shade), as if men and women need to learn where and how to show themselves off. But the next opposition is one internalised by women: 'Bred to disguise, in Public 'tis you hide' (*Lady*, 203). At this key point, gender suddenly appears to become absolutely knowable and specific:

Men, some to Bus'ness, some to Pleasure take;
But ev'ry Woman is at heart a Rake;
Men, some to Quiet, some to public Strife;
But ev'ry Lady would be Queen for life.
(*Lady*, 215–18)

The lines themselves privilege men by putting them first and giving them balanced, even-handed options, pausing at the commas to make choices; women don't even get the 'caesura' or pause in the centre of their lines. And though Pope has announced that a mere two 'Ruling Passions' 'divide the kind', 'The Love of Pleasure, and the Love of Sway' (*Lady*, 207–10), here he appears to undermine even that distinction (unless there is a difference to be drawn between 'Woman' and 'Lady', as there is between the 'Lady' of the title and the 'Women' she describes in line 2). But it is interesting that Pope chooses 'Rake', traditionally a male form of sexual license, for womens' aspiration, as if really what is being acknowledged in women is not so much inappropriate sexual desire as lack of power. The problem for these women is that there is nothing for them to do outside the domestic sphere, however passion-ate, intelligent, or witty, *except* to play-act in various ready-made roles.

Pope reserves the most accomplished lines in the poem to admonish the female will to power, and consequent mapping of sex onto politics, which the poem is itself half seduced by: 'Yet mark the fate of a whole Sex of Queens!/Pow'r all their end, but Beauty all the means' (*Lady*, 220). As in *Rape of the Lock*, beauty is a finite, transient source of leverage.

Once gone, those who have used it to conquer in the public arena discover that they have condemned themselves to being shadows, non-persons, spectators of their own absence from effective action:

> As Hags hold Sabbaths, less for joy than spight,
> So these their merry, miserable Night;
> Still round and round the Ghosts of Beauty glide,
> And haunt the places where their Honour dy'd.
>
> (*Lady*, 239–42)

This is a social problem, Pope recognises, even as he dances nimbly on the grave:

> See how the World its Veterans rewards!
> A Youth of frolicks, an old Age of Cards,
> Fair to no purpose, artful to no end,
> Young without Lovers, old without a Friend,
> A Fop their Passion, but their Prize a Sot,
> Alive, ridiculous, and dead, forgot!
>
> (*Lady*, 243–8)

Yet the only way out of this catastrophic sequence of diminishing returns is provided by an alternative series of positively balanced qualities, extending over the last fifty lines and becoming, gradually, and with details that disguise it, a portrait of Martha Blount. The Lady whose remark 'Most Women have no Characters at all' (*Lady*, 2) Pope uses to clear the way for his gallery of portraits, is herself granted the only stable female character in the poem. Against the round of dazzling surfaces, Martha's serene self-command is celebrated as an inexhaustible virtue. For a woman self-command is also, of course, self-surrender, as Pope translates the 'ruling passions' of pleasure and power into acceptably feminine paradoxes:

> She, who ne'er answers till a Husband cools,
> Or, if she rules him, never shows she rules;
> Charms by accepting, by submitting sways,
> Yet has her humour most, when she obeys;
>
> (*Lady*, 261–4)

If this is a flattering poetic compromise, Pope aligns it with God's artistic labours, distantly recalling the making of Eve in *Paradise Lost*:

Heav'n, when it strives to polish all it can
Its last best work, but forms a softer Man;
Picks from each sex, to make the Fav'rite blest,
Your love of Pleasure, our desire of Rest,
Blends, in exception to all gen'ral rules,
Your Taste of Follies, with our Scorn of Fools,
Reserve with Frankness, Art with Trust ally'd
Courage with Softness, Modesty with Pride,
Fix'd Principles, with Fancy ever new;
Shakes all together, and produces – You.

(Lady, 271–80)

The 'best kinds of contrarieties', as Pope puts it in his note, do not quite evade the earlier oppositional extremes of female behaviour (the lines are preceded by 'Woman's at best a Contradiction still', *Lady*, 270), nor do they suggest that women can be other than secondary; but they offer as a compliment a kind of option on characteristics initially defined as male. The exchanges and minglings do not take place simply in columns of male and female qualities, rigidly divided, but replace and displace each other, losing the 'Your/Our' markers in a limited field of interchange.

Pope's relations with Martha Blount were almost as close as marriage, but without the powers over her which marriage would have conferred. The conclusion recognises the injustice that married women lost most of their property rights, but can only offer a strictly poetic compensation: Martha is better off without the 'Pelf/That buys your sex a Tyrant o'er itself' (*Lady*, 277–8), because

The gen'rous God, who Wit and Gold refines,
And ripens Spirits as he ripens Mines,
Kept Dross for Duchesses, the world shall know it,
To you gave Sense, Good-humour, and a Poet.

(Lady, 289–92)

In the final arrangement of the four poems, this leads straight into the discussion of riches in the epistles addressed to Bathurst and Burlington. The contrast between these two poems is in some ways less marked than that between *Epistle to Cobham* and *Epistle to a Lady*, since both are addressed to rich aristocrats, and both concern the social application of money. Nonetheless contrast and opposition are again the sources of dynamic sequence.

In *Epistle To Bathurst* **[33–4]**, as with *Epistle to a Lady*, contrasting extremes appear both threatening and curiously liberating. The poem opens with a disagreement: Bathurst holds the view that money ('Gold') is Heaven's joke on mankind, randomly distributed, randomly malign. Pope ascribes to himself a more providential view in which avarice is countered by prodigality in a sort of pumping operation: 'Then careful Heav'n supply'd two sorts of Men,/To squander these, and those to hide agen' (*Bathurst*, 13–14). But this won't quite solve the problem, for money is stranger than this positive/negative, absent/present model can envisage: its operations are mysterious, in a way which commodities themselves are not, and Pope indulges in the whimsical fantasy of life without money (35–64), where bribes would be obvious (a hundred oxen, a thousand jars of oil) and even the most profligate wastrel would be unable to 'squander all in kind'. Yet even gold appears solid compared with credit, as the story about the 'Patriot' leaving the king's chamber with a concealed but bursting bag of guineas indicates (65–8). Credit, on the other hand, is bizarrely free-floating, surreally displacing any principle with magical and dreamlike power:

> Blest paper-credit! last and best supply!
> The lends Corruption lighter wings to fly!
> Gold imp'd by thee, can compass hardest things,
> Can pocket States, can fetch or carry Kings;
> A single leaf shall waft an Army o'er,
> Or ship off Senates to a distant Shore;
> A leaf, like Sibyl's, scatter to and fro
> Our fates and fortunes, as the winds shall blow:
> Pregnant with thousands flits the Scrap unseen,
> And silent sells a King or buys a Queen.
> (*Bathurst*, 69–78)

The financial revolution which had invented all this paper money – the Bank of England, 1694, the institutionalisation of the National Debt, the growth of insurance of all kinds – is here demonised as a kind of self-producing, uncontrollable semiotic event, disconnecting power from intention in a travesty of providence: everything is equal under that economy which anonymously and at no-one's direction 'silent sells a King or buys a Queen' (*Bathurst*, 78). Giving this full rein, indeed driving it even beyond the limits of hyperbole, Pope sets himself a problem not dissimilar to that laid down in *Epistle to a Lady*: how to tame in poetry that which appears unstable and unpredictable. Part of Pope's answer is to restore non-monetary content to the foreground of the poem. Riches cannot buy you health, offspring, life, or body, Pope reminds us in a series of severe moral examples; he goes on to ridicule from a high moral position the various fears, dependencies and fantasies by which individuals envisage their relation to money (109–24). But the lines on Peter Walter, who hopes 'this Nation may be sold' (*Bathurst*, 126), and Sir John Blunt, principle architect of the South Sea Bubble which burst stupendously in 1720 **[25]**, and who is here envisaged in ironic encomium as attempting to put a stop to party disagreements by buying both sides (135–52), indicate that the problem requires a large-scale answer.

Accordingly Pope rewrites the alternating rhythm of avarice and prodigality into a grand scheme; half-quoting lines from the *Essay on Man*, Pope installs near the centre of his poem a cosmic view of the flow of money:

"Extremes in Nature equal good produce,
"Extremes in Man concur to gen'ral use."
Ask we what makes one keep, and one bestow?
That POW'R who bids the Ocean ebb and flow,
Bids seed-time, harvest, equal course maintain,
Thro' reconcil'd extremes of drought and rain,
Builds Life on Death, on Change Duration founds,
And gives th' eternal wheels to know their rounds.
(*Bathurst*, 163–70)

The circulation of money is as natural as the changing of the seasons, as stable as the relation between life and death or between one rhyme and another. Pope illustrates this symmetry in the stories of Old Cotta and his heir (179–218). In a section singled out by Joseph Warton **[153]** for its brilliant vividness, Pope envisions Old Cotta's hall as all but deserted, over-run with weeds (which Cotta eats), cold, guarded by a starving mastiff: an eerie, almost medieval vision of a ruin. His son, however, 'mistook reverse of wrong for right' (*Bathurst*, 200) and bankrupted himself in feasting all and sundry and funding the Hanoverian regime. These are both travesties of nature, extreme wanderings from the seasonal sequence providence ordains; not only does Cotta live off nettles and cress ('soups unbought', *Bathurst*, 184), thus disconnecting his estate from productive agriculture and the wider economy, he fails in his social duties as a landlord (191–94). His son, by contrast, feeds everyone with 'slaughter'd hecatombs' and 'floods of wine', upsetting natural balances in a thoroughly modern way; he cuts down the woods ('The Sylvans groan'), offloads his sheep ('Next goes his Wool'), and in the ultimate crime, 'sells his Lands' (*Bathurst*, 210–12). From these contrary extremes it is then possible to deduce a providentially-ordered central way, represented initially by Bathurst himself (223–8), and subsequently in the story of 'the Man of Ross' (249–80), celebrated for funding civic utilities and for his paternalist care for local people, all on a moderate income. These examples are in sharp contrast to the immense and dirty wealth of those criminals whose careers Pope cites and annotates in earlier lines of the poem (20), as well as to the restoration rake-poet Villiers, 'lord of useless thousands' whose death in rags Pope goes on to describe (*Bathurst*, 299–314).

Thus the poem seems architecturally designed to offer symmetrical contrasts of unstable but dynamic relations to wealth revolving around a core of stable civic practice; Sir Balaam's fall through the catastrophic corruptions of money closes the poem with absolute technical and moral mastery, aligning it with a biblical contempt for riches. Nonetheless, that story is itself introduced as a kind of retreat from troublesome questions about money (335–8), and not every extreme in the poem can be easily 'reconcil'd' (*Bathurst*, 168). Most of the villains of the piece are Whig-inclined, if not actually henchmen of the ministry, but the poem cannot state this openly; Bathurst and the Man of Ross here are examples of civic virtue based on the rural values of Pope's undisclosed political allegiance. Before the Man of Ross gets around to dividing the bread ration, paying for orphans to be apprenticed, and healing the sick, he is celebrated for reorganizing the landscape itself along magical-biblical lines: his virtue is derived from a supposedly pre-political 'nature' (253–62). Young Cotta's mistake, by contrast, is to devote his landed inheritance to 'GEORGE and LIBERTY', the Hanoverian cause, always aligned in Pope's imagination with an inability to appreciate landed virtues. Balaam has all the lineaments of a joyless Whig businessman, whose acknowledged virtues are easily corrupted (not by failure, but by success) into an overweening self-sufficiency: finally compromised by his lubricious wife's gambling debts, the Whigs desert him but pillage his fortune for 'the Crown': 'The Devil and the King divide the prize,/And sad Sir Balaam curses God and dies' (*Bathurst*, 401–2). The Whig King is here aligned with the Devil in a fantasy of Tory revenge for years of harassment by Whig politicians: the 'Coningsby' who 'harangues' against Balaam (*Bathurst*, 397) was a key player in the impeachment of Pope's friend Robert Harley in 1715 [19]. One element of the poem is thus a nostalgic retrieval of a mythic state whereby money could only be properly distributed on the basis of landed security, against a 'modern' situation full of embezzlement, fraud and forgery.

But there are difficulties in the more transcendent argument about uses of money within a providential scheme; if providence ordains an overall balance, where is the moral basis for criticizing or recommending individual spending patterns? To move from *Bathurst* to *Burlington* **[33]**, as we do in Pope's rearrangement, is to approach the question from a different angle. Here, we enter a world where the power that money confers appears strangely divorced from the intentional actions of those that possess it. In *Bathurst* money is always forceful, it does things, whether positive or negative; in *Burlington* the proper connection between money and power often seems severed and in need of appropriate restoration. Neither the miser nor the prodigal, the economic motors of *Bathurst*, can actually enjoy, use or 'taste' their wealth. The prodigal cannot internalise his property: 'Not for himself he sees, or hears, or eats;/Artists must choose his Pictures, Music, Meats' (*Burl*, 5–6); when he buys works of art, 'Think we all these are for himself? no more/Than his fine Wife, alas! or finer Whore' (*Burl*, 11–12). There is a loss of agency: other people choose what he eats, his buying is all vicarious and externalised towards those with a focused idea of their collections, even sexual relations turned into a matter of relatively priced and prized commodities which are also the property of others ('fine' and 'finer' are particularly ironic adjectives, derived from the language of connoisseurship). 'Taste', one of the concepts signalled in the first version of the poem, posits a literal root for the metaphorical sense of intellectual pleasure: but the prodigal cannot even eat according to his own desire.

The idea of property turning into show is metamorphosed through the examples of Virro, Visto and Bubo (13–22) into the supposed solidities of architecture and gardening. Aspiration to 'taste' only produces 'show', a self-satirising demonstration of *lack* of taste: 'A standing sermon, at each year's expense,/That never Coxcomb reach'd Magnificence!' (*Burl*, 21–22). Burlington is introduced now as the arbiter of architectural theory, responsible for the recovery of the classical orders of architecture, civic designs based on roman models, grand symmetrical forms against the baroque love of intricate detail and ornament. But the celebration of Burlington's achievements is muted: only one couplet is actually assigned to the main point ('You show us, Rome was glorious, not profuse,/And pompous buildings once were things of Use', *Burl*, 23–4). Even this 'show' will probably do no more than spawn tasteless imitations, random excrescences, which faintly cloud the picture of Burlington's own positive contributions with all-too visible grotesqueries (29–32). Publication of elaborate volumes, themselves 'monumental' in scope, is not enough to prevent wastrels starving 'by rules of art'.

Pope comes to the rescue by tactfully ascribing to Burlington the sentiment that 'more needful than Expence' (the outward 'show'), and more primary than taste (the process of internalization) is 'Sense', an inbuilt faculty of appreciation, which like Taste conveniently grounds its metaphorical meaning of intellectual order in bodily feeling. Sense is a 'Light, which in yourself you must perceive' (*Burl*, 45), Pope proposes, in a line which might be acknowledging Burlington's self-awareness *or* more generally advocating self-study for the wider readership – for Pope is subtly turning the ground of taste and sense towards his own special area of landscape gardening. In the section that follows (47–70), Pope positions himself as instructor (the recipient of the instruction might again be Burlington, or it might be the general reader).

> Consult the Genius of the Place in all;
> That tells the Waters or to rise, or fall,
> Or helps th' ambitious Hill the heav'ns to scale,
> Or scoops in circling theatres the Vale,
> Calls in the Country, catches opening glades,
> Joins willing woods, and varies shades from shades,
> Now breaks, or now directs, th' intending Lines;
> Paints as you plant, and, as you work, designs.
>
> (*Burl*, 57–64)

Pope's garden (an example of the shift away from geometric patterning towards softer, curved lines and 'natural' planting) takes over from the neoclassical symmetries of architecture. The landscape appears (like Belinda in *The Rape of the Lock*) to conspire in its own transformation into art. Pope is doing more than telling us to cooperate with our landscape environment, rather than impose on it, when we make our gardens (though this is an important point). It is rather that proper imaginative power actually dissolves the relation between agency and object: the 'Genius of the Place' instructs and aids the landscape in its operations (as the Man of Ross did in *Bathurst*), actively furthering ('Scoops', 'Calls in', 'catches') what the landscape itself desires ('willing woods'), bracketing human action with its own prior agency ('Paints as you plant, and, as you work, designs'). In effect the landscape does it all for you; 'Parts answering parts shall slide into a whole', like some magically dreamed-up poem where 'Spontaneous beauties' simply line up to be admired (*Burl*, 66–7).

It is possible to sin against these theoretical recreations of *Windsor-Forest*: Villario completes a garden which appears perfectly in line with the checks and balances advocated by Pope, but which is left to the

instructed reader to enjoy because he does not actually like it (79–88);
Old and Young Sabinus rush to extremes of open and closed vistas in a
strange transformation of the avarice and profligacy which
characterised Old and Young Cotta in *Bathurst* into landscape terms
(89–98). But at the centre of Pope's vision is Timon's villa (99–168),
itself a massive set-piece collecting together all the negative satiric attri-
butes of false taste which are locally distributed through the rest of
the poem (a sort of arrogant totality in itself) **[33]**. Timon suffers from
a problem of scale:

> Greatness, with Timon, dwells in such a draught
> As brings all Brobdignag before your thought.
> To compass this, his building is a Town,
> His pond an Ocean, his parterre a Down:
> Who but must laugh, the Master when he sees,
> A puny insect, shiv'ring at a breeze!
>
> (*Burl*, 103–8)

The more grandiose the scheme, the more diminished the 'Master';
this garden hubristically claims superhuman draughtsmanship. Timon's
landscape is all about control, imposition, art, a symmetry which
disfigures:

> No pleasing Intricacies intervene,
> No artful wildness to perplex the scene;
> Grove nods at grove, each Alley has a brother,
> And half the platform just reflects the other.
>
> (*Burl*, 115–18)

It is precisely the couplet art of symmetry which rejects the formal
pattern of landscape. The order of symmetry was for houses; the order
of variety for landscape. As often in Pope that which is over-symmetrical
becomes grotesquely contradictory:

> The suff'ring eye inverted Nature sees,
> Trees cut to Statues, Statues thick as trees,
> With here a Fountain, never to be play'd,
> And there a Summer-house, that knows no shade;
>
> (*Burl*, 119–22)

Pope contrives these horrors to have a certain incongruous beauty,
('There Gladiators fight, or die, in flow'rs') as if the poetry's guidance

through the scene reclaims unintentional pleasures from the disasters of taste. But this only emphasises the disconnection between intention and result so far as Timon is concerned.

Pope has two answers to these perversions of power. One justifies the situation in a way familiar from *Bathurst*: 'Yet hence the Poor are cloath'd, the Hungry fed' (*Burl*, 169): a fool and his money stabilise the economy, as the adage might run. Another answer runs deeper:

> Another age shall see the golden Ear
> Imbrown the Slope, and nod on the Parterre,
> Deep Harvests bury all his pride has plann'd,
> And laughing Ceres re-assume the land.
>
> (*Burl*, 173–6)

This mythic revenge restores Roman agrarian values to the land: Ceres is the Roman goddess of agriculture. There have been many candidates for the 'original' of Timon's villa, since government hacks put it about that it was specifically intended to satirise Cannons, the mansion of the Duke of Chandos; others include Houghton, Sir Robert Walpole's vast monument to himself in Norfolk; Blenheim, Marlbrough's breathtakingly self-aggrandizing palace near Oxford; and Chatsworth in Derbyshire. They are all Whig palaces: in Pope's imagination, the Country gets its own back here.

Laughing Ceres ushers in the prophetic coda, which sees the land as the dynamic origin of all monetary and aesthetic virtues. There is less sense of providential ordering here than in *Bathurst*: it is up to individuals to produce money the right way, and use it wisely. Bathurst and Burlington are models of planting and building, but the real template is more archetypal still:

> His Father's Acres who enjoys in peace,
> Or makes his Neighbour glad, if he encrease;
> Whose chearful Tenants bless their yearly toil,
> Yet to their Lord owe more than to the soil;
> Whose ample Lawns are not asham'd to feed
> The milky heifer and deserving steed;
> Whose rising Forests, not for pride or show,
> But future Buildings, future Navies grow:
> Let his plantations stretch from down to down,
> First shade a Country, and then raise a Town.
>
> (*Burl*, 181–90)

This is the way things ought to be done: the landlord himself acts as paternalistic steward of the soil, looking after the tenants (who create his wealth), using his land to nurture farm animals which thus become valuably 'milky' and 'deserving', and finally running, in the substitute form of his estate's produce, wood, the country and its empire: a dazzling Tory version of Young Cotta's misplaced Hanoverian project.

Only after this mythic regeneration of country values is installed does Pope allow Burlington to occupy any sort of controlling role: 'You too proceed!', he charges the Earl, as if the Earl and his money were somehow absent from what has gone before. The finale looks triumphalist, with Burlington apparently in godlike control of stone forms like harbours which themselves reach out to control 'the roaring Main' (*Burl*, 199–202). But coming at the edge of the poem, there is something marginal as well as elemental about the contest between water and stone, fluid and solid. The 'Imperial Works' (an architecture which promotes imperial expansion) are a kind of challenge to Burlington, who is perhaps not quite a straightforward representative of architectural virtue. No doubt Pope positioned the *Epistle to Burlington* at the end of his sequence because the final upsurge of architectural power is more forward-looking than the precipitate fall of Balaam which ends the *Epistle to Bathurst*; yet that power may itself not be without a certain equivocal hyperbole.

Further Reading

The *Epistles* have for some time been regarded as at the core of Pope's moral endeavours. Rogers (1955) and Dixon (1968) offer standard introductory readings of the poems in historical context. Morris (1984) reads the poems as reflecting a complex and intelligent purpose; more hostile accounts of the 'ideology' the poems promulgate can be found in Brown (1985). The individual poems have occupied a diverse role in criticism, with much less on *Epistle to Cobham* than the others (though a good account of that poem's 'argument' can be found in Sitter 1977), and with *Epistle to a Lady* more or less fenced off in gender issues (though Parkin 1965 offers a sensitive account of 'time' in the poem) **[171–81]**. The *Epistle to Bathurst* has attracted a good deal of critical attention. Wasserman (1960) defends the poem's unity of argument as a sort of secular sermon in which *concordia discors*, the clash of opposites which constitutes an overall harmony in the cosmos, is combined with Aristotelian *mediocritas*, which sees virtue as the mid-point between opposing vices. But several critics have argued that the poem is more morally ambiguous in its view of monetary disorder, even complicit, overall, with the laissez-faire economics it locally satirises, than it can comfortably acknowledge (Erskine-Hill 1972b; Nicolson 1994; Brown 1985, 108–17). Barrell and Guest (1987) see the poem as even more fundamentally riven by the contradictory forces of 'economic amoralism' and Christian-based satire; they also argue that certain practices of composition and of reading trained Pope's contemporaries to ignore or synthesise such contradictions in the ideological interests of the emergent capitalism with which the poem engages. In a different vein, Engell (1988) interestingly aligns literary and monetary concerns in the poem, with writing becoming like money and vice versa. The *Epistle to Burlington*, too, has come to seem less secure in its architectural certainties (Ayres 1990). Ferraro (1996) argues (on the basis of Pope's revisions to the poem in manuscript and print) that Burlington's role as positive *exemplum* is a good deal less central in the later versions than it was in the early versions; that what Burlington represents is more vulnerable to disastrous imitation than is normally assumed; and that something altogether greater than Burlington is being elaborately provided as the true context for Pope's critiques.

(g) *EPISTLE TO DR ARBUTHNOT* (1735) [*TE* IV: 91–127]

Pope advertises the fact that his poem is a patchwork or hybrid, created from several existing fragments and versions **[37]**. As the poem emerges from various levels of publicity – private notes, manuscript circulation, miscellany fragment, letter – so it is *about* the various forms of publicity which writing and writers have to engage with. In his 'Advertisement' Pope gives as the occasion for publication two verse attacks on him: *Verses Address'd to the Imitator ... of Horace*, compiled in 'witty fornication' (Pope's phrase) between Lady Mary Wortley Montagu and Lord Hervey, and Hervey's *Epistle to a Doctor of Divinity from a Nobleman at Hampton Court* which transgressed the boundaries of public and private in that they attacked not only his writing ('of which being publick the Publick judge'), but his 'Person, Morals, and Family' (*TE* IV: 95) **[36]**. The poem is, on the other hand, addressed to a dying friend, and acts as a testimony to that mutual regard. The most obviously autobiographical of Pope's poems, it gives not only a defence of his stance as a writer but a beautifully imagined mythic account of his parentage. Not introspective in the manner of Wordsworth, it defines a personal space which is always under pressure from the selfish probing of the Dunces, but also always made meaningful by the presence of the virtuous.

In some ways, the poem is a miniature, personalised *Dunciad*, with the itch for writing destabilizing all manner of propriety – class, gender, the bourgeois ethics of trade – and invading not just Westminster but Twickenham, a place of holy retirement. Paradoxically, the poem opens with the repeated word 'Shut'. Private space is all too permeable, as Pope characterises it:

> What Walls can guard me, or what Shades can hide?
> They pierce my Thickets, thro' my Grot they glide,
> By land, by water, they renew the charge,
> They stop the Chariot, and they board the Barge.
> *(Arb, 7–10)*

Partly this is comic exaggeration, the first means of rebutting Hervey's assertions that Pope was a friendless outcast: he has only too many so-called 'friends' (a more lasting answer to the charge is registered by the pervasive dialogue with the true friend Arbuthnot, and by the catalogue of those by whom he is 'belov'd' at 135–44). It is also partly designed to idealise the ambiguous space which the poem creates, an 'at home' with Alexander Pope, offered to Arbuthnot/the reader rather than seized by some Dunce (some of the poem's contrary depictions of space oddly resemble those in *Eloisa to Abelard*). 'Twit'nam', as Pope familiarly names his home, may be besieged by refugees from Parnassus (home of the Muses), or Bedlam (the London madhouse) – it is hard to tell the difference, Pope imlies – but poetry itself can offer alternative versions of representative space. The trouble with the Dunces is that not only do they not respect other people's privacy, but they do not respect their own. The drunk parson, 'maudlin poetess' and 'rhyming peer' who beset Pope for advice ('to keep them mad or vain', *Arb*, 22) are *by definition* 'wrong' as writers; aspirant poets should not give up the day job (15–26). Indeed, poetic aspirations are cruelly in contrast to material needs: the 'Man of Rhyme' who walks so casually forth on Sundays and is 'happy' to catch Pope 'just at Dinner-time' is only in jovial mood because he cannot be arrested for debt on a Sunday and Pope will give him a meal (*Arb*, 11–14); another is incongruously 'Lull'd by soft Zephyrs thro' the broken Pane' (*Arb*, 41), and finds himself 'Oblig'd by hunger and Request of friends' (*Arb*, 43) to publish, in Pope's snigger at the way writers pretend to have been encouraged into print by zealous friends. In a succinctly modulated example, 'Three things another's modest wishes bound,/My Friendship, and a Prologue, and ten Pound' (*Arb*, 47–8). In many ways, Pope argues, opposition is better than this kind of friendship, and Pope recalls the opening lines of the poem by getting rid of the most importunate and impoverished (in every sense) Dunce: 'Glad of a quarrel, strait I clap the door,/Sir, let me see your works and you no more' (*Arb*, 67–8).

Better, Pope argues, a foe who can actually bite than a flatterer whose spittle might infect one (106). The desire for opposition continues into a comic self-portrait which deals with the Hervey-Montagu charge that Pope's deformity represented his deformed mind (they write: 'with the Emblem of thy crooked Mind,/Mark'd on thy back, like *Cain*, by God's own hand': Barnard 1973: 272) by constructing a composite statue of bizarre flattery through which Pope's self-knowledge can shine through:

> There are, who to my Person pay their court,
> I cough like *Horace*, and tho' lean, am short,
> *Ammon*'s great Son one shoulder had too high,
> Such *Ovid*'s nose, and "Sir! you have an *Eye-*"
> Go on, obliging Creatures, make me see
> All that disgrac'd my Betters, met in me:
> (*Arb*, 115–20)

Pope is not to be won by flattery any more than he is to be hurt by ridicule of his 'wretched little Carcase' (Hervey/Montagu, in Barnard 1973: 271) **[184–5]**.

Beyond physique lies personality, and Pope leads us inside to a moment of questioning which links poetic with personal origins: 'Why did I write? what sin to me unknown/Dipt me in Ink, my Parents', or my own?' (*Arb*, 125–6). This parody of baptism, with its overtones of original sin, is immediately redeemed by the image of Pope as the poet who is born, not made: 'As yet a Child, nor yet a Fool to Fame,/I lisp'd in Numbers, for the Numbers came' (*Arb*, 127–8). Poetry comes naturally to Pope, and unlike the pestilential Dunces of the opening lines, Pope 'left no Calling for this idle trade,/No duty broke, no Father dis-obey'd' (*Arb*, 129–30). The 'idle trade' suggests that Pope's 'Muse' is not tainted by anything so sordid as money, functioning 'merely' for private consumption, seconding the palliative care of Dr Arbuthnot – 'To help me thro' this long, Disease, my Life' (*Arb*, 132). Pope finds a way of converting the disease/life link which his enemies highlighted into a celebratory union between poetry and medicine, poet and doctor: a sort of self-protecting circle to which we gain privileged access. The circle is widened, as it must be, when Pope goes on to ask 'But why then publish?' (*Arb*, 135). The answer is that the publication that matters has already happened, for Pope's early friends would all 'tell me I could write' (*Arb*, 136): the list of early critics (Granville, Walsh, Garth, Congreve, Swift and so on) is here arranged in a decorous gallery of supporters who combine private friendship with a sort of publication circle. The request of such friends to publish (in contradistinction to the hack's imaginary friends at 44) cannot be denied.

Surmounting 'venal' critics like Gildon and Dennis by not answering them (151–4), and 'verbal' critics such as Theobald and Bentley by converting their pedantic attention to trifles into a sort of curious insect life such as a man of taste might observe in a museum (169–70), Pope leads to the first of the three satiric portraits which, with the contrasting self-portraits, form the argumentative core of the poem. In a vast conditional sentence (beginning 'were there One', *Arb*, 193), Pope sketches a different and more important kind of literary corruption. This 'One' has everything going for him, in the same way that Pope has: 'Blest with each Talent and each Art to please/And born to write, converse, and live with ease' (*Arb*, 195–6). His problem is a self-regarding authority which can make no authentic contact with anyone outside himself, especially anyone who resembles himself:

> Shou'd such a man, too fond to rule alone,
> Bear, like the *Turk*, no brother near the throne,
> View him with scornful, yet with jealous eyes,
> And hate for Arts that caus'd himself to rise;
> (Arb, 197–200)

His critical views are not open (whether positive or negative) but poisonously covert: 'Damn with faint praise, assent with civil leer,/ And without sneering, teach the rest to sneer' (*Arb*, 201–2); like the Dunces whose open enmity is better than false friendship, and unlike Pope, this 'One' is compromised by combinations of qualities which are mutually corrupting:

> Willing to wound, and yet afraid to strike,
> Just hint a fault, and hesitate dislike;
> Alike reserv'd to blame, or to commend,
> A tim'rous foe, and a suspicious friend ...
> (Arb, 203–6)

He is throned (like the hack/spider of 89–94), self-pleasing amid his own flattery: 'Like *Cato*, give his little Senate laws,/and sit attentive to his own applause' (*Arb*, 209–10). The *Cato* reference hints at the identity which Pope is about to reveal: 'Who but must laugh, if such a man there be?/Who would not weep, if *Atticus* were he!' (*Arb*, 213–14). As with the two other portraits, Pope does not quite reveal identity: Atticus is close enough to 'Addison' **[18]** for the identification to be obvious, yet as Pope has promised in the Advertisement a decent veil is retained. But as Pope's note to these lines suggest there is a complex argument going on here about publicity, for the portrait was already in controversial circulation as an example of Pope's ingratitude to friends; Pope is here constructing a sort of reverse self-portrait in which aspects ascribed to his own personality (jealousy, secretiveness, fear) are corralled into an alter ego who can be contrasted with his own self-image to follow. The manner of the lines' insertion here, as a satiric set-piece, also *exemplifies* the art of satiric characterisation which Pope's Addison was too timid to engage in.

Sandwiched between this portrait and the next is a segment contrasting Pope's position with Addison's. Pope established his contrary kingdom precisely in the absence of clubbish courts:

> I sought no homage from the Race that write;
> I kept, like *Asian* Monarchs, from their sight:
> Poems I heeded (now be-rym'd so long)
> No more than Thou, great GEORGE! a Birth-day Song.
> (*Arb*, 219–22)

Pope's '*Asian* Monarchs' are greater, nearer God's invisibility, than Addison's jealous '*Turk*' (*Arb*, 218), and the further ironic comparison with George II, a supremely insolent piece of chumminess, pointedly conjoins the false and empty world of routine panegyric (the fulsome odes the Poet Laureate, Cibber, was supposed to produce each year for the philistine George) with the flattery which Pope has already rejected.

Flattery is for patrons, and in the 'Bufo' section (231–48) Pope changes the register into amused condescension towards the desperate scramble for reward which the patronage system engendered. Another throned figure ('Proud, as *Apollo* on his forked hill,/Sate full-blown *Bufo*, puff'd by ev'ry quill'; *Arb*, 231–2), the bloated Bufo is 'Fed with soft Dedication all day long' in a glorious transformation of the written word into pre-digested baby-food. Bufo (the latin name means 'Toad', for Pope is stepping up his abusiveness) likes it, in a more dangerous way than Addison. Bufo is a caricature of noble patrons who modelled their largesse on the Roman noble Maecenas who gave Horace the Sabine farm on which he could display his independence. For Pope, whose Twickenham version of the Sabine farm had been won not from patronage but from the Homer translation, this reciprocity no longer applied and the description of one's patron as a latterday Maecenas was simply a cheap cliché (*'Horace* and he went hand in hand in song', *Arb*, 234). Again, the language is one of politeness and poetic aspiration, but what the poets really want is cash, or food: the poets 'first his Judgment ask'd, and then a Place' (*Arb*, 237–244). As this picture has become more bodily in accent (the patron gets fed on dedication while the aspiring 'Bards' lack real food) than that of Atticus, so the importance of the scene is greater: Atticus was confined to his 'little senate', but Bufo thinks he's Apollo, god of poetry, and moreover is capable of wielding patronage in the political sense of being able to award a 'place', a safe government job.

Again, the portrait is designed to offer discriminations. Bufo's comic situation should recall to mind Pope's at the start of the poem: but whereas Pope is harassed by those importuning him for help ('My Friendship, and a Prologue, and ten Pound', *Arb*, 48), Bufo thrives on it. Patrons have their uses, for they may draw the crowd from Pope ('May Dunce by Dunce be whistled off my hands!', *Arb*, 254), and tend to leave alone true poets (Dryden, 245–8, and Gay, 256–60). Closing another door, Pope leaves Bufo to his role and depicts himself as enjoying the greater ease of independence: 'Above a Patron, tho' I condescend/ Sometimes to call a Minister my Friend', as he puts it with mock grandeur (*Arb*, 265–6). Against the concealed contention between poet and patron, Pope suggests that he is so comfortable with his own relation to poetry and criticism that he need not have the relation at all – he 'Can sleep without a Poem in my head,/Nor know, if *Dennis* be alive or dead' (*Arb*, 269–70). This is a pose, of course – Pope knew perfectly well that Dennis had died very recently, but affects not to have noticed – but it is important here to establish the primacy of ordinary living as the basis for verse. 'Heav'ns! was I born for nothing but to write?', he queries (*Arb*, 272), echoing his earlier image of himself as lisping in numbers, but now suggesting that the born poet needs to do more than simply reel off verses. Silence has its virtues, and Pope cannot 'chuse but smile' at those who imagine every new poem must be by him – poor critics, who pay him the wrong sort of compliment again with their rumours and guesses (275–82). From this position of untouchable retirement Pope swivels towards more serious exponents of libellous misrepresentation, in the public repudiation and truth-telling he unleashes upon 'Sporus'.

The third portrait intensifies images from the other two. 'Sporus' was a boy castrated, dressed as a woman and 'married' by the Emperor

Nero; in 1735 he is Lord Hervey, supporter of Walpole, confidant of the Queen, and a flamboyant bisexual. He is also many of the things Pope was alleged to be – insect-like, venomous, impotent, scandalous, dirty: in the *Verses* Pope figures as a 'fretful *Porcupine*', 'angry little Monster', a wasp, and (in a barbed quotation from Pope's own *Epistle to Burlington*) 'a puny Insect shiv'ring at a Breeze' (Barnard 1973: 271). 'Sporus' is a clear attempt to alienate all the unfavourable qualities ascribed to Pope into a demonic alter ego who destabilises poetry, politics, gender, and self. Arbuthnot vainly suggests that satire is harmless in the case of so insubstantial a thing as Sporus – '"Who breaks a Butterfly upon a Wheel?"' (*Arb*, 308); but Pope takes the butterfly image and works it up and down with icy efficiency in order to prove the covert toxicity of the creature – the decorative, ineffectual nature of the insect is itself offensive:

> Yet let me flap this Bug with gilded wings,
> This painted Child of Dirt that stinks and stings;
> Whose Buzz the Witty and the Fair annoys,
> Yet Wit ne'er tastes, and Beauty ne'er enjoys,
> So well-bred Spaniels civilly delight
> In mumbling of the Game they dare not bite.
> $\qquad\qquad\qquad\qquad$ (*Arb*, 309–14)

Sporus is an insect without a sting or bite, whether satiric or sexual; civility becomes a meretricious way of avoiding engagement and expression. Hervey wore make-up, but had no teeth: surface flamboyance and inner impotence are superbly caught in these images. 'Mumbling' also suggests poor literary utterance, and in the following lines Pope takes an image which Hervey and Montagu had contrived for Pope, reverses it, aligns it with Milton and shows which combatant can really write. Hervey/Montagu:

> When God created Thee, one would believe,
> He said the same, as *to the Snake of Eve;*
> To Human Race Antipathy declare,
> *'Twixt them and thee be everlasting War.*
> $\qquad\qquad\qquad$ (Barnard 1973: 271)

Pope turns this 'antipathy' around:

> Whether in florid Impotence he speaks,
> And, as the Prompter breathes, the Puppet squeaks;

Or at the Ear of *Eve*, familiar Toad,
Half Froth, half Venom, spits himself abroad,
In Puns, or Politicks, or Tales, or Lyes,
Or Spite, or Smut, or Rymes, or Blasphemies.

(*Arb*, 317–22)

As a politician, Hervey tells Queen Caroline ('*Eve*') what Walpole ('the Prompter') wants her to hear; as a poet, he 'spits himself abroad', in an egotistical display of toothless but poisonous lather ('Half Froth, half Venom') in which blasphemy is the same as rhyme and puns the same as politics. Nothing has stable identity, not even gender:

His Wit all see-saw between *that* and *this*,
Now high, now low, now Master up, now Miss,
And he himself one vile Antithesis.
Amphibious Thing! that acting either Part,
The trifling Head, or the corrupted Heart!
Fop at the Toilet, Flatt'rer at the Board,
Now trips a Lady, and now struts a Lord.
Eve's Tempter thus the Rabbins have exprest,
A Cherub's face, a Reptile all the rest;
Beauty that shocks you, Parts that none will trust,
Wit that can creep, and Pride that licks the dust.

(*Arb*, 323–33)

Hervey's sexual identity is all performance and gesture, and no authentic essence ('Now trips a Lady, and now struts a Lord'); his mind and writing are like a couplet gone wrong ('His Wit all see-saw ... Now Master up, now Miss'), and the 'vile Antithesis' which Pope gives as 'he himself' comes *outside* the couplet to which it notionally belongs, in a third rhyming line, as if Hervey's contradictions cannot be balanced out within a couplet pattern but engender an overloaded triplet **[182–4]**.

It is against this summation that Pope sets the record of his entire career, with a series of defiant, discriminating negatives:

Not Fortune's Worshipper, nor Fashion's Fool,
Not Lucre's Madman, nor Ambition's Tool,
Not proud, nor servile, be one Poet's praise
That, if he pleas'd, he pleas'd by manly ways;

(*Arb*, 334–7)

After the gender ambivalences of Sporus we are given Pope's 'manly ways', and manly ways indicate an heroic poetry which considers flattery shameful, truth superior to 'Fancy's Maze', Virtue better than Fame. Pope defines himself against the whole range of corrupt social practices into which Sporus pours his energies (362–7).

Yet Pope has more still to offer, and seeks in the last fifty lines to modulate his voice once again into something more apparently private. The other author of the *Verses* was Lady Mary Wortley Montagu, and Pope devotes a mere two lines to her, and not even really lines of attack but self-inculpation: 'Yet soft by Nature, more a Dupe than Wit,/*Sapho* can tell you how this Man was bit' (*Arb*, 368–9). Perhaps answering the contention that Pope was 'No more for loving made, than to be lov'd' (Barnard 1973: 271), this is a quite unexpected and dangerous admission, as if Pope publishes the fact that Lady Mary could embarrass him by revealing some of their earlier flirtatious relations ('bit' here means something like 'smitten' or 'cheated'); it translates the loveless-ness ascribed to Pope in the *Verses* into a reminder to Lady Mary of that earlier relationship, an exposure of the grief attached to it, and a self-portrait of the supposedly venomous satirist as 'soft by Nature'. It is this last aspect with which Pope ends the poem. Answering the charge that his birth was 'obscure', Pope chooses the calmest of tones to give an idealised portrait of his father, a patriot of 'gentle Blood (part shed in Honour's Cause,/While yet in *Britain* Honour had Applause)' (*Arb*, 388–9), who kept out of all controversy ('The good Man walk'd innoxious thro' his Age', *Arb*, 395), in a true indication of 'gentle Blood'. The elegiac depiction of his dying mother, nursed with all imaginable piety, returns us to the domestic scene, an independence which is not loneliness, the door shut against the world, but open to the sympathetic reader.

Further Reading

Modern critics have tended to regard the poem as one of Pope's most skilful attempts to portray 'the poet in the poems', or to follow and explicate the turns and modulations of that image (Rogers 1973b; Hotch 1974; Donaldson 1988). The literal truth of the record, is of course as open to question as it is carefully constructed, and the multiplicity of roles, voices and positions can be made to look contradictory rather than complementary. Materialist criticism points out that Pope omits from the poem all mention of his own engagement with the book trade, presenting instead a wholly mythic account of himself as a poet born not made (Hammond 1986). Such critiques, however, have not seriously dented the poem's position as Pope's most complex, meaningful and dynamic *apologia* for his role as poet in society.

(h) *IMITATIONS OF HORACE* (1733–40) [*TE* IV]

The *Epistle to Dr Arbuthnot* offers an autobiographical image of the platform from which the critique of society in *Epistles to Several Persons* is launched; but in his poetry of the 1730s Pope increasingly utilised the Roman satirist Horace as mentor, sounding board and model. The series of poems published in the Horatian mode between 1733 and 1738 presents a great range of voice (there are lyrics, as well as epistles and satires), giving Pope the opportunity to try out in extended form the many tonal variants he had deployed in *To Arbuthnot*: domestic, filial, fraternal; witty, ironic, self-mocking; bitter, angry, cold. Imitations of Donne and Swift (and, in a double-bluff, of Pope himself) are woven into the sequence. Taken as a whole the series selects the values of retirement, friendship, independence, and poetry itself from Horace's oeuvre, and conspicuously ditches Horace's imperial panegyric and 'insider' status: the only patron Pope can come up with to match Horace's Maecenas is Bolingbroke, the 'Patriot' outsider in permanent internal exile. Horace's Sabine farm, the place of his sober economy, is a gift from the noble patron Maecenas; Pope's Twickenham is more hard-won, and less protected. **[35–7]**

The first poem in the series (*The First Satire of the Second Book of Horace, Imitated* **[35]**) was occasioned, Pope tells us, 'by the Clamour raised on some of my epistles. An answer from Horace was both more full, and of more Dignity, than any I could have made in my own person' (*TE* IV: 3). But he goes on to make the point that both Horace and Donne (who had also imitated Horace) 'were acceptable to the Princes and Ministers under whom they lived', a condition which, he implies, has disappeared from the current literary scene; in presenting the Latin text opposite the English version (his habit throughout), Pope makes it immediately obvious that his poem is not far short of twice the length of Horace's (he also used typographical emphasis to show up particular deviations from his model). The additions greatly enrich the irony of the self-presentation:

> There are (I scarce can think it, but am told)
> There are to whom my Satire seems too bold,

Scarce to wise *Peter* complaisant enough,
And something said of *Chartres* much too rough. ...
Tim'rous by Nature, of the Rich in awe,
I come to Council learned in the Law.
You'll give me, like a Friend both sage and free,
Advice; and (as you use) without a Fee.

(*Sat. 2.i*, 1–4, 7–10)

The pretend head-shaking, the conversational interjections, the casual naming of individuals satirised by Pope, the little dig at (most) lawyers' appetite for fees – all these are extensions of Horace's more direct scenario. The fake piety of 'Tim'rous by Nature, of the Rich in awe' sets up a seductively non-satiric persona, in need of professional help. Pope stresses the unofficial nature of the consultation (omitting Horace's report that some have accused his satire of stretching *ultra legem*, beyond the law), for though it is part of his overall concern to distinguish satire from libel, and to establish satire as a quasi-legal sanction in itself, at this point the pose is one of engaging bemusement. There follows a series of exchanges between the prudential lawyer (Pope's friend William Fortescue, a court insider and confidant of Walpole), who advises rest, sleep, drugs, sex – anything to take the mind off writing – and the wheedling poet, who, it seems, just can't keep his mouth shut. This gradually mutates into a discussion of what poetry can be under a royal family who 'scarce can bear their *Laureate* twice a Year' (*Sat. 2.i*, 34); those who go down the route of patronage and panegyric produce noisy nonsense (23–8) while the king trusts to 'History' for 'Praise' – a somewhat ironic hope, Pope implies.

The central section of the poem (45–100) quietly shifts gear: Pope takes centre stage, initially defending poetry as no more than a personal amusement, like drinking or eating, then as a form of self-expression, before swivelling round to a startling revision of the standard metaphor of satire as social mirror:

In me what Spots (for Spots I have) appear,
Will prove at least the Medium must be clear.
In this impartial Glass, my Muse intends
Fair to expose myself, my Foes, my Friends ...

(*Sat. 2.i*, 55–8)

The self-deprecation is no longer ironic, but actually a guarantee of honesty: foes and friends are linked by the equations of alliteration in a 'glass' which makes no distorting distinctions because it does not spare the 'self' which writes. Self-criticism becomes self-celebration as the exigencies of the public's obsession with Pope remind us (he contends) of his essential, and virtuous, centrality:

> My Head and Heart thus flowing thro' my Quill,
> Verse-man or Prose-man, term me which you will,
> Papist or Protestant, or both between,
> Like good *Erasmus* in an honest Mean,
> In Moderation placing all my Glory,
> While Tories call me Whig, and Whigs a Tory.
>
> (*Sat. 2.i*, 63–8)

Moderation gets you called an extremist only by extremists: honest, uncorrupted expression is bound to issue in an unmediated truth unaffected by ties of any literary or political form. It is not quite straight-faced, and Pope goes on to evince some characteristic sharp practice. Arguing that he is 'too discreet' to wield satire against all and sundry, he claims 'I only wear it in a Land of Hectors,/Thieves, Supercargoes, Sharpers, and Directors' (*Sat. 2.i*, 71–2), lines replete with the kind of ready irony Pope was *already* famous for: while thieves and sharpers (cheats) are sitting targets, proscribed by law, supercargoes are officers who embezzle the cargo in their trust and the supposedly neutral word 'Directors' conjures in actuality the whole litany of abuse against the South Sea Directors of 1720 **[25]** and the ensuing sense that to be that high up the professional tree was to be automatically corrupt. That it is made to rhyme with 'Hectors', a cant name for bullies ironically derived from the most stalwart of the Trojan heroes, indicates something of the allusive stimulus embedded in apparently off-the-cuff remarks.

This off-setting of absolute moral positions by covert displays of skilful insinuation continues through the poem. The satire which pickles the enemy for ever is likened to the unforgiving manoeuvres of politicians – one of whom, Walpole, is Pope's major target ('But touch me, and no Minister so sore', *Sat. 2.i*, 76). The lawyer can only respond to the poet's defiance by a resigned shrug and a warning to watch out for assassins (101–4), which the poet takes as an opportunity to recast the whole sense of what 'law' is. If the law fails to regulate the state, the poet can become a vigilante, not so much *ultra legem* as *supra legem*, above the law, dispensing a satiric justice which is every bit as rough as circumstance requires: 'arm'd for *Virtue* when I point the Pen,/Brand the Front of shameless, guilty Men' (*Sat. 2.i*, 105–6). Suddenly poetry is a Jove-like assault on the world, carried out by an untainted satirist who outstrips his models (Horace, Boileau, even Dryden, 111–14) by being 'Un-plac'd, un-pension'd, no Man's Heir, or Slave?' (*Sat. 2.i*, 116). At a high rhetorical moment, the position of satirist is all but dehumanised, principle so high that it can hardly attain syntactic connection with the world:

> TO VIRTUE ONLY and HER FRIENDS, A FRIEND,
> The World beside may murmur, or commend.
>
> (*Sat. 2.i*, 121–2)

Having claimed this highest of moral grounds (which Horace actually ascribes to his lawyer friend Trebatius), Pope climbs down from it a little, sketching his retirement from the 'distant Din' of the world among some other 'friends of virtue', grafting satiric honesty onto the homely pleasures of gardening and feasting in a glorified echo of his previous argument about the innocence of pleasure (125–32). The request for advice has become a speech in defence ('This is my Plea, on this I rest my Cause-', *Sat. 2.i*, 141), approved by the lawyer, albeit with the caution that 'Laws are explain'd by Men – so have a care' (*Sat. 2.i*, 144). With an engagingly comic imitation of a lawyer's fussy exactitude, Pope has his lawyer show him the statute book and remind him of the law which might be cited against his own independent satiric 'law' (145–8). This brings us down to earth. But Pope's parting shot is poised between a hopeful innocence about satire and a devious bamboozling of his lawyer:

> *P. Libels* and *Satires!* lawless Things indeed!
> But grave *Epistles*, bringing Vice to light,
> Such as a *King* might read, a *Bishop* write,
> Such as Sir *Robert* would approve – *F.* Indeed?
> The Case is alter'd – you may then proceed.
> In such a Cause the Plaintiff will be hiss'd,
> My Lords the Judges laugh, and you're dismiss'd.
>
> (*Sat. 2.i*, 151–6)

We know that Pope preferred to think of his work in this light; writing to Swift, who (ever the *provocateur*) was happy to think of his satires as 'libels', Pope says 'I would rather call my satires, epistles. They will consist more of morality than of wit, and grow graver, which you will call duller' (*Letters* III: 366). But he can hardly have thought that 'Sir *Robert*' [Walpole] would approve of anything he was about to write, or that the King would read it, and the close of the poem seems close to ironising the lawyer friend – as if in invoking Sir Robert, however ironically, the lawyer's canny carefulness simply evaporates. It is possible that the lawyer is also acting ironically, participating in Pope's knowing wink about the foibles of great men: but the end of the poem sets up a sort of reading problem for the series, between 'open' statements and 'closed' ones, requiring the key of irony to decode them.

This variation in tone, in which moral urgency is protected from overbalancing into pomposity by a comic sense of self, pervades the Horatian poems, though the balance is different in each instance. Contrast between excesses and artifices at court, and natural appetites of country life, inform *The Second Satire of the Second Book of Horace Paraphrased* **[37]**, which also contains a charmingly downbeat self-portrait encapsulating much of Pope's sense of moral place at this time:

> In *South-sea* days not happier, when surmis'd
> The Lord of thousands, than if now *Excis'd*;
> In Forest planted by a Father's hand,
> Than in five acres now of rented land.
> Content with little, I can piddle here
> On Broccoli and mutton, round the year;
> But ancient friends, (tho' poor, or out of play)
> That touch my Bell, I cannot turn away.
> (*Sat. 2.ii*, 133–40)

Pope indicates an indifference to the vagaries of the money market; to be deemed 'Lord of thousands' by a spurious stock-market is no happier state than to 'piddle ... On Broccoli' under Walpole's punitive tax regime: the important thing is the simple exchange of friendship. Even the loss of paternal acres is not a problem for the man of inner self-mastery. Pope jokes about property's tendency to 'slide' (no matter how architecturally stable) into the hands of 'a Scrivn'ner or a City Knight' through fraud or law, and counsels staunchly 'Let us be fix'd, and our own Masters still' (*Sat. 2.ii*, 167–80).

As the series progresses, moving away from the satires to the epistles, this fixed self becomes increasingly autobiographical. *The Second Epistle of the Second Book of Horace* **[40]** is unusually poignant in tone and contains a rare and very carefully moderated account of Pope's upbringing and tribulations under anti-Catholic legislation:

> Bred up at home, full early I begun
> To read in Greek , the Wrath of Peleus's Son.

Besides, my Father taught me from a Lad,
The better Art to know the good from bad: ...
But knottier Points we knew not half so well,
Depriv'd us soon of our Paternal Cell;
And certain Laws, by Suff'rers thought unjust,
Deny'd all Posts of Profit or of Trust: ...
For Right Hereditary tax'd and fin'd,
He [Pope's father] stuck to Poverty with Peace of Mind;
And me, the Muses help'd to undergo it;
Convict a Papist He, and I a Poet.
                                    (*Ep. 2.ii*, 52–5, 58–61, 64–7)

Poetry has here become the equivalent of the paternal religion for which the true patriot suffers – though it is also a main economic resource, as Pope in a rare confession signals: 'But (thanks to *Homer*) since I live and thrive,/Indebted to no Prince or Peer alive' (*Ep. 2.ii*, 68–9). Where Horace had been educated at Athens, Pope has a more literary nurturing; Homer had been primarily a text of moral learning, associated with the father (in a section very close to the Horatian source), but in translation the fathering author (or Popean text) has become the very source of equanimity, a self-education in 'the equal Measure of the Soul' (205). But apparent poise comes tinged with the knowledge of the duncely, bathetic jostle of history, as Horace's advice 'Learn to live well' becomes framed by the metaphor of play-acting:

Walk sober off; before a sprightlier Age
Comes titt'ring on, and shoves you from the stage:
Leave such to trifle with more grace and ease,
Whom Folly pleases, and whose Follies please.
                                    (*Ep. 2.ii*, 324–7)

The trace of Macbeth's 'poor player, that struts and frets his hour upon the stage, and then is heard no more', casts an ominous shadow across this most inward of the Horatian poems.

In *The First Epistle of the Second Book of Horace, Imitated* **[40]**, Pope returns to his grand manner with the fiercest irony of the series. Horace's poem is addressed to the Emperor Augustus, writing with what Pope calls 'a decent Freedom' to him, 'with a just Contempt of his low Flatterers, and with a manly Regard to his own Character' (*TE* IV: 192), in defence of the utility of poetry to society. Pope shares many of these aims. But while Horace was genuinely in contact with the court of Augustus, and could celebrate a ruler whose powers included literary appreciation, Pope had no chance at all of addressing George II, who was notoriously dismissive of literary culture. Though George's second name was Augustus, in a rather hopeful tribute to the imperial ideal which plays directly into Pope's irony, he had very little of Augustus's political abilities, and all the compliments to princely qualities which Pope translates from Horace become flagrantly ironic when ascribed to George. The opening of the poem is a ringingly false panegyric:

> While You, great Patron of Mankind, sustain
> The balanc'd World, and open all the Main;
> Your Country, chief, in Arms abroad defend,
> At home, with Morals, Arts, and Laws amend;
> How shall the Muse, from such a Monarch, steal
> An hour, and not defraud the Publick Weal?
>
> (*Ep. 2.i*, 1–6)

Embedded in this we can see standard opposition claims: that Walpole's government failed to protect British interests abroad through military means, that the only form of 'patronage' it knew was systematic bribery and corruption, and that this corruption extended itself through the whole cultural and moral landscape. It is irony on a grand scale, compounded in the ensuing potted history of the British monarchy and its martial achievements (7–30).

The history of poetry, and the history of the state, are closely interwoven in the poem: Pope views poetry from the point of view of history, and then overlays this with history viewed in the eyes of poetry, searching for a stable basis for status in authorship, power in verse (69–160). His position, like Augustus's, is always hedged about with irony; he derides the 'Poetick Itch' which has seized the nation: 'Sons, Sires, and Grandsires, all will wear the Bays,/Our Wives read Milton, and our Daughters plays' (*Ep. 2.i*, 169–72), but specifically includes himself (as Horace did) in this comic malaise (175–80). Pope advises Augustus to pay no attention to this harmless hobby-horse on the ironic grounds that it keeps everyone quiet and politically inactive (179–200). But the last hundred lines of the poem have a further contrast to offer. The theatre is seen as a literary space particularly prone to fickle changes of taste and absurd pandering to the mob. Where money is all, morality is irrelevant: 'But fill their purse, our Poet's work is done,/Alike to them, by Pathos or by Pun' (*Ep. 2.i*, 294–5); and the 'many-headed Monster of the Pit', that is the crowds in the cheap seats, takes on an ominous ability to run the show, calling for farce, cheap spectacle, bawdy jokes, the appropriation of martial costume into the easy heroics of actors. Against this, Pope offers to 'instruct the times,/To know the Poet from the Man of Rymes' (*Ep. 2.i*, 340–1), suggesting (still with the bounds of theatrical poetry) the power of real literary skill – the 'pathos' to which the rhymester is indifferent:

> 'Tis He, who gives my breast a thousand pains,
> Can make me feel each Passion that he feigns,
> Inrage, compose, with more than magic Art,
> With Pity, and with Terror, tear my heart;
> And snatch me, o'er the earth, or thro' the air,
> To Thebes, to Athens, when he will, and where.
>
> (*Ep. 2.i*, 342–7)

Pope renounces this dramatic ground (as Horace had), but claims its emotional force. Teasingly pointing out the foibles of non-dramatic poets (going on too long, moaning about lack of appreciation, writing epistles to the King, and so on, 356–71), Pope amuses himself by casting himself as potential (but impossible) poet laureate, 'I' enroll your triumphs o'er the seas and land' (*Ep. 2.i*, 373). Reminding Augustus that Kings depend on poets for the transmission of their image to posterity, Pope for a moment does a very good impersonation (with help from Horace) of straightforward royal panegyric:

> Oh! could I mount on the Maeonian wing,
> Your Arms, your Actions, your Repose to sing! ...
> How barb'rous rage subsided at your word,
> And Nations wonder'd while they dropp'd the sword!
> How, when you nodded, o'er the land and deep,
> Peace stole her wing, and wrapt the world in sleep...
>
> (*Ep. 2.i*, 394–5, 398–401)

But compared with the eulogy of Anne in *Windsor-Forest* [62–3], the irony is impudently plain: Pope had mounted on the Maeonian (Homeric) wing, by translating Homer for his own purposes rather than panegyric, and George had done (according to those of Pope's persuasion) nothing whatsoever in Arms or Action (though 'Repose' was appropriate enough); when Augustus nods it is not the imperial nod of Zeus, which signifies assent or command, but nodding off, asleep, while the rest of Europe goes onto a war footing. Small wonder then that Pope acknowledges in a way that Horace cannot, 'Besides, a fate attends on all I write,/That when I aim at praise, they say I bite [satirise]' (*Ep. 2.i*, 408–9). With perfect aplomb masquerading as humility, Pope concludes his letter to the king with a refusal to flatter, and a reminder that 'A vile Encomium doubly ridicules;/There's nothing blackens like the ink of fools' (*Ep. 2.i*, 410–11).

Subsequent Horatian essays retreated slightly from this daring mode; the series explores the mutability and strangeness of mental life in order to comment on the wayward trajectories of the court, money, property, and desire. But Pope rounded off the series with a pair of dialogues, in Horatian manner but not tied to particular poems, which first appeared under the title *One Thousand Seven Hundred and Thirty Eight* and were later rechristened as *Epilogue to the Satires* **[40]**. In these we return to the dialogue form of the first Imitation, and there is a similar progression from low-key, comic manoeuvring to high-powered satiric denunciation. The Friend who talks with Pope opens with an ironic challenge: 'Not twice in twelvemonth you appear in Print,/And when it comes, the Court see nothing in't' (*Epil. i*, 1–2). This is Pope wrong-footing criticism, since there was everything for the Court to 'see' if it looked hard enough. But the 'impertinent Censurer' (Pope's note to line 1) has another axe to grind about the whole concept of Horatian imitation, which is that Horace's stance was essentially palliative:

> But *Horace*, Sir, was delicate, was nice;
> *Bubo* observes, he lash'd no sort of *Vice*:
> *Horace* would say, Sir Billy *serv'd the Crown*,
> Blunt *could do Bus'ness*, H-ggins *knew the Town*,
> In *Sappho* touch the *Failing of the Sex*,
> In rev'rend Bishops note some *small Neglects*,
> And own, the *Spaniard* did a *waggish thing*,
> Who cropt our Ears, and sent them to the King.
> (*Epil. i*, 11–18)

The Friend recasts in miniature the whole of Pope's enterprise, rewriting it in a supposedly more ingratiating style which he takes to be truer of Horace. For Pope of course this renders Horace no more than a sort of Court puppet, of the kind the whole series denounces, and the Pope-figure does not really respond to the actual point at hand, leaving it an open question how far Pope has departed from his model.

'Pope' enters the poem in response to the key-word, 'Sir ROBERT' (*Epil. i*, 27), picking up a suggestion that he go and see him with a backhanded compliment precisely drawn from Walpole's private life, where he is 'uncumber'd with the Venal tribe' and can 'win without a

Bribe' (*Epil. i*, 31–2). Coolly setting himself up as the Top Bard who knows all there is to know about the First Minister, Pope listens unmoved to the Friend's bland catalogue of those he may satirise without danger (including in a characteristic manoeuvre some 'honest' Whigs, who voted against Walpole, 39), only to unleash a tirade of objects (people, crimes, vices) which require the satiric opposition which readers of the series will know Pope has evinced. In an impressive tirade which silences the mealy-mouthed Friend, Vice is imagined as a triumphant, destructive empress, not unlike Dulness, adored by the whole of British society with the exception of its uncrowned laureate poet (141–72).

The second dialogue momentarily inverts the relation between Friend and Pope by making the Friend more earnest and giving Pope comic-defensive lines in which satiric imagination, often accused of being libellous, cannot outstrip social actuality:

> Vice with such Giant-strides comes on amain,
> Invention strives to be before in vain;
> Feign what I will, and paint it e'er so strong,
> Some rising Genius sins up to my Song.
> (*Epil. ii*, 6–9)

In a more agitated, if still comic, vein of debate, the hapless Friend tries to allot Pope an acceptable level of target, without success (10–62). Pope points out (with a customary barb) that his satire is not all negative: 'God knows, I praise a Courtier where I can' (*Epil. ii*, 63); 'Ev'n in a Bishop I can spy Desert' (*Epil. ii*, 70). But praise is confessedly directed towards Opposition heroes: 'But does the court a worthy Man remove?/That instant, I declare, he has my Love' (*Epil. ii*, 74–5), and Pope resists the courtly requirement for 'random Praise' (*Epil. ii*, 106) as much as he berates the 'spur-gall'd Hackney' and 'new-pension'd Sycophant' who write in defence of Walpole (*Epil. ii*, 140–2) and whose Courtly 'Perfume' smells only too disgusting to the honest poet (*Epil. ii*, 182–4) **[186]**.

Pope seems to be seeking an object for anger, which eventually resolves itself into something which is hardly personal at all: 'Ask you what Provocation I have had?/The strong Antipathy of Good to Bad' (*Epil. ii*, 197–8). Pope internalises the charge, implicit in the bold black/white opposition, that the claim is too large, in the last and least comic of the self-presentations:

Fr. You're strangely proud. *P.* So proud, I am no Slave:
So impudent, I own myself no Knave:
So odd, my Country's Ruin makes me grave.
Yes I am proud; I must be proud to see
Men not afraid of God, afraid of me:
(Epil. ii, 205–9)

In a further apocalyptic vision, Pope addresses 'Ye tinsel Insects! whom a Court maintains' and pledges 'The Muse's wing shall brush you all away' (*Epil. ii*, 220–3). We have moved a long way from the interdependence of satirist and victim proposed in Pope's opening lines (6–9), where satiric invention seemed almost to conjure social enactment; Pope now claims a kind of Noah-like status against a flood of 'insuperable corruption and depravity of manners' (his note to line 255). A saving irony is still precariously preserved, as the Friend, despairing of bringing Pope to heel, counsels him to go on with further '*Essays on Man*', as more politically innocuous than satire (255). But the last poem of all (*1740. A Poem*), a thorough-going political diatribe which Pope did not publish and which he wrote partially in hieroglyphics to resist the scrutiny of government spies, indicates something of the desperate climate in which Pope saw himself prior to revision of *The Dunciad* **[169]**.

Further Reading

This extreme position ('Yes, the last Pen for Freedom let me draw,/ When Truth stands trembling on the edge of Law', Dialogue II, 248–9) has not always commanded reverence from commentators. For Fabricant (1988) for example, the presentation of poetic self as poet-hero is a signal of unbalanced solipsism and unfocused bellicosity – a kind of aggressive narcissism, in effect, lacking the more sharply-defined and rational opposition which characterises *The Dunciad*. But Pope's Horatian persona as a whole includes self-deprecation, a sense of oddness, irony about the limitations of physique, and a certain pathos (Parker 1990). Arguments about the satiric persona have also included questions about Pope's appropriation of Horace: Weinbrot contends that Pope began to doubt the witty, conversational Horace as a model because of the Roman poet's affiliations with Augustus, known to historians as somewhat more autocratic than Horace could acknowledge: during the 1730s Pope transferred his allegiance to the more turbulent satirists, Juvenal and Persius, ending, in the *Epilogue to the*

Satires, in 'overwhelmingly Juvenalian-Persian elevation and gloom' (Weinbrot 1982: 331). Erskine-Hill (1983) has however argued for a more complex understanding of Pope's Augustanism, which (with some ambivalence) retained a fundamental trust in Horace's independence and wisdom. Very detailed studies of Pope's Horace by Stack (1985) and Fuchs (1989) have tended to confirm that however Pope deviated from his model (and the deviations are always part of the point), his view of Horace remained substantially appreciative.

(i) *THE DUNCIAD* (1728–42)
[*TE* V]

It is in many ways an error to speak of 'The' *Dunciad*, as if it were unitary, for part of its point is its extraordinary responsiveness to a changing literary and cultural environment. There are four main versions:

(a) *The Dunciad: An Heroic Poem. In Three Books* (1728), with a false 'Dublin' imprint and shabby format; **[28–30]**
(b) *The Dunciad Variorum* (1729), with voluminous mock-critical apparatus and a more detailed text; **[31–2]**
(c) *The New Dunciad* (1742), a first version of what became book IV of the poem; **[43]**
(d) *The Dunciad, In Four Books* (1743), a final full version in four books with a new hero, the poet laureate Colley Cibber, replacing the old one, Lewis Theobald, and extended commentaries and appendices **[44]**. It is this version, as the poem to which Pope returns at the end of his career, the poem in which he engages his energies most completely, which will be examined here. The poem is a continuing site for the collision between the aristocratic and heroic culture of epic and the political and literary culture of mass production; the mock-heroic form allows Pope to superimpose a highly contemporaneous vision of London onto the timeless morphology of epic in comic and disturbing ways.

Book One opens with a conventional-sounding epic formula:

The Mighty Mother, and her Son who brings
The Smithfield Muses to the ear of Kings,
I sing.

(*D*, I: 1–3)

Everything about this is epic except the word 'Smithfield', the London meat market where (as Pope's note to line 2 tells us) Bartholomew Fair was held, 'whose shews, machines, and dramatical entertainments, formerly agreeable only to the taste of the Rabble, were, by the Hero of this poem and others of equal genius, brought to the Theatres of Covent-garden, Lincolns-inn-fields, and the Hay-market, to be the reigning pleasures of the Court and Town'. Precisely aligning this potted cultural history with the reigns of George I and II ('Still Dunce the second reigns like Dunce the first', *D*, I: 6), Pope gives us a nutshell version of the poem's action: Dulness regains empire over the human mind by leading the exponents of contemporary culture from their dingy lodgings in the penumbra of the philistine City towards the seat of government in the West End.

Pope's note to line 1 reminds us that 'the *Mother*, and not the *Son*, is the principal Agent of this Poem'. In classical epics, heroes (Achilles, Odysseus, Aeneas) are guided and protected by their divine mothers (Thetis, Athena, Venus) towards performance of heroic duty; but what Dulness promotes in her offspring is finally the reverse of epic action. The epic which primarily informs the design of the poem is, as Pope's notes indicate, the Aeneid, in which Aeneas escapes from a defeated Troy to found a new empire in Rome. The empire of Dulness, in moving from the City to the Court, is performing an ironic version of this overarching action. In its cosmological allusions, however, *The Dunciad* also alludes heavily to Milton's *Paradise Lost*, as in the mock genealogy of Dulness herself:

> In eldest time, e'er mortals writ or read,
> E'er Pallas issu'd from the Thund'rer's head,
> Dulness o'er all possess'd her ancient right,
> Daughter of Chaos and eternal Night:
> Fate in their dotage this fair Ideot gave,
> Gross as her sire, and as her mother grave,
> Laborious, heavy, busy, bold, and blind,
> She rul'd, in native Anarchy, the mind.
>
> (*D*, I: 9–16)

Dulness's lineage echoes *Paradise Lost* II: 894–6, where Satan, having left his domain of Hell, must pass through the 'Eternal anarchy' of 'eldest Night,/And Chaos'. Milton's vision of noxious chemical elements is incorporated here into the body of the 'fair Ideot', in contrast with Pallas (Athena, goddess of wisdom and art) who emerges fully-armed from the head of the king of the gods, Zeus ('the Thund'rer'). Milton's poem also envisages a war between the creative Godhead, who creates the world by speaking and whose 'son' (Christ) is the Divine *logos* or creative word, and Satan, whose creativity is a bestial and mechanistic travesty of the *logos* (he gives birth to Sin from his own head and copulates with his daughter to produce Death). The 'Mighty Mother' has some of the lineaments of Milton's Sin, though she is also a composite allusion to various dark mother-goddesses associated with night, fertility, and the underworld (Cybele, Isis, Ceres, Persephone) **[179]**.

Pope's goddess is housed in 'The Cave of Poverty and Poetry' (*D*, I: 34), close to Bedlam (the lunatic asylum) and Grub Street (spiritual and sometimes literal home of hack writers). The 'high' mythological home is also the matrix of 'low' cultural production, such as 'hymning Tyburn's elegiac lines' (*D*, I: 41), where Pope nicely dignifies the wretched verse ascribed to those executed at Tyburn. Dulness is not unproductive; as the note to line 15 decodes the allegory, 'Dulness ... includes ... Labour, Industry, and some degree of Activity and Boldness: a ruling principle not inert, but turning topsy-turvy the Understanding, and inducing an Anarchy or confused State of Mind'. But creativity here is a womb-like space producing on its own without the intervention of Zeus-like intelligence:

> Here she beholds the Chaos dark and deep,
> Where nameless Somethings in their causes sleep...
> How hints, like spawn, scarce quick in embryo lie,
> How new-born nonsense first is taught to cry,
> Maggots half-form'd in rhyme exactly meet,
> And learn to crawl upon poetic feet.
>
> (*D*, I: 55–6, 59–62)

Chaos meets Grub Street ('Grub' means both 'ditch' and 'larva'), as Pope spins an apparently unstoppable fantasy of poetic copulation and unauthored linguistic mayhem:

> There motley Images her fancy strike,
> Figures ill pair'd, and Similies unlike.
> She sees a Mob of Metaphors advance,
> Pleas'd with the madness of the mazy dance:
> How Tragedy and Comedy embrace;
> How Farce and Epic get a jumbled race;
> How Time himself stands still at her command,
> Realms shift their place, and Ocean turns to land.
>
> (*D*, I: 65–72)

It is like watching evolution speeded up: the spawn, embryo, and maggot of literary hints become image, figure and simile, capable of bizarre procreation; literary forms jumble and hybridise; geology and nationhood become unstable counters of exchange.

The productions of the 'Grub-street race' (D, I: 44) are *seen* in vision: Pope's compressed syntax superimposes a complaint about stylistic errors, or cheerfully inaccurate writing ('Here gay Description Aegypt glads with show'rs', D, I: 73) onto the surface of the poem itself, so that we experience as event what is being satirised as badly-constructed writing. The vision is, however, distanced by a critique of Dulness's disfiguring aesthetic:

> All these, and more, the cloud-compelling Queen
> Beholds thro' fogs, that magnify the scene.
> She, tinsel'd o'er in robes of varying hues,
> With self-applause her wild creation views;
> Sees momentary monsters rise and fall,
> And with her own fools-colours gilds them all.
>
> (D, I: 79–84)

Pope here inverts Newtonian optics, the physics of light which clarifies and divides, into a mock-epic subversion of intelligence: 'cloud-compelling' is very nearly an exact epithet of Zeus (the 'Thund'rer' whom Homer calls 'cloud-gathering') but Dulness's clouds are marshalled precisely to obfuscate, distort and discolour what would otherwise be clear.

Dulness chooses Lord Mayor's day (with a possible allusion to the Coronation Day of George II) to elect a King in place of the deceased City Poet, Elkanah Settle. Lord Mayors, like Kings, had their ceremonial verses, flagrant instances of poetry surrendering to political flattery (I: 85–94). Dulness reviews the 'succession' of City poets (a kind of mock-heroic version of the succession of kings) in terms which recall the shapeless mutations of matter from her earlier vision ('growing lump', D, I: 102). The succession leads her to Cibber and his 'monster-breeding breast' (D, I: 108). Named 'Bays' here, by allusion to the laurel wreath figuratively worn by the Poet Laureate, Cibber is pictured in a parody of epic anger; having lost at gambling, he seems to embody the uncontrollably self-propagating tendencies of matter even as he internalises Satan's fall through Chaos in *Paradise Lost* (II: 927–42):

> Swearing and supperless the Hero sate,
> Blasphem'd his Gods, the Dice, and damn'd his Fate.

Then gnaw'd his pen, then dash'd it on the ground,
Sinking from thought to thought, a vast profound!
Plung'd for his sense, but found no bottom there,
Yet wrote and flounder'd on, in mere despair.
Round him much Embryo, much Abortion lay,
Much future Ode, and abdicated Play;
Nonsense precipitate, like running Lead,
That slip'd thro' Cracks and Zig-zags of the Head;
All that on Folly Frenzy could beget,
Fruits of dull Heat, and Sooterkins of Wit.

(D, I: 115–26)

This characteristically alarming vision, in which recognisable comic actions (gnawing the pen) coexist with nightmare images of literature as bodily excrescence and mental waste, continues into Pope's account of the Hero's library, in which books become animate, material, even edible (I: 127–54). Above all they are flammable, in the travesty sacrifice which accompanies Bays's petition to Dulness, a near-blasphemous boast of Cibber's malign activities (underpinned by very selective quotation from his *Apology* in the notes) (I: 155–256). Like his unacknowledged model, Satan, Cibber glories in his 'brazen Brightness' and 'polish'd Hardness' (*D*, I: 219–20), metallic metaphors for superficial confidence which melt easily into the underlying metaphor of material heaviness ('our head like byass to the bowl', *D*, I: 170).

Cibber matches Dulness: his monsters answer hers, his materialism is equated with hers, his superficial and dazzling performance suits hers, his inability to distinguish prose from verse is mirrored in hers. Cibber is 'form'd by nature Stage and Town to bless,/And act, and be, a Coxcomb with success' (*D*, I: 109–10); he is all performance **[182–3]**. As he weeps to set fire to his altar (in a parody of Priam's tears at the destruction of Troy, here close to the hypocrisy of acting: 'a Tear ... Stole from the Master of the sev'nfold Face', *D*, I: 243–4), Dulness puts out the fire with a particularly cold and heavy specimen of Grub-Street writing (I: 257–60) and arrives in full comic majesty ('Her ample presence fills up all the place;/A veil of fogs dilates her awful face', *D*, I: 261–2) to summon Cibber to her 'sacred Dome' (*D*, I: 265) and anoint him King, with opium, in a blasphemous dual parody of the baptism of Jesus and of the coronation of a king (I: 287–92). The anointing with the narcotic opium is ominous, for Cibber has little to do from this point on. The 'Great Mother' (*D*, I: 269) is the real ruler here and the point is made in terms which crystallise the various hints in the poem that Dulness bears more than a passing resemblance to George

134

II's Queen Caroline, widely held to be, with Walpole, the real power in the land. In her wish to be a 'Nursing-mother' and 'rock the throne' (a neat conflation of political destabilization and maternal fondness), Dulness parodies the biblical passage in the Coronation liturgy which signalled that queens were meant to be 'nursing mothers'; while her stated programme (I: 311–18) matches the standard anti-Walpole charges (absolutism, reliance on standing armies and court placemen, 'screening' the king from the people and from law), the gendering of Dulness turns corruption into a malign version of motherhood which returns the adult male to smothered, infantile quiescence.

At the opening of Book II, Cibber is seated on a throne which alludes complexly to Milton's Satan, the coronation of George II, and the mock-coronation of Richard Flecknoe, hero of Dryden's *Mac Flecknoe*, an important literary-political source with which the poem sees itself as allied.

> High on a gorgeous seat, that far out-shone
> Henley's gilt tub, or Fleckno's Irish throne ...
> Great Cibber sate: The proud Parnassian sneer,
> The conscious simper, and the jealous leer,
> Mix on his look: All eyes direct their rays
> On him, and crowds turn Coxcombs as they gaze.
> His Peers shine round him with reflected grace,
> New edge their dulness and new bronze their face.
>
> (*D*, II: 1–2, 5–10)

Satan's power was always for Milton partly the power of the supreme actor, his heroism that of a vaunting braggart; Cibber's trade-mark expressions as an actor are here Satanised by allusion to the opening of Book II of *Paradise Lost* as the Dunces travesty the malign energy of Milton's devils.

The book as a whole is concerned, however, to remove Cibber from an active role and demonstrate the kinds of activity his 'Peers' engage in. The games proposed by Dulness to celebrate Cibber's coronation are modelled on the funeral games of Virgil's *Aeneid* (book V), which are themselves modelled on the funeral games in book XXIII of the *Iliad*: they are thus associated with death, a dark aspect of the most riotously comic section of the poem. In the first game, two booksellers (Pope's old enemy, Edmund Curll, and his erstwhile publisher, Bernard Lintot) are made to race for possession of a poet – an allegory of the book-trade tyranny Pope had escaped. Pope contrives a revengeful accident for Curll:

Full in the middle way there stood a lake,
Which Curl's Corinna chanc'd that morn to make:
(Such was her wont, at early dawn to drop
Her evening cates before his neighbour's shop,)
Here fortun'd Curl to slide; loud shout the band,
And Bernard! Bernard! rings thro' all the Strand.
Obscene with filth the miscreant lies bewray'd,
Fal'n in the plash his wickedness had laid:

(*D*, II: 69–76)

Like the epic phantom, this has a classical precedent (Virgil's runner Nisus slips on the blood of sacrifice in *Aeneid* V), but the point is clearly made, despite the decorous language ('lake', 'chanc'd', 'fortun'd'), that the filth is directly traceable to the victim himself. The crime for which Curll is punished here is the publication of youthful letters by Pope which had been passed to Curll by Henry Cromwell's mistress Elizabeth Thomas (charmingly dignified into 'Curl's Corinna') **[11–12]**; but Pope is also repaying Curll for what he takes to be a truly epic and 'dauntless' (*D*, II: 58) career in turning literature into commerce, as he details in a poised note (to line 58). Pope also draws on Curll's widespread reputation for obscene publications (the ironic 'Curl's chaste press' of *D*, I: 40), and associates bodily malfunction with corrupt creativity generally. Curll is not abashed by his fall; he prays to Jove, who happens to be sitting on the celestial privy where it is his custom to use the prayers of mankind for toilet paper ('Amus'd he reads, and then returns the bills/Sign'd with that Ichor which from Gods distills' as Pope puts it with high euphemism, *D*, II: 91–2). But Curll's prayer is granted special attention through his ongoing liaison with Cloacina, the Roman goddess of the sewer, who selects Curll's petition for the royal treatment. The worlds of epic deities and London street culture are promiscuously fused, as Pope suggests that Curll gets his literature from dark sexual forays along the Thames docks: 'Where as he fish'd her nether realms for Wit,/She oft had favour'd him, and favours yet' (*D*, II: 101–2). Jove having 'sign'd' the prayer, Curll is in his element:

Renew'd by ordure's sympathetic force,
As oil'd with magic juices for the course,
Vig'rous he rises; from th' effluvia strong
Imbibes new life, and scours and stinks along;

(*D*, II: 103–6)

The bookseller derives a weird sexual kick ('Vig'rous he rises') out of bodily waste in what is probably the most elegant excremental vision in literature [185–6].

The first 'poet' offered for enslavement to a bookseller by the Goddess turns out to be a phantom of the kind the book trade occasionally used to disguise responsibility or to insinuate high-class authorship (as Dulness explains, II: 131–40). But Curll also wins the next contest, for the more substantial body of Eliza Haywood, author of scandalous memoirs and novels. The Goddess proposes:

> "Who best can send on high
> "The salient spout, far-streaming to the sky;
> "His be yon Juno of majestic size,
> "With cow-like udders, and with ox-like eyes.
> "This China Jordan let the chief o'ercome
> "Replenish, not ingloriously, at home."
>
> (D, II: 161–6)

Translated, this epic proposition means that he who can piss the furthest wins the breeding machine (already presented with 'Two babes of love close clinging to her waist', 158, indicating actual bastard children *or* illegitimate literary productions); the loser gets a chamber pot. Not surprisingly, Curll wins again: the rival bookseller Osborne wets his own face and goes off happily enough with the chamber pot on his head, while Curll's brazen self-confidence results in truly epic urination: 'Thro' half the heav'ns he pours th'exalted urn;/His rapid waters in their passage burn' (D, II: 179–84). Curll's productions are all productions of the body, waste, filth, corruption: the paradoxical burning of the waters is a marker of venereal disease, caught, as the note delicately puts it, 'in unhappy communication with another'.

Pope pursues this degradation of literature to infantile physical pleasures in a tickling contest (II: 191–220), and a 'braying' competition displaying 'the wond'rous power of Noise' (D, II: 221–68). But in the end he returns to the Duncely element of mud. Taking an insalubrious route round Bridewell prison 'To where Fleet-ditch with disemboguing streams/Rolls the large tribute of dead dogs to Thames' (D, II: 271–2), the Goddess asks the Dunces to dive in the mud to show 'who the most in love of dirt excel,/Or dark dexterity of groping well' (D, II: 277–8). Fleet ditch was an open sewer running into the Thames; though Pope comically transforms pollution into something which almost shares the heraldic colouring of the rivers in *Windsor-Forest* ('The King of dykes! than whom no sluice of mud/With deeper sable blots the silver flood', *D*, II: 273–4), the association between Fleet street (a key area of the book trade) and its nearby sewer allows Pope to rewrite Curll's personal obsession with filth on a much grander scale.

In diving into the mud, the Dunces are also testifying to their commitment to low rather than high, dark against light, bathos ('depth') against sublime. Pope deposits various literary enemies in the swamp with due comic grandeur – none more so than Jonathan Smedley, who returns from his underworld voyage like a river god, 'in majesty of Mud' (*D*, II: 326):

> First he relates, how sinking to the chin,
> Smit with his mien, the Mud-nymphs suck'd him in:
> How young Lutetia, softer than the down,
> Nigrina black, and Merdamante brown,
> Vy'd for his love in jetty bow'rs below,
> As Hylas fair was ravish'd long ago.
>
> (*D*, II: 331–6)

Pope imputes to Smedley an autoerotic fascination with filth (at the same time, he risks readerly identification with that fascination through his careful detail): the 'suck'd', and 'softer than the down' are Smedley's apprehension of a sexual caress from 'Nut-brown maids' (*D*, II: 337) who appear to be animated excrement ('Merdamante' means something like 'shit-loving'). Smedley's further voyage along a 'branch of Styx ... That tinctur'd as it runs with Lethe's streams,/And wafting Vapours from the land of Dreams' (*D*, II: 338–40) suggest an intoxicating inhalation of sewer gas which Smedley receives as divine inspiration.

But lethargy is the state which Dulness values most, and the book concludes with all the critics failing to stay awake during a reading of the dullest of contemporary poets. The crude materialism of Book II is succeeded by a psychological exploration, expanding the Smedley's ludicrous underworld vision into a full-scale parody of Aeneas's visit to the underworld in *Aeneid*, book VI: But whereas Aeneas goes physically underground, Bays's trip is internal, a dream, induced by Dulness's potions in a disturbing fusion of the roles of mother and lover: 'But in her Temple's last recess inclos'd,/On Dulness' lap th' Anointed head repos'd' (*D*, III: 1–2). The status of what Bays is about to dream is made problematic by the poem's comparisons with madmen and other visionaries, not excluding poets; he is conveyed downwards 'on Fancy's easy wing' (*D*, III: 13), led by a 'slip-shod Sibyl' (*D*, III: 15), suggesting the rickety nature of his imaginative vision.

Here the book trade parodies epic conceptions of reincarnation:

> Here, in a dusky vale where Lethe rolls,
> Old Bavius sits, to dip poetic souls,
> And blunt the sense, and fit it for a skull
> Of solid proof, impenetrably dull:
> Instant, when dipt, away they wing their flight,
> Where Brown and Mears unbar the gates of Light,
> Demand new bodies, and in Calf's array,
> Rush to the world, impatient for the day.
> Millions and millions on these banks he views,
> Thick as the stars of night, or morning dews,
> As thick as bees o'er vernal blossoms fly,
> As thick as eggs at Ward in Pillory.
>
> (D, III: 23–34)

The pushy confidence of duncely poets is insisted on, alongside their nightmarish thronging; the lines encompass the direct comedy by which Thetis's 'dipping' of Achilles to render him invulnerable is turned into a sort of mechanical process of case-hardening, the transforming fantasy of poets ushered into the light by disreputable booksellers (Brown and Mears) in 'Calf's array' (cheap bookbindings), and the tasteful epic similes which run without warning into the brutal light of day of a London scene ('As thick as eggs at Ward in Pillory').

Recalling Aeneas's encounter with his father Anchises, Pope stages the encounter between Bays and his poetic forbear, Elkanah Settle, who wonders with rapture at the possible material embodiments of his son's soul through time (III: 43–66). The notion of lineage and fatherhood, here as in Book I, is a way of classifying enemy literature as all of a family, as well as condemned to physical status, so much material endlessly reproduced. When Settle grants Bays a prophetic vision of the triumph of Dulness over science he emphasises knowledge's vulnerability to simple, brutal destruction: books, cities, and people get burnt (III: 67–112). The account derives a kind of perverse magnificence from Adam's vision of redemptive Christian history at the end of *Paradise Lost*, itself based on Anchises' prophecy of the glories of Augustan Rome; at the same time it betrays its limited and local focus by celebrating the new armies Dulness is lining up in London. Augustan Rome was destroyed by armies of Goths and Vandals (III: 83–94), then by superstition (III: 101–12); Britain has already had its superstition (III: 113–22), and now come the armies, those same 'millions' thronging the bookshops (D, III: 127–38).

After a number of characteristic vignettes of this roll-call, Dunces who are both frivolous *and* threatening, sublime *and* bathetic, classic *and* Grub-Street, Pope grants Bays a pantomime apocalypse:

All sudden, Gorgons hiss, and Dragons glare,
And ten-horn'd fiends and Giants rush to war.
Hell rises, Heav'n descends, and dance on Earth:
Gods, imps, and monsters, music, rage, and mirth,
A fire, a jigg, a battle, and a ball,
'Till one wide conflagration swallows all.
Thence a new world to Nature's laws unknown,
Breaks out refulgent, with a heav'n its own:
Another Cynthia her new journey runs,
And other planets circle other suns.
The forests dance, the rivers upward rise,
Whales sport in woods, and dolphins in the skies;
And last, to give the whole creation grace,
Lo! one vast Egg produces human race.

(D, III: 235–48)

In one sense, what Pope is mocking here is the taste for cosmic spectacle in the 'low' theatrical entertainments of his time: Theobald's *Rape of Proserpine* (1727), is implicated as the source of the 'monstrous absurdity' whereby Hell rises and Heaven descends (note to III: 237). The conflagration is based on that underworld fantasy, and on Settle's own spectacular (and to Pope, ridiculous) *Siege of Troy* (1707); the 'sable sorcerer' episode is based on pantomime versions of the Faust story. More widely, Pope caricatures in these chaotic manoeuvres aspects of duncely writing which contravene the rules of nature: whales sporting in woods (III: 246) recall the absurdities mocked in Horace's *Ars Poetica* which Pope had drawn on in the *Essay on Criticism* **[49–57]**. But at the back of it all lies the possible decreation implicit in any creative act, the idea that by representing God's world amiss you can do it a blasphemous injury. The Miltonic sublime turns God into the original poet and Satan into the original parodist: the Dunces are firmly of the devil's party. The boundaries of the vision are very nearly transgressed: this is Pope imagining Bays having a vision of selected highlights from duncely shows with such sequence and momentum that a theatrical pantomime nearly becomes a genuine apocalypse. The vision of orchestrated chaos is comically intense, so that, momentarily, we share it as something (almost) rich and strange **[158–9]**.

We are allowed to escape from the full identification with disaster which fascinates Bays: seeking a source for such wonders, Bays is told 'Son; what thou seek'st is in thee! Look, and find/Each Monster meets his likeness in thy mind' (D, III: 251–2), confirming the powerful pathology to which he is subject, and we are not. Hell's pantomime continues in Settle's prophetic descriptions (III: 253–72), but the stagey nature of their construction becomes more comically evident. John Rich, manager of Lincoln's-Inn-Fields (where some of these shows took place), is characterised as a 'matchless Youth' whose 'nod these worlds controuls', but his epic status is undermined by timely reference to what gets thrown at him in the theatre:

> Angel of Dulness, sent to scatter round
> Her magic charms o'er all unclassic ground:
> Yon stars, yon suns, he rears at pleasure higher,
> Illumes their light, and sets their flames on fire.
> Immortal Rich! how calm he sits at ease
> 'Mid snows of paper, and fierce hail of pease;
> And proud his Mistress' orders to perform,
> Rides in the whirlwind, and directs the storm.
>
> (D, III: 257–64)

All this would-be Zeus controls is an illusory universe, considerably less real than the paper and peas the booing audience rain down on him.

Settle's rapturous account of the future of Dulness's empire envisages 'low' theatricals merging with 'high' culture, ''Till rais'd from booths, to Theatre, to Court,/Her seat imperial Dulness shall transport' (D, III: 299–300). Again the merger is aligned with death: 'Pluto with Cato thou for this shalt join,/And link the Mourning Bride to Proserpine' (D, III: 309–10; Cato was a severe neoclassical play by Addison [16], The Mourning Bride a tragedy by Pope's friend Congreve; they are fused by Dulness with underworld pantomimes). But this vision disappears through the 'Iv'ry Gate', traditionally associated with false dreams, as Pope's spoof note points out, leaving open the possibility of redemption; his competing notes to lines 5 and 6, one citing the vision as a 'chimera of the dreamer's brain' and the other pointing to the fulfilment of the prophecies in Book IV, puts into play the different interpretations of the book, which were of course still open in the three-book version of 1728–29. The Dunciad, in Four Books comes after the decade of Horatian satire, however, and shares the darkening vision of those poems.

Bays appears never to awaken from his rapturous dream on his mother's lap (IV: 20): the final condition of Dulness is loss of consciousness, and Bays is as unheroic in action as George II is in kingship (Pope's note indicates). Book IV gestures towards an extinction which can scarcely be withstood even by the poet whose normal working habit was to inscribe his own survival through poetry:

> Yet, yet a moment, one dim Ray of Light
> Indulge, dread Chaos, and eternal Night! ...
> Suspend a while your Force inertly strong,
> Then take at once the Poet and the Song.
> (D, IV: 1–2, 7–8)

Miltonic Chaos is still faintly comic ('inertly strong'), but the book as a whole, in its length, density, and sometimes suffocating difficulty, can be taken to mimic the drift towards gravitational entropy that Dulness represents.

At a moment of malign cosmic influence (IV: 9), the 'Seed of Chaos' (Dulness) rises 'To blot out Order, and extinguish Light,/Of dull and venal a new World to mold,/And bring Saturnian days of Lead and Gold' (*D*, IV: 14–16). In doing so she fulfils both the prophecy of I: 28 and gives material body to the pantomimic fantasies of (un)creation in Book III: Book IV is a sort of Royal interview in which Dulness reviews and rewards her supporters. Dulness sits in emblematic majesty, a nightmare parody of the iconographic celebrations of monarchs that Pope drew on in *Windsor-Forest*, with abstract virtues like Morality, Poetry and Logic made material, punished and chained at her feet (IV: 21–44). The way from allegory to satire is paved by the figure of Opera, personified here as a beguiling foreign harlot who entices the aristocracy away from poetry towards the effeminate spectacles of the opera house. Opera, for Pope, was an illegitimate form of entertainment which relied wholly on sound independent of sense, thus violating a cardinal precept of the *Essay on Criticism*. (It was also the one art form which the foreign king George II enjoyed, and was associated with effeminacy because of the prominence of *castrati* in heroic roles.) Opera silences the enchained Muses, drowning them out with artificial sound with no end in view other than self-celebration (IV: 45–71). This materialization of culture is also prophetic.

Dulness summons her followers through 'Fame's posterior Trumpet' (*D*, IV: 71), a formulation characteristically invoking resonances both epic and rude, but the Dunces arrive in dark parody of Newtonian physics:

None need a guide, by sure Attraction led,
And strong impulsive gravity of Head:
None want a place, for all their Centre found,
Hung to the Goddess, and coher'd around. ...
The gath'ring number, as it moves along,
Involves a vast involuntary throng,
Who gently drawn, and struggling less and less,
Roll in her Vortex, and her pow'r confess.

(D, IV: 75–8, 81–4)

Within the comic cod-science it is also possible to see the lineaments of the smothering mother, infantilizing her offspring. What follows is in effect a catalogue of cultural vices, beginning naturally with bad writers, patrons, pompous officials proud of their 'culture' (IV: 91–118). But the catalogue is much expanded from the more literary interests of the first three books. Pope (by his own account freely self-educated among the trees of Windsor Forest) imagines the reign of Dulness beginning in infancy, with an education which separates words from things, sound from sense, and turns mental life into a Blakean prison – a schoolmaster speaks:

Then thus. "Since Man from beast by Words is known,
Words are Man's province, Words we teach alone. ...
We ply the Memory, we load the brain,
Bind rebel Wit, and double chain on chain,
Confine the thought, to exercise the breath;
And keep them in the pale of Words till death.
Whate'er the talents, or howe'er design'd,
We hang one jingling padlock on the mind:

(D, IV: 149–50, 157–62)

The picture of mental talents bound at Dulness's feet with which the book begins (IV: 21–44) is here given a literal explanation – and a political force, since schoolboys go on to be politicians, and kings have been known to act like schoolmasters (IV: 165–88).

A 'sable shoal' of academics then swamps the floor like cattle ('Thick and more thick the black blockade extends,/A hundred head of Aristotle's friends', D, IV: 191–2), headed by the textual critic Richard Bentley in the mock-epic guise of Aristarchus (an Alexandrian commentator and editor). Aristarchus commends his own efforts in Dulness's service as a heroic battle to demean ancient culture into shreds: 'In ancient Sense if any needs will deal,/Be sure I give them

Fragments, not a Meal' (D, IV: 230, echoing the Goddess's commands to critics, IV: 119–26). His pedantic attention to the letter rather than the spirit itself approaches unintelligibility:

> 'Tis true, on Words is still our whole debate,
> Disputes of *Me* or *Te*, of *aut* or *at*,
> To sound or sink in *cano*, O or A,
> Or give up Cicero to C or K.
>
> (D, IV: 219–22)

Bentley's philological minuteness is characterised by Pope as a perverse fragmentation of classical heritage into mere phonemes: the first line of Virgil's *Aeneid* ('*Arma virumque cano*', 'Arms and the Man I sing', itself the prime source behind the singing of *The Dunciad*) becomes here a matter of trivial pronunciation; Bentley can't work out whether to pronounce the name of the great Roman orator as Cicero or Kikero (Pope, in another guise, appears to encourage the pronunciation of Cibber as Kibber). Academic discourse is as much lumber as the heavy books of Bays's study:

> For thee we dim the eyes, and stuff the head
> With all such reading as was never read:
> For thee explain a thing till all men doubt it,
> And write about it, Goddess, and about it:
>
> (D, IV: 249–52)

The pointless repetitiveness enacted here extends the 'padlock' of school education into adulthood.

Individuation is resisted. As if to prove the point that 'With the same Cement, ever sure to bind,/We bring to one dead level ev'ry mind', (D, IV: 267–8) Bentley and the pedants have to make way for an unnamed but representative 'Pupil', returning from his further education on the European 'Grand Tour' with his tutor, his whore, and his companions. The Pupil's career is presented as a disfiguring parody of Aeneas's upbringing and adventuring: protected by Dulness's 'kind cloud' as Aeneas was made invisible in Carthage by his mother Venus (though Dulness's cloud is a cloud of ignorance, a lack of exposure to proper formative influences), the 'young Aeneas' traverses Europe in a blaze of self-regarding frivolity quite opposite to the epic intent of Virgil's hero. In theory the Grand Tour allowed students to complete their classical education by visiting the sites of classical civilisation; in practice, Pope suggests, it continues the erasure of classical values already visible in the cultures which have replaced the earlier ones: 'All Classic learning lost on Classic ground;/And last turn'd *Air*, the Echo of a Sound!' (*D*, IV: 321). While Bentley turns classical culture into fragments, the Italians have turned it into opera, the '*Air*', i.e., Aria, or song from an opera, which the 'Heir' hums in an unconscious pun. The presence of a whore (a sort of literal embodiment of the 'Harlot form' of opera) guarantees this mental corruption will have bodily effects down the generations, as the tutor promises in his vision of the 'sons of sons of sons of whores' propping up Dulness's empire (*D*, IV: 331–4).

Next in line come a number of satiric victims whose education has turned into obsessive self-directed study. The quarrel between Annius, a dealer in (and faker of) antiquarian curiosities (coins, statues, mummies), and Mummius, one of his customers, affords Pope an opportunity to satirise the psychological and economic roots of collecting (IV: 347–97). Annius and Mummius are reconciled: the energies which might break apart Dulness's empire become cosily collaborative. The same thing happens when two further 'students' (one of gardening, one of insects), arrive to dispute in infantile fashion about their hobbies. Again, Dulness views both kinds of narrow-minded obsession as equally favourable to her cause, and their squabble, which suggests a certain intellectual liveliness, is patched up into the anaesthetic doziness which she most esteems (IV: 437–58). It is the reverse of the questing, cosmic vision of *Essay on Man*, which seeks to place the details of the material universe in a theological and ethical framework: here, Dulness wants to channel mental energy into obsessive and singular pursuits, 'See Nature in some partial narrow shape,/And let the Author of the Whole escape' (*D*, IV: 455–6).

Pope continues this ominously counter-theological process in the ensuing account of theologians and philosophers. Here too the processes of materialism have a task: against those who humbly seek God through common sense and careful study ('to Nature's Cause thro' Nature led', *D*, IV: 468), the 'gloomy Clerk' (*D*, IV: 459), argues from preconceived notions of God to the imperfections of the world which in turn cause doubts about the existence of God. Philosophers seek nothing less than to materialise God, indeed, into 'some Mechanick Cause' (*D*, IV: 475). It is a matter of superimposing a sense of self on the world, and thus allying oneself with the Satanic claim to be one's own 'author': 'See all in *Self*, and but for self be born' (*D*, IV: 477–80). Dulness herself is idolised as 'Wrapt up in Self, a God without a Thought' (*D*, IV: 485).

The condition aimed for is finally one of sleep, the self-centred abandon which characterises Bays's dozy presence throughout the last book. The figure of Silenus (a satyr from Virgil's *Eclogues* who sings the praise of drink, here representing a government journalist) commends the appropriately educated throng to Dulness's breast (IV: 515), then introduces a 'WIZARD OLD' whose mysterious *'Cup'* reduces them to swinish, infantile pleasures. This wizard is unlike the pantomime sorcerers of Book III: he has direct political power and cogency. The 112-line passage (IV: 493–604), perhaps the most obscure in the whole poem, parodies initiation rites of ancient 'Mysteries' under a metaphor for political corruption: the *'Cup'* represents bribes and pensions, used by Walpole's regime to anaesthetise the political will of anyone given to Opposition. All 'drinks' of this kind lead to a poisonous loss of principle: 'Lost is his God, his Country, ev'ry thing;/And nothing is left but Homage to a King!'(*D*, IV: 523–624). Dulness awards the gifts of 'Firm Impudence, or Stupefaction mild' (*D*, IV: 530) to guard her devotees from any useful form of self-knowledge, as a classical goddess might award a hero a weapon. Classical magic and biblical miracles are turned into a riot of corrupt festivity, with luxurious rituals of French cookery (IV: 549–664) looking like a blasphemous parody of the communion service.

Dulness attempts to send her approved apostles out to 'MAKE ONE MIGHTY DUNCIAD OF THE LAND' (*D*, IV: 604), thus claiming the poem as the poet had indicated at the start of the Book (IV: 8), but interrupts herself with a yawn before which 'All Nature nods: /What Mortal can resist the Yawn of Gods⁇' (*D*, IV: 605–6). This epic action has some very immediate, contemporary consequences: the Church authorities fall asleep first (IV: 607–10), followed by parliament and the armed forces (IV: 611–18), as effective action of any sort is lost. The 'Muse' is invited to relate the process in detail (IV: 619–26), but is apparently interrupted by Dulness in person, claiming not only the song but the poet, again as announced at the start of the Book. We are returned to the emblematic level of the start of the Book, as a Miltonised Dulness comes to extinguish the cosmic lights of Art, Truth, Morality, Religion and Philosophy:

> She comes! she comes! the sable Throne behold
> Of *Night* Primaeval, and of *Chaos* old!
> Before her, *Fancy*'s gilded clouds decay
> And all its varying Rain-bows die away.
> *Wit* shoots in vain its momentary fires,
> The meteor drops, and in a flash expires.
>
> (*D*, IV: 629–34)

In a final nightmare vision, Chaos (Dulness's father) returns to occupy the place of Creation:

Lo! thy dread Empire, CHAOS! is restor'd;
Light dies before thy uncreating word:
Thy hand, great Anarch! lets the curtain fall;
And Universal Darkness buries All.

(D, IV: 653–6)

In the 1728/9 *Dunciad* this final narrative had been installed in the hero's vision at the end of Book III as a prophecy, and was framed by a couplet which signalled it as a mere dream; here, the prophecy is fulfilled, and the creating word of God ('Let there be light') is erased by the fiat of uncreation.

Pope apparently used to read these final lines with sombre emphasis. Erskine-Hill (1972a: 66) comments that 'In the fiction of *The Dunciad* there is no consolation, absolutely nothing'; Pope's own death was less than a year away at publication. As a final vision, a last tilt at Walpole, it approaches an epic tone in which the 'mock' element is virtually absent. There is, however, a tiny reminder of the possible tawdriness of Dulness's apocalypse: 'The hand, great Anarch! lets the curtain fall' recalls the cheap theatrical effects of the Dunces in the first three books, and as such gives the final extinction a trace of comic wobbliness. Moreover, though these lines are the end of the *poem*, they are not the end of the *book*.

The publication history of *The Dunciad*, with its multiple formats and ability to incorporate new material across the decades, gives it a special status in Pope's writing **[195–7]**. The overt parody of textual scholarship, and covert compilation of actual information and defensive material, which Pope had begun in the three-book *Dunciad Variorum*, was extended considerably in the four-book text: the spoof classical edition has the subliminal function of presenting the modern poem as something equivalent to Horace or Virgil. Not all of what Scriblerus does in the notes is riotously parodic, and his discussion of the poem's epic nature does promote *The Dunciad* as epic of its time, by one who had truly mastered the epic vein. The 'Testimonies of Authors' (normally in a classical edition a chorus of praise, such as had prefaced Pope's *Works* of 1717) is here a set of quotations from attacks on Pope designed to justify the poem as retribution rather than the initiation of conflict; but it is also a chorus of praise from various worthies, including many of the Dunces themselves. Appendix II is a straightforward bibliography of attacks on Pope 'with the true Names of the Authors' identified.

Appendix VI presents 'A Parallel of the Characters of Mr. Dryden and Mr. Pope, As drawn by certain of their Cotemporaries'; here Pope compares on facing pages attacks on him with attacks on the by now unimpeachable Dryden and finds considerable solidarity with the earlier poet: both are traduced as rebels, illiterates, cheats, asses and apes, and so on. The work of the poem, that is to say, continues outside the poem itself, and the sombre ending of the mock-epic is somewhat lightened by the textually-based joke of the mock-book.

Further Reading

Criticism of the poem took some time to emerge from the controversy it aroused: complaints about the personal nature of the satire, and the pathology of the satirist, were in a sense the poem's lifeblood and Pope managed to incorporate controversy into the texture of the poem in an ongoing signal of his authorial power. In the twentieth century, Johnson's view that it was one of Pope's 'greatest and most elaborate performances' (Johnson 1905: 145) has been amply ratified [157–9]. Williams (1955) established the basic geographical pattern of the poem's reference (its parody of Lord Mayor's Day celebrations), and its socio-logical transformations of living individuals. He examined in detail the nature of the poem's ongoing citation and incorporation of the *Aeneid* and *Paradise Lost* as standards of heroic and theological activity which the Dunces invert. Williams's geographical work has been very substantially revised and extended by Rogers (1972) to indicate the profundity of its local reference and sociological specificity and by the same critic (1985) to clarify the poem's allusions to the coronation of George II: Rogers also extends Williams's analysis of the semantic use (and abuse) of personal names and identities in the poem (1974b). Despite its reputation for scabrous personal bitterness, Leavis (1976: 94) argued that Pope takes such pleasure in the creation of his 'marvel-lously organised complexity of surprising tropes, felicitously odd images, and profoundly imaginative puns', that the poem's actual mood, in some instances 'might fairly be called genial', and that episodes such as those which satirise collectors and scientists in Book IV indicate something of Pope's own private attraction to those sciences. Jones (1968) argued that Pope has a much greater sense of involvement with his Dunces than initially appears: the 'strangeness' of the poem Jones relates to its 'psychomachic' elements of ambiguous attraction; Pope is not simply bearing the standard for culture against the barbarians but responding to, ordering, exorcising his attraction to the world of unrestricted play which Dulness represents: 'what Pope as a deliberate satirist rejects as dully lifeless his imagination communicates as obscurely energetic – states of being densely, but often unconsciously, animated' (637). Even the apocalyptic conclusion has its elements of poetic and readerly pleasure, as Pope repudiates but also responds to the vitality of anarchy: 'what destroys the world completes the poem' (647). Such a line has also led to more hostile assessments of Pope's relation to what he attacks: Brown (1985) manages to read the poem as a perverse celebration of the energies of an economic system it ostensibly demonises, and Stallybrass and White (1985) argue that Pope is inevitably tainted and compromised by the very forms of bodily excess which he renders so grotesquely vivid. The gendering of Dulness has also been brought more into question in recent years **[179]**.

PART III

CRITICISM

(a) POPE AND POETRY

Pope was right enough to declare with studied casualness that 'The life of a Wit is a warfare upon earth' (*PW* I: 292), for there was little in contemporary criticism of his poetry which was not motivated by opposition and envy. Nonetheless, Pope's actual publishing career was immensely successful and he was unquestionably the leading poet of his day: Warburton's edition of his works (1751) accorded him the status of a classic. But it was not long before depreciation began to set in, partly because Pope's hard-won facility in verse produced many imitators, and partly because his complete dominance of the poetic scene was intimidating for successors who would do more than imitate. Cowper claimed that Pope had corrupted poetry by making it easy: he 'Made poetry a mere mechanic art,/And every warbler has his tune by heart' (Bateson and Joukovsky 1971: 121–2). The poet and scholar Joseph Warton produced the first major critical work on Pope in 1756, revising it through several versions and adding a second volume in 1782 (Barnard 1973: 379–407, 508–21); and though he paid due tribute to Pope's abilities, he advanced the fatal case that Pope was in effect a moralist rather than a poet, that he lacked 'a creative and glowing IMAGINATION': 'the Sublime and the Pathetic are the two chief nerves of all genuine poesy. What is there very sublime or very Pathetic in POPE?'. It was a damaging question, despite the fact that Warton kept (almost by accident) finding examples of exactly that which he claimed that Pope lacked. In *The Rape of the Lock*, according to Warton, 'POPE principally appears a POET; in which he has displayed more imagination than in all his other works taken together' (Barnard 1973: 399); the *Elegy to the Memory of an Unfortunate Lady* he found 'as it came from the heart, is very tender and pathetic' (400); *Eloisa to Abelard* was 'truly poetical, and contains ... strong painting' (404). The *Essay on Man* almost made him change his mind: 'I feel myself almost tempted to retract an assertion in the beginning of this work, that there is nothing transcendently sublime in POPE. These lines have all the energy and harmony that can be given to rhyme' (513). But in his conclusion, Warton argued that basically Pope's work was didactic, moral, and satiric, 'and consequently, not of the most *poetic* species *of poetry*'; 'He gradually became one of the most correct, even, and exact poets that ever wrote', but 'Whatever poetical enthusiasm he actually possessed, he withheld and stifled' (520).

Pope did not lack defenders. Arthur Murphy vigorously debunked the category of 'Invention' which Pope was supposed to lack as mere singularity and affectation, and asserted 'The three great primary branches of composition are finely united in the writings of Pope; the imagination is delighted, the passions are awakened, and reason receives conviction; there is poetry to charm, rhetoric to persuade, and argument to demonstrate' (Barnard 1973: 447–52). Samuel Johnson took a measured view of the controversy in allowing a good deal of Warton's particular criticisms of Pope, but dissenting from the overall assessment that Pope was merely the poet of 'Good Sense'. In a remarkable testimony to Pope's power, Johnson writes:

> Pope had likewise genius; a mind active, ambitious, and adventurous, always investigating, always aspiring; in its widest searches still longing to go forward, in its highest flights still wishing to be higher; always imagining something greater than it knows, always endeavouring more than it can do.
>
> (Johnson 1905: 217)

Pope, in fact, had everything:

> Pope had, in proportions very nicely adjusted to each other, all the qualities that constitute genius. He had Invention, by which new trains of events are formed, and new scenes of imagery displayed, as in the *The Rape of the Lock*, and by which extrinsick and adventitious embellishments and illustrations are connected with a known subject, as in the *Essay on Criticism*; he had Imagination, which strongly impresses on the writer's mind, and enables him to convey to the reader the various forms of nature, incidents of life, and energies of passion, as in his *Eloisa, Windsor Forest*, and the *Ethick Epistles*; he had Judgement, which selects from life or nature what the present purpose requires, and, by separating the essence of things from its concomitants, often makes the representation more powerful than the reality; and he had colours of language always before him ready to decorate his matter with every grace of elegant expression, as when he accommodates his diction to the wonderful multiplicity of Homer's sentiments and descriptions.

'After all this', Johnson proposes, 'it is surely superfluous to answer the question that has once been asked, Whether Pope was a poet? otherwise than by asking in return, If Pope be not a poet, where is poetry to be found?' (Johnson 1905: 247, 251).

This was, however, precisely the question which was asked in the coming generation of Wordsworth and Coleridge, when Pope was accused of sticking to the low ground of ethical writing (when he should have been exploring the heights of mental life). The Romantics sought a new definition of the poet's role in society, a less theologically-controlled view of Nature, and a return to earlier, more magical models of English poetry (Shakespeare and Spenser in particular). Pope's translation of Homer was decried as a poisonous source of 'poetic diction' and artificial language, his versification was deemed to be monotonous and 'sing-song' and Pope was demoted to the ranks of non-poets: 'Pope is a satirist, and a moralist, and a wit, and a critic, and a fine writer, much more than he is a poet' (the influential critic Francis Jeffrey; Bateson and Joukovsky 1971: 178). De Quincey claimed: 'I admire Pope in the very highest degree; but I admire him as a pyrotechnic artist for producing brilliant and evanescent effects out of elements that have hardly a moment's life within them' (230).

Griffin (1995) has reexamined the literary history of 'Romanticism' and argues that Wordsworth's depreciation of Pope is not a neutral judgment but a functional separation of his own poetic identity from Pope's dominant mastery; the separation also leaves a number of traces of anxiety in Wordsworth's self-formulation. 'Romanticism' itself is founded on a negation of Pope, on the attempts of writers like Joseph and Thomas Warton, Edward Young, and William Cowper, to free themselves from Pope's poetic dominance. The literary history of early nineteenth-century England was more complex than a sudden and revolutionary sweeping away of the poetry of reason by the poetry of powerful feeling, for Pope continued to be a major poetic presence, admired even by those who would disparage him, such as Hazlitt. For Hazlitt, Pope was a master of the 'artificial style', not the sort of poet who 'gives the utmost grandeur to our conceptions of nature, or the utmost force to the passions of the heart'; he was rather 'a wit, and a critic, a man of sense, of observation'. And yet,

> within this retired and narrow circle how much, and that how exquisite, was contained! What discrimination, what wit, what delicacy, what fancy, what lurking spleen, what elegance of thought, what pampered refinement of sentiment! It is like looking at the world through a microscope, where everything assumes a new character and a new consequence, where things are seen in their minutest circumstances and slightest shades of difference; where the little becomes gigantic, the deformed beautiful, and the beautiful deformed.

For Hazlitt, Pope's best work was the 'filigree' of *Rape of the Lock*, where 'The balance between the concealed irony and the assumed gravity is as nicely trimmed as the balance of power in Europe. The little is made great, and the great little. You hardly know whether to laugh or weep' (Bateson and Joukovsky 1971: 195–6).

But the stoutest defender of all was Byron, who asked: 'If you search for passion, where is it to be found stronger than in the epistle from *Eloisa to Abelard* ... ¿'. Byron found in Pope (and Dryden) all the 'invention, imagination, sublimity, character' that could be wished, and denounced the envious depreciation of contemporary poets:

> It is this very harmony, particularly in Pope, which has raised the vulgar and atrocious cant against him – because his versification is perfect, it is assumed that it is his only perfection; because his truths are so clear, it is asserted that he has no invention; and because he is always intelligible, it is taken for granted that he has no genius. We are sneeringly told that he is the 'Poet of Reason', as if this was a reason for his being no poet. Taking passage for passage, I will undertake to cite more lines teeming with *imagination* from Pope than from any *two* living poets, be they who they may.
>
> (Bateson and Joukovsky 1971: 202)

Byron claimed he would 'show more imagery in twenty lines of Pope than in any equal length of quotation in English poesy, and that in places where they least expect it', instancing the Sporus portrait from *Epistle to Dr Arbuthnot*: 'Now, is there a line of all the passage without the most forcible imagery ... ¿ Look at the variety, at the poetry, of the passage – at the imagination: there is hardly a line from which a painting might not be made, and *is*' (Bateson and Joukovsky 1971: 208). But his claims for Pope were also founded on the very point for which Warton had initially decried him, that of being 'the moral poet of all civilisation; and as such, let us hope that he will one day be the national poet of mankind' (Bateson and Joukovsky 1971: 206–7).

But moralistic biographies of Pope tended to emphasise his spite, meanness, hypocrisy, and badness of heart, a sense of inauthenticity which tainted criticism as a whole. Matthew Arnold's famous essay of 1880, on the question 'Are Dryden and Pope poetical classics?' maintained their subjugation in the literary hierarchy: 'We are to regard Dryden as the puissant and glorious founder, Pope as the splendid high priest, of our age of prose and reason, of our excellent and indispensable eighteenth century. For the purposes of their missions and destiny their poetry, like their prose, is admirable'. But: 'do you ask me whether such verse proceeds from men with an adequate poetic criticism of life, from men whose criticism of life has a high seriousness, or even, without that high seriousness, has poetic largeness, freedom, insight, benignity?'.

Answer, No: 'Dryden and Pope are not classics of our poetry, they are classics of our prose' (Bateson and Joukovsky 1971: 249–52). This is, of course, to define poetry in a certain unquestioning way and then to miss everything in the poetry which might approximate to the definition. Interestingly, Arnold wrote this rallying cry *against* what he took to be a resurgence in interest and respect for the eighteenth century and a growing disrespect for the authority of Wordsworth and Coleridge. In the twentieth century, with Modernism displacing the emotional cast of Victorian and Romantic poetry, Pope was ripe for reassessment.

Some of this came in biographical terms: Sherburn (1934) offered a sympathetic and properly-researched biography of the first part of Pope's career, and the same scholar edited Pope's correspondence in 1956, providing an immense store of new material for students of Pope, alongside the battery of scholarship presented in *The Twickenham Edition of the Poems of Alexander Pope* (1939–69). Ault (1949) took Pope's side in many of the controversial and murky issues of his poetic career. General critical revival began with Warren (1929), which took Pope seriously as 'critic and humanist'. But the best of the early work was in the area of 'practical criticism'. In 1930 the poet Edith Sitwell roundly denounced as deaf those who took Pope's couplets to be unvarying and monotonous and showed, by means of close reading, how variable Pope's texture was, and how significant its variety was (Sitwell 1930). In the same year Empson invented, elaborated and celebrated the poetic effects of 'ambiguity', and Pope was one of the authors whose verbal textures appeared much the richer. Quoting, for example, a couplet about Dulness, 'Where, in nice balance, truth with gold she weighs,/And solid pudding against empty praise', Empson proceeds to track our implied readerly weighings and vacillations:

Neither *truth* nor *gold*, neither *praise* nor *pudding*, are to be despised, and the pairs may be connected in various ways. A poet is *praised* by posterity for attending to what Pope called *truth*; whereas *gold* and *pudding* are to be gained by flattery. *Gold* may be the weights of the balance with which *truth* is *weighed*, so that the poet will tell any lie that he decides will pay; or all four things may be alike and equally desirable, so that, though the author is hungry and sensible, he is also *truthful* and anxious for his reputation; his proportion of *praise* and *pudding* has to be worked out with honest care. This spectacle, in its humble way, is taken to be charming; so that this version is contemptuous but without the bitterness of the first one. For these versions, *praise* is that of good critics, and it is *empty* beside *pudding* in a sense that would sympathise with the poet's hunger, or as an imagined quotation from him so as to bring him into contempt. But it might be *empty* as unjustified, as being the *praise* of (that is, from or to) the rich patrons who had bought the compliments; *gold* then takes on the suggestion of contempt, never far from it in Pope's mind, and means 'shoddy poetical ornament'; *pudding* is paired with *truth*, in the natural order of the antitheses, and means either the cheap food which is all he would be able to buy, or the *solid* reality of his dull but worthy writings. At any rate, the epithets *solid* and *empty* contradict the antithesis 'venal' and 'genuine'; it is gay and generous of Pope to have so much sympathy with *pudding*; and it is this detachment from either judgment in the matter (the *truth* such men could tell, the *praise* they could win, is nothing for Pope to be excited about) which makes the act of *weighing* them seem so absurd.

(Empson 1961: 126–7)

Less virtuosic, but equally appreciative, was the work of F. R. Leavis. Reacting against the emotionalism and fake solemnity which he saw as poisonous to the literary culture of the late nineteenth century, Leavis (1972) reinvented Pope as a late metaphysical, the agent who transformed the 'line of wit' inherited from Donne and Jonson into the meaningful and authentic correctness of Augustan values. Leavis refuses to see these values as some sort of arid formalism, mere arrangement of words and metre; 'Politeness was not merely superficial; it was the service of a culture and a civilisation, and the substance and the solid bases were so undeniably there that there was no need to discuss them' (76). 'When Pope contemplates the bases and essential conditions of Augustan culture his imagination fires to a creative glow that produces what is poetry even by Romantic standards. His contemplation is religious in its seriousness' (81). Pope's handling of seemingly opposed modes (insolence, elegance, majesty, the ludicrous, pathos) is not only a sign of wonderful versatility, but is the mark of a truly creative engagement with the world. His seriousness, experienced in surprising variety of tone and imagery, is not the solemnity of the Victorians (to whom Pope seemed frivolous, rationalistic, or disgusting), but 'a play of mind and a flexibility of attitude' which demand a corresponding 'play of the critical intelligence in the reader' (71). The art is the feeling:

There is, indeed, evidence in the satires of strong personal feelings, but even – or, rather, especially – where these appear strongest, what (if we are literate) we should find most striking is an intensity of art. ... His technique, concerned as it is with arranging words and 'regulating' movements, is the instrument of fine organization, and it brings to bear pressures and potencies that can turn intense personal feelings into something else.

(80, 82)

Leavis's response to the Twickenham edition of *The Dunciad* was to celebrate the poem's 'astonishing poetry' (Leavis 1962, 91), its sureness of transition between Miltonic grandeur, Augustan values, and imaginative wit. Again he sees an underlying sense of order as a kind of depth rather than repressiveness: 'As the antithesis of triumphant Chaos it informs the prophetic vision of the close with that tremendously imaginative and moving grandeur' (92–3). Leavis disputes the value of the label commonly applied to Pope, that of satirist, by discovering a kind of genial appreciation within satiric attack, a 'predominance of creativeness, delighting in the rich strangeness of what it contemplates' (94). *The Dunciad* offers not ordered progress but a 'packed heterogeneity' (95):

> What fascinates him are effects of fantastic incongruity; effects that at the same time seem to evoke a more exciting reality than that of common sense. ... The relation between his interest in these qualities and his concern for Augustan order constitutes one of the most striking aspects of his genius. ... there is nothing repressive about the Order that commands his imagination. His sense of wonder has been richly and happily nourished, and can invest what offers itself as satiric fantasy with the enchantment of fairy-tale...
>
> (95–6)

Tillotson (1938) offered a more comprehensive sense of Pope's worth as a poet, grasping the nettle of his supposed 'correctness' and glossing it under four aspects: Nature, Design, Language, and Versification. Tillotson finds positive virtues in all these areas of Pope's art, but perhaps particularly in the language, which he considers to have 'an almost surreptitious conciseness' and a brilliantly condensed forcefulness (103). In versification too Tillotson celebrates Pope's virtuosity of effect: in rhyme and particularly in manipulation of the couplet, he sees Pope as essentially offering a kind of poetic responsibility which the reader trusts, within which effects of surprise are continually expected and exploited: he uses to the full 'the privilege of variety when once uniformity has been established' (132). The complex variations of effect (sudden bathos, sudden sublime, irruption of conversational idiom, tensions between high and low) are deployed across a couplet art which is nothing like mere music or clever trickery. Its antitheses, inversions, parallellisms, balances and imbalances, pauses and deferrals are all harnessed to the expression of a moral or creative *content*: 'a vision of men and things which is as elaborate as intense' (131). This line was followed by a number of critics: Mack (1949) was a classic exposition of the ways that verbal devices played around with the surface meaning of poems; Parkin (1955) provided a more strictly formalist account of the technical devices of Pope's work: implied dramatic speaker, irony, parallelism, paradox, metaphor, and tonal variation are considered as they function in the individual poem and in his work as a whole (3).

Pope was now established as a poet whose work repaid analysis along formal lines towards the discovery of essence and meaning. Tillotson's subsequent book on Pope (1958) transferred its attention from manner and form to content and analysed a number of the different senses that 'Nature' has in Pope's work. To a large extent, Pope studies have been marked by a search for unified thematic content, though this can mean a variety of things. For Wilson Knight (1955), Pope's work is quasi-religious in seriousness: he discovered 'profound metaphysical importance' in Pope's 'vision' of the world: 'In Pope religion and society, God and politics, spirit and body, converge. His world is compact, but burning: within its present humanity lies its eternal catholicism' (14). Rogers (1955) saw Pope's work primarily in relation to the world it was criticizing, as does Dixon (1968). For Brower (1959), however, it is Pope's classicism which provides the metaphysical context for the poetry, and his reading constitutes a very full and persuasive reconstruction of the 'poetic voices that Pope heard as he wrote'. What Pope alluded to, what he changed from conspicuous sources, what he left out, what he left unacknowledged, can be rediscovered to provide an enriching intertextual field in which to read the poetry. The saturating presence of classical writers like Virgil and Horace grounds the poetry in an aesthetic and moral order. Thomas Edwards (1963) sees Pope's work as attempting to mediate between the 'dark estate' of the actual world and ideal visions of imagination and intellect; a precarious but humane balance eventually gives way to satire and disorder. For Spacks (1971), the imagery of the poetry can be read in terms of recurrent patterns to yield a moral discipline: Pope's images 'are means of conveying his ideas about the value of ethical control, or they embody principles of aesthetic control'. Keener (1973) also sees Pope's work as a unity, possessing overall design. Lerenbaum (1977), however, shows that Pope's desire to put his work into a consistent philosophical framework could not be sustained against his pragmatic and flexible practice as a writer (Rogers 1995 offers a more recent commentary on this aspect).

For other critics, the content of Pope's work is an exploration of subjectivity and world: Pope's conception of himself in relation to literary tradition is presented in Russo (1972); his self-fashioning through letters and their publication is examined by Winn (1977) and Jones (1990). The most important of these accounts, however, is Griffin (1978), an analysis both of the 'poet-protagonist' who figures so conspicuously in the poems, and whose private poetic and psychological concerns emerge into the poems in somewhat more clandestine fashion.

> By reestablishing and clarifying the nature of this intimate link – not quite an identity – between "Pope" and Pope ... we can recover some of the personal energy that invigorates Pope's greatest poems and makes them vividly self-expressive products of an imagination intrigued with and often at odds with itself, and yet more sharply at odds with the world.
>
> (xiv)

Jackson (1983) offers a difficult but richly suggestive account of Pope's work as a unity, relates the imagistic patterns of Pope's major works as an expanding and reflexive vision, to be read almost as myth, as one might read Milton or Blake. 'Pope's central subject of order and disorder (the breaking away from and returning to divine design) necessitates sustained acts of mythopoesis that over and over again invoke metaphors of division, possession, obsession, and usurpation, which in turn are opposed by figures of unity, freedom, dedication, and authority' (12). However disjunct *Eloisa to Abelard* is from the *Essay on Man* in generic terms, as 'myth they are interdependent parts of a unified vision, which is forged by extending the initial design into further and more elaborate contexts' (13). The poems invert and reinvent each other in startling ways; the poetry 'displaces and reconstitutes its own myths, thereby signifying its principle of growth and vitality' (18). The poetry is always, as Johnson had claimed, questing and aspiring; 'His dramas are those of man fulfilling or subverting the divine design, and thus they commonly focus on the authority that may (or may not) be invested in such recurrent terms as *knowledge* or *power*': 'At its most intense, Pope's poetry confronts the ego brimming over with the ambition to flood the possibilities that lie at the periphery of perception, to become its own image of itself, to fulfil itself in various acts of transgression that constitute a raid on the possible. It is for such reasons that Pope enters his own dramas of internal subversion and betrayal, alert to those confusions of identity and purpose that baffle the aspiring ego' (18). Pope stands between Milton and Blake because of his nervously vigilant sense of impending fall: 'Pope's entire existence as a poet depends upon summoning criteria that contextually contain and limit the performing self while simultaneously indicating that such a performance is self-consumptive ... his primary vision is the forms of alienation precipitated by the egotistical sublime' (177). Hence his rejection as a mere tool of restrictive law by the romantics.

Most critics of the 1980s were in some way or other committed to an idea of Pope's imaginative vision. Morris (1984), one of the most solid and appreciative humanist accounts of Pope, is interested in the flux and reflux of themes and images from a more traditional perspective; he finds an ultimate unity of purpose and theme in Pope in his privileging of refinement and his continual attempts to promote 'the correction of nonsense by sense' (12). In a different way from Jackson, he sees the 'visions and revisions which mark his work – including its blindnesses, lapses, failures, and contradictions – ultimately compelling and coherent' (13). Pope's relation to emotion, passion and unreason has attracted some comment; Shankman (1983) studies his *Iliad* translation as a key document in 'the Age of Passion'; Fairer (1984) sees Pope as attracted by the possibilities of a roving and passionate imagination but always keen to establish mental and moral control; Ferguson (1986) sees Pope rather as exalting emotion with a conscious extravagance, valuing the strengths of urgent response and the discordant elements of mental life. Damrosch (1987) offers a Pope who is concerned with the problem of representing experience at the beginning of the modern age; Lockean developments in psychology suggested that knowledge might be a merely private, mental affair, and Pope is seen as committed both to the details of lived experience and to pre-Lockean certainties about the nature of perception and identity.

Humanistic accounts of Pope continue to be produced. Plowden (1983) extends the field of Pope's classical reading; Quintero (1992) revisits Pope's classical inheritance and attempts to reconstruct the 'rhetorical sensibility' which Pope expected of his readers, and defends the coherence and structure of the works (up to *The Dunciad* of 1729) by reference to literary codes derived from classical models which were implicitly available in Pope's day and which have now become more or less invisible. But there is increasingly a sense that Pope's work can be (or ought to be) viewed from something other than the perspective of an 'ideal contemporary', capable of reading each work 'With the same Spirit that its Author *writ*' (*EC*, 234). The great waves of political and feminist criticism, which give short shrift to authorial intention and humanistic coherence, have not left Pope untouched; nor has that branch of materialist criticism which reads significance into the 'sociology of the text', or the actual forms in which literary works are produced. It will be appropriate therefore to review some main developments in these more specialised fields.

(b) POLITICS

'Still Dunce the Second Reigns Like Dunce the First'

Pope's supposed political allegiances were always a ready handle for his enemies. His name itself offered a convenient opportunity to associate his poetry with Catholic absolutism, as in *Pope Alexander's Supremacy and Infallibility Examin'd* (1729; see Guerinot 1969: 166–70). John Oldmixon's *The Catholick Poet* (1716) succinctly demolishes Pope's *Iliad* translation with the charge that 'This Papish dog ... has translated HOMER for the Use of the PRETENDER' (Guerinot 1969: 40). Such comments as these, so obviously deriving from vested interests, were largely ignored in later reception of Pope's work: the poetry has been taken more or less at its own estimation, as the work of one who attempted to transcend party divisions and speak from a principled independence. More recently, however, political (and politicised) analysis of Pope's oeuvre has become a distinctly animated area of study.

Mack (1969) began the work of reanalysing Pope's later career (1731–43) in political terms. In a volume plentifully illustrated with pictures of Pope's house and garden and satirical and political engravings, Mack sought the 'enabling myth' (vii) of Pope's Horatian stance, his appropriation of Horace's rural virtues of independence, frugality, and hospitality into a focused image in the house and grotto at Twickenham. Finding that 'certain aspects of Pope's abode and life at Twickenham become luminous with implication' (25), Mack describes the way Pope turned a forced exclusion from London into the 'pursuit of politics from the vantage of retirement' (116). 'Twit'nam', as Pope familiarly calls it in *Epistle to Dr Arbuthnot*, was both a place of retreat and psychological safety, and a sign of his success in overcoming political obstacles. From this platform it was possible to indict Walpole's regime in the Horatian poems **[119–30]** and revised *Dunciad* **[130–49]**, to the extent that Pope could figure himself and Walpole as 'mighty opposites', warring for the soul of Britain. The garden and grotto 'supplied a rallying point for his personal values and a focus for his conception of himself – as master of a poet's "kingdom," a counter-order to a court and ministry that set no store by poets' (232). Though the throne of Augustus is no longer filled by a virtuous and responsible ruler, 'there remains an alternative center, and a power of a different kind: the poet-king-philosopher in his grotto ... Under his magisterial wand ... lords and rich men, ministers and society-wenches, kings, courtiers, Quakers, clowns, and good Ralph Allens move through the paces of an intricate satirical ballet, which combines the features of reality and dream' (236).

A complementary guide to these movements can be found in Erskine-Hill (1975). Arguing that 'Literature is at once a social action, a product of society, an imitation of society and a criticism of society', Erskine-Hill finds that Pope's work fulfils 'each of these roles equally clearly' (4). The *Epistle to Burlington* [105–9], for example, is a social act in that it is like conducting a conversation which is designed to be overheard; it is a product of those economic and political forces which brought into being wealthy aristocrats who transformed their landed estates; it imitates social life in the visit to Timon's Villa, and criticises that Villa and its values by comparison with an expressed noble ideal. Erskine-Hill argues that Pope is more engaged than most poets in the social and political reality of his time:

> Perhaps no body of verse in the language expresses such detailed and specific concerns with the people and events of its time as his later epistles and satires. These poems are filled with proper names and allusions. Pope seems to derive from the very acts of naming and allusion a peculiar and various poetic energy which, while certainly communicated to the reader, may yet remain somewhat mysterious.
>
> (Erskine-Hill 1975: 5)

In order to explore the poetic force of these mysteries, Erskine-Hill offers detailed miniature biographies of six individuals from Pope's 'social milieu', including his close Catholic and Jacobite friend John Caryll, the Whig-inclined Ralph Allen, and the original of the 'Man of Ross' from the *Epistle to Bathurst*, among heroes; and Peter Walter, attorney and money-lender, and Sir John Blunt, financial projector, among villains. These form 'a balanced selection of evidence as to the nature of late seventeenth and early eighteenth-century society' (9) to which Pope's work can be seen as a response. Erskine-Hill reads the poetry in themed relationship to the individuals: images of false stewardship of the land and of national corruption are opposed to redeeming visions of the country house ideal, and of civilisation in general, grounded in Pope's awareness of these divergent biographies.

Analyses of Pope's political affiliations have become more specific and far-reaching as the historiography of politics in the period has itself become more dynamic. The period was once seen as one of relative political stability; this view stressed the basic acceptance of the 'Glorious Revolution' of 1688, which displaced the Catholic autocrat James II in favour of a constitutional monarchy, and saw politics as a matter of the shifting loyalties and individual personalities of those involved. The two-party system of Whig and Tory (which derives from the political debates surrounding the Revolution) appeared to be of less pressing importance. To some commentators, groupings of a 'Court' party (valuing the City, financial institutions, trade) against a 'Country' party (valuing land and agriculture as the basis of national wealth) appeared more useful as indicators of political thought (Kramnick 1968). 'Country' values implied that the only true political path was public-spirited action by men of landed property to preserve civil society; the true citizen is he who possesses an actual stake in the land and is thus established as both independent of financial corruption and responsible for the localised order of society. Such a citizen is of obvious relevance to the Pope of the Horatian period, when the whole question of the politicisation of culture was in vigorous debate (Goldgar 1976). Even *The Essay on Man* has its political aspect (Hammond 1984; Erskine-Hill 1988).

But the most contentious and provocative area of recent political study has been the rediscovery of Jacobitism as an active political force. The adherents of the exiled Stuarts were for a long time regarded as hopeless idealists, doomed to defeat. But recent research indicates that Jacobite activity, and fear of Jacobite activity, underlies much of the political agenda in Pope's lifetime, and there have a number of modern attempts to co-opt Pope to the Jacobite cause, or to defend him from it. In 1972 John Aden could offer Pope as initially reluctant to enter the political field at all, courted by both parties. Events after the death of Anne in 1714, however, gradually pushed him into political action: harassment of Catholics, the exile of Bolingbroke and impeachment of Harley, the trial of Atterbury, and the banishing of Swift to Ireland, affected Pope's relation to the political scene profoundly, and as Walpole's power increased Pope was ineluctably aligned with opposition politics. The returned Bolingbroke provided a political theory of non-partisan civic duty and loyalty to the mixed nature of the constitution which offered an attractively positive identity to one of Pope's pro-scribed religion, and he was able to voice opposition views on the Walpole administration without openly renouncing the principles of

1688 (Aden 1972). But six years later Aden revisited Pope's early, pre-*Dunciad* work with a sort of political geiger-counter, detecting anti-1688 sentiments coded into such apparently innocuous pieces as the *Pastorals, Essay on Criticism,* and imitations of Chaucer. Pope himself wrote *A Key to the Lock,* as if by a Whig commentator, translating the action of *The Rape of the Lock* **[17, 65–76]** into a political allegory; but this appears to be less a joke than a deflection of attention from the actual political allegory encoded in the poem. The translations from Statius, and in particular the translations of Homer, afforded Pope considerable opportunity for covert comment on power, the succession of kings, foreign invaders, the uses of political argument, and the significance of war: perhaps Pope did translate at least some details of Homer for the use of the Pretender after all. Aden begins to make a serious case for Pope's Jacobite sympathies:

> By birth and breeding, to be sure, Pope was, if not at least a nominal Jacobite, certainly a Stuart loyalist. Whatever the shortcomings of that House (and he was not unaware of them) it was the most congenial to his needs and instincts. Though Anne was clearly his ideal, better a Stuart in any case than an unknown factor, especially an alien, more especially if a Protestant champion, and more especially still if a Whig appointment.
>
> (Aden 1978: 178).

Aden argues that Pope's loyalism was 'based on dynastic convictions and a deep distrust of interruption, violent or otherwise', and that this dislike of disruption allowed him to accept the revolution as a fact even though he disapproved of it in principle, and to withhold support for any sort of militant Jacobitism.

Erskine-Hill (1982) has made the strongest general case for actual Jacobite content in Pope's work, reading the images of rape, seizure, invasion and restoration in *Rape of the Lock* and *Windsor-Forest* as metaphors for William III's occupation of the English throne, and suggesting that Pope might not have been averse to reversing Walpole's command of culture by a Stuart Restoration. In 1984, the same critic offered a reading of the card-game in *Rape of the Lock* **[65–76]** as a possible (if untidy) political allegory, perhaps speaking to those in the Jacobite coterie attuned to resonances of colour, gesture and allusion. Brooks-Davies (1983) argued that *The Rape of the Lock* constituted a slightly different sort of Jacobite allegory, based on the iconography of magical, redemptive, but absolutist kingship. In Brooks-Davies (1985) he produced a startling allegorical interpretation of *The Dunciad* **[130–**

49] which saw the poem through the light of post–1688 Jacobite propaganda: in a poem published on the fortieth anniversary of the Revolution, 'Dulness is England choosing an unlawful successor to the kingdom' (Brooks-Davies 1985: 3); the elected heir is not so much Theobald or Cibber as William III and his Hanoverian colleagues. Allusions to Virgil and Milton are not just there for mock-epic gravity but for dense political allusion; the rituals of coronation in the poem can be read as a highly-charged parody of biblical narratives, aligning William with Saul and the 'true' king with an absent David (96). Because most Jacobite propaganda was (for obvious reasons) highly coded, Brooks-Davies has to delve very deep to align the poem with Stuart values: he links signs and symbols in the poem with the mystery cults of mother-goddesses such as Isis and Ceres and to alchemical cryptograms to discover a hidden pattern of allegiance to true lines of succession against false ones. The poem also reaches back emotionally to a true 'nursing mother' in the figure of Anne, which Pope holds out, in a knowingly futile gesture, as a model to the exiled Stuart king. For this is 'emotional Jacobitism', and Pope is master of the irony of producing a covert Jacobite epic when it is far too late:

> Equally preposterous is Pope's evident commitment to the Stuarts as an ideal while, except for Anne, rejecting almost all that they represented in terms of administrative inadequacy. In other words, his Jacobite *Dunciad* offers little, if any, consolation to the naïve adherent of the king over the water, and whatever nostalgia there is in the poem is immediately qualified by dizzying and exuberantly witty caveats.
>
> (Brooks-Davies 1985: 140)

The book is, confessedly, more an exploration of a private mythology, shaped by Jacobite culture, than a political programme (viii).

Erskine-Hill (1996) has returned to the Jacobite question, revisiting the poems for further evidence of a 'political vein in their stone' (94). He emphasises, for example, the prominence of political identities among the animated cards of the game in *Rape of the Lock* **[65–76]**, Canto III:

> To say the least this is full of political observation and activity: '*Spadillio* first, unconquerable Lord' (l.49), 'The hoary Majesty of *Spades*' (l.56), 'The Rebel-*Knave*, who dares his Prince engage' (l.59), 'mighty *Pam* that Kings and Queens o'erthrew' (l.61), 'The *Club*'s black Tyrant' (l.69), 'Th' embroidered *King* who shows but half

his Face' (l.76), 'the *Queen of Hearts*' (l.88), and 'The *King* unseen' (l.95) draw from the game a maximum amount of political variety and excitement. When Pope adds the card-game, treated in this way, to a poem already making political allusion and deploying political language, he does so to warn the reader approaching the climactic action of the poem that this act can be seen in a political light. The card-game, in fact, supplies a political context for the forthcoming rape.

(Erskine-Hill 1996: 78)

Consequently, Belinda's active resistance to the rape (her lack of acquiescence in Clarissa's palliating advice) takes on a political significance, as does her repeated cry 'Restore the Lock'. *The Dunciad*, though concerned with bad writing as well as bad ruling, is based on the *Aeneid*'s powerful 'myth of loss, exile, wandering and restoration' which had already been established as part of Jacobite rhetoric (106). While Pope prudently chooses a mode of 'comic obliquity' to phrase anti-government sympathies, there is a strong implicit identification of an absent king in waiting in the later work. However, as Erskine-Hill puts it elsewhere, 'the jury is still out' on the extent of Pope's Jacobitism (Erskine-Hill 1998: 24).

The notion of Pope as Jacobite, emotional or active, has not been received with complete acquiescence. Much of what Pope has to say about previous Stuart rulers is surprisingly critical: the man who can ridicule the pedantry of James I (in *The Dunciad*, IV: 175–88), and declare in 1735 that his reign 'was absolutely the worst reign we ever had – except perhaps that of James the second' (Spence 1966: 242) is not perhaps a natural Jacobite. Chapin (1986) sees Pope as committed to an Erasmian model of ecumenical catholicism and the pragmatic politics of a non-partisan 'Patriot King'; he was anti-Williamite but also anti-Stuart, often rather rude about monarchs generally, and was temperamentally hostile to the kind of submission to absolute authority, however magical, entailed in Jacobitism's 'Divine-Right' theory of kingship. Downie (1990) is unconvinced by the theory of Pope's Jacobitism, because insufficient attention has been paid to Pope's Whiggish associates and leanings (the vocabulary of 'Liberty' in the poetry might be open to such a reading). Pope did *not* establish himself in a protective Jacobite enclave, but consorted with active Whigs (and Jacobite-hunters) such as Ralph Allen; the 'Jacobite background' is no more (and in some ways less) convincing than a Whig background. His rhetoric of 'order, hierarchy and stability' is conservative but not even definitively Tory, let alone Jacobite (19). Dickinson (1988) sees

Pope as attempting to stick to his own stated programme of a virtuous, non-partisan independence, while acknowledging his strong sympathies with the Tories – though even here Pope cannot be unambiguously a Tory because he could not be committed to the defence of the Church of England (12). Dickinson concedes that Pope may have had nostalgic links with Jacobite versions of history, but declares that any Jacobitism in the verse 'rarely rose above the level of innuendo' (12) and that there is no evidence that Pope was in any sense actively working towards the diplomatic end of a Stuart restoration.

Dickinson concentrates instead on Pope's overt links with the 'Country' opposition to Walpole (after a period of apparent friendliness with the minister himself) and the economic forces which (according to the theory) corrupted stable civic virtues into a baseless opportunism. Pope was courted by the 'Patriot' group opposed to Walpole, and was to an extent active in their programme to cultivate Frederick, Prince of Wales, as a figurehead, but he grew increasingly suspicious of the motives of the groups leaders. This last area has been developed in detail by Christine Gerrard (1990 and 1994). Pope was certainly attracted by the overtures of the Patriot group, and even went so far as to give Frederick a puppy from his dog Bounce, celebrating the gift in a charming 'Heroick Epistle'; but he never aligned himself with the group to the extent of writing the required Patriot epic. Pope's friendship with Bolingbroke, who had strong if intermittent links with Jacobitism, was always a sticking point for the Whig segment of the Patriot opposition, but Gerrard doubts that Pope's work of the 1730s could be seen as merely cloaking some more subversive Jacobite agitation (87). After the collapse of the Opposition, Pope's unpublished diatribe *1740* **[129]** sprayed abuse all around the spectrum of power: 'Pope's satiric scattergun leaves no political group untouched. This is the most cynical poem he ever wrote' (Gerrard 1994: 91–2); its dynastically ambiguous appeal for a saviour 'Patriot King' (in Bolingbroke's phrase) scarcely seems an achievable ideal.

The divisiveness of these readings of Pope's poetry as political statement is a sign of the elusiveness and ambivalence of the poems themselves: it is possible to argue them into a variety of allegiances. Another way of reading the poems politically also emerged in the 1980s in the wake of developments in literary theory. Formalist assessments of the literary text as essentially autonomous, organic, self-contained structures yielded to Marxist demands that criticism address the social and political 'unconscious' of texts; and rather than settle for a sophisticated paraphrase of authorial intention, modern literary theory insisted on opening texts for aspects which escaped or subverted authorial guarantees of meaning. A small spate of politically hostile accounts of Pope appeared, beginning with Brown (1985), which not only refused to accept the patrician values of Pope's poetry but suggested that the poetry itself shows reluctant signs of fracture even as it tries to present itself as timelessly unified. Brown reads the poems as

> documents of the ideological structures of the period, and if we read them not for what they claim to say but for what they fail to recognise, what they rationalise away, what they carefully conceal, and for the complex process by which they conceal it, we can begin to identify a new basis on which to understand their significance.
>
> (3)

The poetry's surfaces, so committed to aesthetic wholeness, are fundamentally divided and contradictory: reading *Windsor-Forest* alongside *The Dunciad* leads Brown to subvert the ostensible values of each poem, so that the former becomes 'an exposure of the violence of accumulation in imperialist culture' and the latter 'a celebration of the prolific energies of early English capitalism' (156).

Taking his cue from Marx, Hammond (1986) reads the works against their surface grain to discover the workings of the ideology which was invisible to Pope, that set of ideas and practices which operated 'to disguise historically-specific social and cultural phenomena as natural, permanent and unalterable properties of the world we live in' (3). Criticism thus has to read the gaps, the silences, and the discontinuities in literary works, looking for what Pope cannot or does not see in the world he presents and the choices he makes. Pope's claim to moderation and independence is placed alongside his subversive opposition to Walpole's ministry and his allegiance to quite specific forms of political organisation: 'Virtue' is not so much a neutral appeal as a relative, political concept. The autobiographical *Epistle to Dr Arbuthnot* is read for its 'unconscious' disclosure of the material basis for the independence he celebrates; and *The Dunciad*'s mythology of hack writers is tested for class bias and set against Pope's own status as a beneficiary of the commodification of culture. The works are unable to smooth out such contradictions and tensions fully.

Hammond remains committed to the materiality of history and culture and disdains that form of extreme philosophical scepticism about the unity of the human subject and the pertinence of historically-based truths which is known as deconstruction (7–8). But in the same year, Atkins (1986) provided a sustained account of Pope through the eyes of deconstruction. Analysing the oppositional stance of the poetic voice and its uses of the couplet form of binary opposition to establish truth and identity by negating otherness and falsehood ('The strong antipathy of good to bad'), Atkins contends that Pope's differentiations are always contaminated by elements of similarity and that Pope's negated victims have a habit of showing up in supposedly purified areas of self-presentation.

It is possible to find contradiction in Pope without completely demolishing his credentials. Nicholson (1994) describes the various trials the Scriblerians (especially Pope) had in negotiating the new opportunities for investment and monetary manipulation afforded by the development of banking and the stock market: all were in theory opposed to a system which appeared to allow for fraud and delusion on a grand scale, and which appeared to reconstruct the way individuals conceived of themselves and their agency in new and anti-social directions; yet all were investors to some degree, who sought monetary profit from the rise of capitalism. Similar kinds of 'simultaneous' meaning, sometimes figuring as contradiction, have informed gender-based criticism, to which we now turn.

(c) GENDER AND BODY

'In Sappho touch the Failing of the Sex'

Pope grew up in a closely-protected environment in which women (mother, aunt, nurse) to some extent dominated. Though unmarried, and probably mostly celibate, Pope embraced a kind of Restoration rakish culture in his early poems and letters [10–12]. Though always conscious that his unusual frame reduced his sexual chances, he had significant quasi-romances with Lady Mary Wortley Montagu and the Blount sisters; the friendships with Lady Mary and Teresa went badly awry, but Martha Blount was still a close friend in his last years, and was the major beneficiary of his will. He was close to many other women of noble rank. The mysterious 'Amica' appears to have invented a romance with Pope on the basis of his poetry [19–20, 44]. Female friends were often the named recipients of his poems (they were also the recipients of some of his most carefully self-implicating letters): as well as *The Rape of the Lock* and *Epistle to a Lady*, we have the 'Epistle to Miss Blount, with the works of Voiture', and 'Epistle to Miss Blount, on her leaving the Town, after the Coronation'; 'To Belinda on the

Rape of the Lock', 'Impromptu, to Lady Winchelsea', 'To a Lady with the Temple of Fame', 'To Mrs M. B. on her Birth-day' 'Verses to Mrs Judith Cowper', and other occasional verses of the kind. Pope was tireless (and perhaps, officious) in his attempts to protect his female relations and aid them financially.

Women constituted, as Pat Rogers puts it in a brief but suggestive survey of Pope's female friends, 'an order only too symbolic' (Rogers 1972b: 136). *Eloisa to Abelard* and *Elegy to the Memory of an Unfortunate Lady* are clearly attempts to work out in individualised instances issues related to the gendering of women; *Sapho to Phaon* 'represents' a strong woman strongly. Many of Pope's abstract concepts or semi-mythological deities are also female: the largely negative forces of Fortune and Fame are (partly because of their classical etymology) figured as fickle women. Vice appears in similarly gorging and suffocating queenly triumph in the *Epilogue to the Satires* (Dialogue I). The representation of Dulness as monstrous goddess and travesty-mother has been much explored in recent feminist criticism (Ingrassia 1991; Francus 1994). Nature is more positively figured as female, as are the Muses of poetry, and Virtue (though etymologically, virtue is connected with maleness). Gender clearly has a part to play in Pope's imaginative world.

Many (mostly male) critics have argued that Pope's deformities and his political marginalisation led him to have a special empathy with the situation of women in his era. Certainly Pope could not take 'manliness' for granted, as his letters show: masculinity had to be won, constructed, acquired through mastery of the pen, through the compensations of satiric conquest. There is plenty to show that Pope recognised that much of what reduced the autonomy of women was cultural rather than natural. He writes in the 'Epistle to Miss Blount, with the Works of Voiture'

> Too much *your Sex* is by their Forms confin'd,
> Severe to all, but most to Womankind ....
> Still in Constraint your suff'ring Sex remains,
> Or bound in formal, or in real Chains;
> *(TE* VI: 62–5)

He recognised that the cultural imperative to marry could be utterly disastrous for women. Nonetheless Rogers points out succinctly that for all his relative disadvantages, as a man Pope still had more automatic independence than any woman of his age (Rogers 1972b: 138). Like Pope, eighteenth-century women could not go to university or take civil office. But they were much more hemmed in than Pope in terms of what they could do, for they were not regarded as autonomous, but subject to male keeping. One of the main areas in which the odds were stacked against them was literature itself: only women of aristocratic status like Anne Finch, Countess of Winchilsea, and Lady Mary Wortley Montagu could gain significant respect, while successful playwrights and novelists like Aphra Behn, Susannah Centlivre and Eliza Haywood tended to be regarded as vulgar and transgressive. But literature was also one main field in which gender was produced, the binary divide between male and female, with its oppressive, positive-negative internal hierarchy, made to seem natural, anatomically-determined and unchallengeable.

Feminist theory of the last two decades has made a number of radical inroads into this 'naturalness': by reclaiming and revaluing the work of women writers, by uncovering the historical and cultural systems of misogyny and subjection, by analysing and contesting mythic constructions of 'the feminine', by refusing the authority of the male gaze which constructs female portraits only to criticise them (as in *Epistle to a Lady*) and by challenging the essentialism by which anatomical sex is equated with cultural gender. Felicity Nussbaum's *The Brink of All We Hate* (1984) attempted (under the rubric of a particularly disturbing line from Pope's *Epistle to a Lady*) to trace a line of development in anti-feminist satires from 1660 to 1750. Nussbaum's study sets Pope's *Epistle to a Lady* in the tradition of work by Samuel Butler, the Earl of Rochester, Restoration translations of the notorious sixth satire of Juvenal, and Swift. Pope's poems are found to be a good deal less violent and scatological than much of this earlier tradition, though his work still rounds up the usual suspects: women as mutable, pleasure-seeking, self-worshipping, threatening and so on. Against this satiric perspective, the portrait of Martha Blount sets conduct-book regulations for positive female behaviour (self-possession, good humour, sense, domesticity, companionship). To Nussbaum this is an etherealisation, less attractive to feminist sympathies than Swift's realistically wrinkled Stella – in fact barely female in any recognisable way at all. In the end, Nussbaum is ambivalent about Pope's ambivalence:

> Pope subtly exploits the antifeminist tradition and employs most of its assumptions, and in addition he combines that tradition with the impulse towards panegyric. When antifeminist satire begins to blend with romance, however, it brings about its own demise for a time. Pope avoids such an artistic dilemma by keeping both the desirable and the undesirable qualities of the sex alive and magnetically attractive. Women are still the object of satire because of

characteristics inherent in their sex. At the same time he encourages our understanding of women's situation and uses the satiric mode to capture the contradictory impulses women inspire. Within the asexual ideal, he keeps them forever in unresolved conflict.

(Nussbaum 1984: 158)

A year after this Ellen Pollak published *The Poetics of Sexual Myth* (Pollak 1985), a highly sophisticated and entertaining analysis of 'gender and ideology in the verse of Swift and Pope'. Contesting what seemed to her an over-literary emphasis in Nussbaum's book, where individual artistic choices might mitigate the misogyny implicit in available conventions for writing about women, Pollak seeks a more complete dismantling of the 'cultural ideology' which underlies both literary conventions and personal aesthetic choices.

Pollak works from a detailed socio-economic and cultural context to establish the existence of what she terms 'the myth of passive womanhood'. In a period of relative diminution of women's earnings and role in production, conduct books aimed to condition young women into acceptance of a secondary, passive role by figuring assertiveness (especially in women's writing) as futile narcissism. An accompanying idealisation of women as gentle, affectionate, domestic companions for men, entitled to (limited, and essentially ornamental) education and leisure, did not, Pollak argues, have much genuinely libertarian potential since under the guise of affection it supplanted overt misogynistic controls with indirect and hidden ones. Even the most powerful and talented women could be close to despair if they thought about their situation: as Lady Mary Wortley Montagu wrote to her daughter, resignedly, mischievously: 'Let us sing as chearfully as we can in our impenetrable Confinement and crack our Nuts with pleasure from the little Store that is allow'd us' (71). Women were encouraged to accept a spiritualised, decorative role in a myth which incorporated, protectively, its own anxieties about female 'deviance' (figures of prude, coquette, and scold were used to define that which went beyond 'passive womanhood'). These imperatives were presented as 'natural' through a set of literary and cultural devices ('myth') which concealed their historically-determined status.

While Swift ruthlessly and noisily exposed the gaps between the reality of his world and its bourgeois ideals, Pope 'seemed to go out of his way to resolve that dissonance, to rhetorically accommodate the contradictions inherent in his culture's dominant sexual codes and – despite their delimiting character – to make them seem sufficient to experience, fulfilled' (12). Thus in *the Rape of the Lock* **[65–77]** Pope is found to respond to the autoerotic potential of Belinda by confirming her as an object, ineluctably bound to forms of exchange and circulation in which men have the only real power, even as he 'satirises the irrational materialism of bourgeois values that objectify human beings by giving primacy to forms over substance' (12). Belinda (a standard 'type' of deviant) is told to knuckle under to socialisation and marriage by Clarissa, a prude (the opposite standard type), dramatizing 'choice' as a matter of female discussion. But Belinda has already converted herself into an object in the 'toilet' scene, as another negative type (Thalestris, the Amazon queen) reminds her:

> Was it for this you took such constant Care
> The *Bodkin*, *Comb*, and *Essence* to prepare;
> For this your Locks in Paper-Durance bound,
> For this with tort'ring Irons wreath'd around?
> (*RL*, IV: 97–100)

Politically, for Thalestris, the answer is no; ideologically, for the poem, the answer is yes, since the 'nourishment' Belinda has bestowed upon her locks 'to the Destruction of Mankind' (I: 19) actually converts her into a possessable object, the part taken for the whole (in the rhetorical figure known as metonymy), in a playful but ineluctable fusion of outward appearance with inner identity. Belinda's quest for autonomy and subject-status, always close to the horror of female sexual aggression, is doomed from the start; 'By her very mode of being she enacts a self-destruction which, though mediated by the Baron, begins and ends with her' (95). If in the poem she 'remains constantly resistant to the terms of female existence as Pope imagines them' 106), this is just another illustration of his overall point, that resistance is useless. The geniality of the poem, which in the end claims the lock for itself, possessing Belinda's sexuality even as it offers her a compensatory literary 'fame', conceals the ideological brutality with which 'Belinda is put on the scene of Pope's poem in extremes of pride, beauty, and virginity to be humiliated, mutilated, and raped' (106).

Pollak also contests the bourgeois reading of the *Epistle to a Lady* **[96–101]** as a contrast between negative and positive versions of femininity and argues that in effect there is no cogent difference between them, since the whole poem depends on the 'implicit metaphorisation of the female as a work of art' (109). In Pope's vision, women lack meaning, essence, 'character'; they seek the forms of art only to fill them defectively, act only to defeat their own worst intentions, and commit themselves to essentially circular, masochistic pleasures.

Pope's text denies 'character' to women in a more fundamental sense than even its own ironies would suggest. Metaphorically bridging the gap between verbal and visual modes of representation by his use of this key term, Pope establishes an essentially unitary structure of sexual difference – an economy of gender in which woman is not other in an irreducible, but only in an appropriated, sense. She is not the sign of a separate, autonomous otherness, is not a subject, an end in herself, but is 'his other', the *not man* that by opposition gives identity (gives 'character') to man.

(Pollak 1985: 111)

Martha Blount appears to be celebrated as the woman rewarded for operating in accordance with the 'natural' grammar of the gender system. But Pollak argues that the contrast between negative characters and the woman composed of the 'best kind of contrarieties' is only superficially complex, a 'sophisticated rhetorical strategy for obscuring an ideological simplicity, for bifurcating a premise that is univocal' (118). Addressed as quintessentially 'mistress of herself', an authentic woman after all, she is at the same time a composition, already blended, formed by Heaven to be a 'softer man', but nonetheless in essence raw material which 'she' is incapable of ordering herself. The lines to Martha reconstruct her, adding in husband and daughter though she was unmarried and childless, presenting her as:

a fait accompli of mediation, a blended, finished 'work' whose charm and moral perfection are stasis itself. The reward for her goodness is not, as for the Man of Ross, in the active 'ends of being,' but is passively contingent on the blandishments of men: by the patronage of Apollo she is protected from herself; by the patronage of Pope she is immortalised and blessed (281–92).

(Pollak 1986: 120–1)

The poem which gives her identity conceals her: 'buried in the indeterminacy of direct address even as she is personalised by the candor of a private interchange, undeciphered hieroglyph, she is "charactered" both as woman and the artifact of man' (127).

Pollak finds that while Pope and Swift are both committed to a phallocentric view of the universe, Swift's explosive and uncomfortable skirmishes with the ideological system which he cannot actually dismantle offer more pleasure to the feminist reader than Pope's aesthetically flawless accommodation with it. She concludes with some remarks about Pope's colonisation of the female voice in the extreme case of *Eloisa to Abelard* **[77–82]**, where once again she contests the notion that some positive exchange is being offered. What is really being indulged, she contends, is 'not the specificity of a woman's torment, or her display of erotic and emotional intensity, but rather a voyeuristic male appropriation of female eroticism in the service of a phallocentric ordering of desire in which both excess and lack are figured as female' (186).

Critics have tried to rescue the unregenerate Pope for more profeminist positions by various means. Rosslyn finds that in *The Epistle to a Lady* Pope (almost accidentally) finds himself charmed by the evanescence of female character which he satirically decries, that the satiric burden of subjugation is sabotaged by the imaginative expression in which is appears (Rosslyn 1988). Claridge (1988) uses the freely-punning subversive strategies of deconstruction and Lacanian psychoanalysis to retell *The Rape of the Lock* **[65–76]** less in terms of a commitment to 'the cheerful and necessary socialisation of a woman out of virginity' than as a self-undermining victim of a 'covert psychological dynamic', in which Pope seeks actually to virginalise/desex her; it is a contest between Belinda's autoerotic and labile sexual pleasure and Pope's desire to snatch (rape) the phallic sign (the lock) of her creativity – to replace the female power of cantos I–III with the Popean art of cantos IV–V. For her 'the text suggests the inadequacy of Pope's pen to assume authority' over Belinda (129). Treacherously artificial, always threatening to exceed the power of male art to visualise her, Belinda must be infiltrated, voyeurised, scripted; yet she is also phallically strong, a very Samson of the hairdressing world, guarded by gender-bending sylphs, possessing the womb which the men in the cave of spleen envy, capable of infinite desire. She can't be allowed to get away with this:

> The poet has exposed Belinda and made her vulnerable as she loses part of her artfully constructed self, in order to nullify her. Now he will use the artifice of her story to build himself up – to make potent his pen with her stolen phallic power, the rape whose economy drives this narrative.
>
> (Claridge 1988: 137)

The couplet form itself is characterised as a male device of closure and finitude, a form of linguistic control which points to an obsessive fear of female artistic excess. In the end, Claridge claims, Belinda's *jouissance*, 'the uncanny power that seemed to reside in a politically powerless creature' (143), outweighs Pope's conversion of her lock into his penned poem, her sexual creativity into his engendered fame.

Susan Matthews (1990) takes up the issue of the supposed characterlessness of women (as formulated in the *Epistle to a Lady*) and suggests it might be possible to read it as a kind of liberation – by denying women the 'characters' of language Pope excludes them from the symbolic order (equated with the phallic law of the father in Lacanian psychoanalysis) and leaves them in the maternal realm of the imaginary; women novelists, however, found it expedient to avoid such protean types of female character. Steve Clark (1990) pursues the instability of gender definitions and sexual imagery through a range of Pope's work, finding considerable identity between Pope and those characters whose gender seems particularly threatening (Sporus, Atossa). He argues that Pope's voice is not so much manly as desexualised, that it attempts to avoid the pitfalls and contaminations of desire: 'Pope's discursive authority ... appears to be constituted through an exorcism of desire: in this case, the object of repudiation has become a female body invested with a masculine potency' (96). That these gender terms 'may now appear hopelessly indeterminate in relation to his work', Clark hopes, may come to regarded 'as one of its greatest strengths'.

In contrast to these highly theoretical, text-based accounts, Rumbold (1993) gives an accessible and thorough survey of what is known of the actual lives and experiences of the women whom Pope celebrated, stigmatised, or otherwise characterised in his work. By grouping a reading of each major poem with a biographical analysis of one or more of its female protagonists, Rumbold sounds out the contexts from which Pope's constructions of the feminine emerge, and restores a voice to those partially silenced by the effectiveness of Pope's poetic control. Rumbold details Pope's relations with his mother, half-sister, and nurse, the gradual shift in amorous emphasis in his correspondence with the Blount sisters away from the brittle and manipulative Teresa towards the more self-effacing and put-upon Martha ('Patty'), the disillusionment of his fantasticated erotic image of Lady Mary Wortley Montagu in her 'Oriental' guise, and his changing position in relation to widowed and powerful aristocrats such as the Duchess of Buckinghamshire and the Duchess of Marlbrough. Women writers such as Judith Cowper, a more deferential and less threatening literary figure than Lady Mary, and Anne Finch, Countess of Winchilsea, also emerge from the shadows, as do women in Pope's circle involved (covertly or otherwise) in politics: Henrietta Howard, George II's mistress, and Mary Caesar, a Jacobite activist [165–9].

Pope's drawing of boundaries for the behaviour of women could be wilfully crude. His half-sister Magdalen summarises his eventual polarisation of the Blount sisters: '*Patty Bl* the fair one, Mr. *Pope*'s, the other he did not love, call'd Bitch, Hoyden' (112), but such polarities, which characterise some aspects of Pope's work, are revealed here as constructed ones, to be considerably modified in the light of documentary sources, which themselves point to new ways of reading the poems: the correspondence between Pope and Martha, for example, 'shows poignantly how in daily life as well as in *Characters of Women* [*Epistle to a Lady*] he idealised this touchy and indecisive woman along the lines of his archetypal unfortunate lady' (285). While Rumbold does not call into question 'Pope's primary commitment to the rules laid down for men – as writer, public figure, head of the family, friend to his male friends and protector to his female friends – it is easy to see how the opportunities (or disabilities) which enabled him to experience so wide a range of less positive and assured roles ... are connected with his willingness in *Eloisa* and the *Elegy to the Memory of an Unfortunate Lady* to enter into the gloom and passion of female confinement' (43). In those poems particularly, which derive partly from sympathy with women of his acquaintance helplessly oppressed by bad marriages and partly from fascination with the transgressive brilliance of Lady Mary, Pope appears to celebrate female rule-breakers: 'he had transcended the conflict between lady Mary's self-assertion and the dutiful passivity typical of his unfortunate ladies by imagining heroines whose outrageous self-expression was offset by impressive moral strength' (109). Such conflicts could not always be resolved, of course, and the increasing vehemence with which he denounces the creative power of women like Lady Mary in terms of personal filth and sexual aggression point straight towards the gender of Dulness in *The Dunciad* **[130–49]**:

> Indeed, that Dulness herself is female is one of the most important facts about her: if her gender is a source of delight in opening up a world of capricious fantasy akin to the female world of *The Rape of the Lock*, it is also the key to her obscenity as ... she opposes and undoes the work of God the Father ... Her yawn, the formless yet potent opposite of the divine fiat, like her womb-like cave of pullulating literary monstrosities, draws on Pope's fundamental unease about female creativity; yet her very existence at the centre of his own creation testifies to his need for such a creature. To oversimplify, she stands for what his mind abhors and his imagination craves.
>
> (Rumbold 1993: 166–7)

For Rumbold the section of *Epistle to a Lady* **[96–101]** which contrasts the lasting values of Martha's modesty with the dazzling aggression of women like Teresa and Lady Mary (242–9) is a more positive attempt to resolve such a division:

> Teresa and all her glittering kind are conclusively denounced in the idealistic and no doubt unnoticed falsehood that the rising moon distracts attention from the setting sun. In Pope's quixotic defence of the self-effacing female ideal we sense the depth of his desire to respond as vividly to what he conceived of as goodness as to the brilliance which in the end would only disgust him. It is a moving moment, as much for the impasse indicated by the implausible conceit as for its declaration of quietly sustaining love.
>
> (Rumbold 1993: 277)

A useful adjunct to Rumbold's work is Thomas (1994), an account of the wider response to Pope among women writers and readers of his day. The self-educated Pope, deprived of a university education, could in many ways offer a model of literary self-advancement to the 'unlettered' female writer: he acted as their 'classic' author, especially after the 'feminised' Homer translation (19–67), to be read, imitated, quoted, celebrated, appropriated and subverted through the century. Women readers apparently felt more specifically addressed by Pope than by any other male poet, and there exists a whole canon of female responses to Pope's work, covering the social range from aristocratic to demotic. Of course, Pope's mastery of verse technique could be intimidating for his readers, and much of his verse constructs femininity in ways which were hotly opposed by women writers; alternately, some women writers felt Pope was not conservative enough, particularly in the *Essay on Man*, which some took to lack orthodox Christian apologetics. But there was 'recuperative potential' to be discovered in heroines like Eloisa (183), despite the explicitly sexual nature of *Eloisa to Abelard*; there was a model of skill to imitate, innocently, in *The Pastorals*; and most extensively there was an education in the use of 'personae' in the Horatian poems **[119–30]**:

> Perhaps acute awareness of daily feminine role-playing aided them in fabricating personae: women wrote as women writing as Pope writing as Horace. Their frequent responses to Pope's Horatian poems suggest women's longing for a share of cultural authority. It also discloses their belief in Pope's poems as models for authoritative feminine expression.
>
> (Thomas 1994: 226)

Thomas concludes that 'Current analyses implying that contemporary women were somehow victimised by Pope's gendered rhetoric should reconsider the critical acuity with which his female audience often read' (244).

Christa Knellwolf takes her cue from Pope's best kind of femininity, 'a contradiction still', and argues for the critical usefulness of unresolved oppositions as a means of realizing the 'liberatory potential' in the poetry (Knellwolf 1998). She thus finds the poems less aesthetically successful in their ideological work than Pollak does. Starting anti-chronologically with *Epistle to a Lady* **[96–101]**, Knellwolf looks for contradictory impulses towards women as a means to open up the ideology which oppresses them. The constructed femininity in the poem seems to suggest than women are both powerless and threatening, and she argues that this logically impossible combination derives from a contemporary shift in women's relation to cultural production (sometimes referred to as the 'feminisation' of culture; 15). Knellwolf goes on to examine the issue of violence in *Windsor-Forest*, specifically the episode of Lodona, which transforms the female figure into an object which is itself the very 'ground' of representation, or mirror of art. She finds gender politics in unusual places, such as the *Essay on Criticism*, where Pope denounces obscenity and impotence with a vehemence which reinforces his 'engendering' commitment to the symbolic association of creative potency with the virile body. In her treatment of *Eloisa to Abelard*, Knellwolf finds an ambivalent questioning of the conventional association between creativity and potency, though Pope undermines this by reintroducing his own image towards the end. Knellwolf argues that while Pope was unusually receptive to the idea that 'an active sexuality was a positive complement to an active mind' in a woman, but only so long as these qualities were not aggressively used (131). In two chapters on *The Rape of the Lock* **[65–76]**, Knellwolf analyses the contradictory expectations that 'women have to preserve sexual inexperience and simultaneously have to comply with the conventional courtship pattern of a heterosexual relationship' (139). Finding in the construction of Belinda 'a knife-edge between sympathy and censure' (179), Knellwolf relates her alternate trivialisation and heroisation to patriarchal anxieties about the nature of women, and seeks to exploit the dual nature of mock-epic (thoroughly contemporary and polite, thoroughly ancient and martial) to emphasise the subversive visibility which the poem gives to women even as it seeks to negate and subject them. Arguing that Pope's poem shows a deeply analytic concern with the power, limits and distortions of 'representation', Knellwolf finds that in the end, Belinda achieves not the compliment of fame which Pope consciously intends but a certain haunting, indomitable presence which eludes him:

> Pope's objective is to render an image of an existence that is void of meaningful life. Belinda is, nevertheless, not empty: all those elements which are offensive to Pope's understanding of woman may appear like horrid perversions and parodies of that which is good and meaningful, but the abundance of half-real, half-living figures that surround Belinda challenge the notion of emptiness. They may be no more than ghostly reflections and hollow echoes to begin with, but they attain to a certain independence and thus question conventional assumptions about female existence on which the poem is based.
>
> (Knellwolf 1998: 195)

In *The Dunciad* **[130–49]**, Knellwolf finds no coherent subject beyond a vexed enquiry into women's role in the production of culture. The 'Mighty mother', Dulness, has a power which is both erotic and emasculating, intrusive and smothering. As inverter of the creative 'logos' of St John's Gospel into an 'uncreating word' (IV: 654), Dulness negates male creation by female annihilation; yet this also testifies to a kind of actual female power beyond Pope's imagination (212–13). This failure of conclusiveness, with a drift towards uncontainable and contradictory meanings of gender emerging from the equivocal role of the body in creativity, Knellwolf argues, forms a kind of invitation for debate and revaluation in femininst terms.

'He pleas'd by manly ways'

Recent studies of gender have reminded us that men also undergo the experience of gendering; that is, maleness is not simply an anatomical given from which masculinity 'normally' results, but a constructed, learned system of codes and behaviour. In an important study of eighteenth-century sexual ideology, Kristina Straub argues analyses the contrasting uses of a conventional 'schoolboy' figure in the literary war between Colley Cibber, actor and poet laureate, and Pope, in whose unofficial laureate epic *The Dunciad* **[130–49]** Cibber was made to star. The schoolboy is male but not a man, destined to authority yet subject to correction; he is implicated in various rituals of homoerotic discipline. Straub argues that Pope, disabled from obvious exertions of masculinity by his troubled body, rigorously seeks to negate and reject the figure of the schoolboy and define his own mature manliness by opposition to it. Cibber, associated by his profession as actor with 'unmanly' forms of display, plays ambiguously with the figure, sometimes making Pope the boy who must be corrected, sometimes offering himself for corrective judgement, and gaining a measure of literary authority through his self-aware exhibitionism:

> Cibber's schoolboy persona functions in relation to ideologies of sexual identity and literary authority as a sort of door that swings both ways: he opens into a rigidly binary system of heterosexual roles that ground literary authority and sexual dominance in an oppositional, binary structure of gender difference. On the other hand, he also opens into a fluidity of sexual roles that threatens binary gender roles and places literary authority on ambiguous ground. Without being subversive himself, Cibber perpetuates uncertainties about the dominant versions of sexual identity and literary authority that are emergent in the eighteenth century. His schoolboy suggests a fluidity and liminality still barely possible amid the growth of a new ideology of authority and masculinity. Pope's use of the schoolboy trope is more of a slamming than a swinging door. Confronted with his own problems of sexual ambiguity and literary authority, Pope associates deviation from verbal mastery with sexual deviation, and firmly positions both outside newly dominant definitions of masculinity and literary authority.
> (Straub 1992: 78)

The association between sexual and literary authority is sometimes disconcertingly direct in the war between Cibber and Pope: one comic take on the quarrel from 1742 all but has them compare sizes (Guerinot 1969: 301–5). But the implications of such gestures are wide-ranging, as Straub's analysis demonstrates.

Pope's endeavours to write himself into mastery as the British Homer had a more positive goal, but the results of the claim to masculinity were again more ambiguous than he might have desired. Carolyn Williams has placed Pope's versions of Homer in the context of early eighteenth-century gender debates and Pope's 'quest for a masculine role in society' (Williams 1993: 1). Homer, as the great seminal fount of Western literature, and master of the epics of war (*Iliad*) and questing (*Odyssey*), ought to have provided an unquestioned model for a writer concerned about civic and political 'manliness'. Pope grew up among discussions of sovereignty in which the state was often figured as female, with the ruler as a male husband or head; the ruler might be corrupted, however, by contact with 'feminine' tastes or luxurious practices (the opera, in which castrati singers were notable new arrivals, was a particular source of disgust for Pope). With his own manliness in question, Pope's aspirational epic sympathies while a boy, and his subsequent development as supreme verbal athlete, look like an attempt to draw firm gender boundaries where these were perceived to be under threat. The translation itself can be seen as attempting to produce a distinction between manly Greeks and effeminate Trojans which is underplayed in the Homeric text. Yet Pope was accused of 'feminizing' Homer by putting the epics into the music of couplets, and making it 'pretty' (Williams 1993: 76–7). The heroes themselves failed to fit uniform standards of manly conduct (Achilles does nothing except sulk for much of the poem); a complex homoeroticism pervades the relationship between Achilles and Patroclus; even all-powerful Jove appears sometimes rather henpecked by his wife. *The Odyssey* is peopled with deceptive and artful women who overpower everyone except Odysseus, and even positive models of domestic virtue like Penelope (and Andromache in *The Iliad*) require complex attention in order to 'translate' their roles into 'properly' gendered terms. Williams also explores the influence of these epic genderings on Pope's mock-epic versions of war and empire, *The Rape of the Lock* (with Belinda's anomalous Achillean strengths) and *The Dunciad* (with a 'hero' seduced by effeminate arts).

'Such *Ovid*'s nose'

Pope knew better than anyone that the human body was not merely some neutral anatomy but a complex code, another site of the struggles of interpretation. From Dennis onwards, Pope's enemies had 'read' his body as the sign of inner malignity, a deformed mind in a deformed body, spiteful, monkeyish, not quite human, not fully male. As Mack shows (1978), he resorted to a number of defensive self-interpretations: having his portrait painted or sculpted in ways which disguised his 'deficiencies' or drew attention to qualities of mind (Wimsatt 1965); playfully accepting his limitations in letters and converting them into satiric advantage (as in the *Epistle to Dr Arbuthnot*); behaving in a compensatory laddish way; narrating himself as a medical case-history (Nicolson and Rousseau 1968). In the early poems he explores in dark and sometimes grotesque detail the frustrations of disfigured, damaged or imprisoned lovers. In the Horatian poems he seeks comradeship with his audience in a way which seems to displace his demonised figure in favour of an amiable observer-figure; the perverse flattery of his body which he ironically catalogues in *Epistle to Dr Arbuthnot* resists the limiting category of 'disabled' (Mack 1978). Deutsch (1996) shows how often and how astutely Pope made his physical predicament work for him, even to the extent of producing a 'poetics of deformity' in which monstrosity can be read as a literary method and form of conceiving. Pope used the codes of the body in adversarial ways as well, belittling Timon as a 'puny insect' at the supposedly masterful centre of his huge villa, querying the status of the female body in the case of Belinda, identifying the Dunces with their own excremental output. The body should be appropriately clothed and subject to rules of continence, for its signifying potential is always prone to anarchic licence. Yet Pope's work has always itself exploited this licence. Jonathan Smedley complained that Pope and Swift were inclined, like infants, 'To *foul* and *dirt* each Place they came in,/And to play some Pranks, unfit for naming' (Guerinot 1969: 134), perhaps in response to the immersion of Smedley in Fleet Ditch imagined by Pope in *The Dunciad* (Book II). Johnson censured both Swift and Pope for their 'unnatural delight in ideas physically impure, such as every other tongue utters with unwillingness, and of which every ear shrinks from the mention' (Johnson 1905: 242). It is a telling charge, not least for its own ineluctable attraction into a kind of verbal play with the filth which is being rejected.

Since Freud it has become considerably easier to construe a 'delight in ideas physically impure' as not so unnatural after all; Norman O. Brown turned the scatological fascinations of Swift into a bona fide 'excremental vision' in 1959, and Ruth Perry (1981) discussed the links between 'anality' and ethics in Pope's satires. The anal complex is the basic moment of socialisation where the infant learns to control impulse, may be punished for autonomy, resistance and pleasure, and is rewarded for observing certain rules – hence the association between bodily product and parental approval which results in the identification (in psychoanalysis as in satire) of excrement with money. While Swift seeks to remind his culture of the unspoken link between the body 'down there' and the mind 'up here', Pope however consciously used excremental imagery to damn his opponents and indicate his own adult, trained status. Perry cites the traces of Pope's own anality in biographical details such as his miserly retention of his work for years before publishing it, his compositional practice of piecing together 'saved' fragments of expression, his habit of saving paper, the defensive enclosure of his grotto. But these are also linked, intentionally, to an ethical interest in the regulation of human activity: the flow (or the spread) of money, the careful measuring out of one's life and substance, resistance to an infantile coprophilia (exemplified throughout *The Dunciad*. 'That is, the judgements about behaviour implicit in his poems are based on standards like those of toilet training: doing the right thing at the right time, keeping an eye on the social world, getting and spending in right amounts, giving and keeping at the right time' (145). The Dunces are characterised as violators of toilet-training, in that so far from learning when to retain and when to expel their creativity, they simply wallow in their own filth – Curll slips in a 'lake' of urine left by one of his own stooges, but is merely 'reviv'd by ordure's sympathetic force'. The booksellers' idea of a heroic contest is to see who can piss furthest; the Dunces dive into Fleet ditch and indulge in fantastic mythic relationships with faeces. The muckily physical collector Mummius, in book IV of *The Dunciad*, is made to wait for his coins until Annius can pass them in a kind of anal birth which signifies a quite improper form of expulsive/retentive relation, a conversion of the proprieties of property into something which is merely excrement.

While there is clearly pleasure in the writing of all this, since Pope takes immense pains to couch these filthy anecdotes in the purest euphemisms available, he can argue that they form a kind of genuine satiric vision: they *mean* something, as opposed to being mere filth. The satire itself moderates its aggressive impulses, restrains, directs, and contains them in exquisitely balanced form. Pope himself takes the argument up in the *Epilogue to the Satires*, Dialogue II, where he describes his disgust at the way empty-headed courtiers recycle each other's 'wit' like the Westphalian hogs eating each other's excrement (a well-known animal myth of the time). The friend responds:

> *Fr.* This filthy similie, this beastly Line,
> Quite turns my Stomach – *P.* So does Flatt'ry mine;
> And all your Courtly Civit-Cats can vent,
> Perfume to you, to me is Excrement.
> *(Epil. ii, 181–4)*

To the adult, discerning temperament, moral repugnance to false use of language is viscerally disgusting, much more so than the poetic use of obscene images which that disgust motivates and justifies. The unsocialised Dunces, conversely, have no means of regulating their appetite or judgement at all, simply floating around in undifferentiated infantile pleasures. Satire is a form of late toilet training, in this analysis.

Stallybrass and White (1985) discuss Pope's images of the 'grotesque body' in relation to a new division of social space, located principally in the coffee-houses which proliferated after the Restoration and which were in Pope's day the sites of a serious, productive leisure. There was no alcohol, no gambling, no festivity, but talk, discussion, exchange of views – a bourgeois 'public sphere', as it has become known, which banished carnivalesque, festive, or libidinous elements in the interests of polite, disciplined 'commerce' (either in the sense of financial business, as with the several insurance companies that were formed from such social meeting-places, or in the sense of the 'commerce of letters' whereby the practice of literary criticism came to prominence). In a similar way, they argue, Pope demonised the 'low-Other' of the irrational body and its festive entertainments into a polar opposition to rational discourse. But this exertion upon the 'grotesque body' was always nevertheless contaminating:

> Hence the apparent paradox that writers who were the great champions of a classical discursive body including Dryden, Swift and Pope spent so much time writing the grotesque, exorcising it, charging it to others, using and adopting its very terms whilst attempting to purify the language of the tribe. The production and reproduction of a body of classical writing required a labour of suppression, a perpetual work of exclusion upon the grotesque body, and it was that supplementary yet unavoidable labour which troubled the identity of the classical. It brought the grotesque back into the classical, not so much as a return of the repressed as a vast labour of exclusion requiring and generating its own equivocal energies. *Quae negata, grata* – what is denied is desired: Augustan satire was the generic form which enabled writes to express and negate the grotesque simultaneously. It was the natural site for this labour of projection and repulsion upon which the construction of the public sphere depended.
>
> (Stallybrass and White 1985: 91)

For Stallybrass and White, while the Augustan project fought 'to cleanse the cultural sphere of impure and messy semiotic matter, it also fed voraciously and incessantly from that very material. It nourished and replenished its refined formalisms from the symbolic repertoire of the grotesque body *in the very name of exclusion*' (104). Thus *The Dunciad* **[130–49]** persistently demonises those who 'mediate' low and high, body and mind, by bringing 'the Smithfield Muses to the ear of Kings', corrupting high culture with the riotous demotic entertainments of street theatre. Under Theobald/Cibber, 'Tragedy and Comedy embrace;/... Farce and Epic get a jumbled race' (*D*, I: 67–8), reducing creativity to an anarchic hybridisation of bodies which ought to be kept hierarchically apart. For Stallybrass and White, however, Pope's doomed project forms 'a closure of identity which in attempting to block out somatic and social heterodoxy is fated to rediscover it everywhere as Chaos, Darkness and "Mess"; ... The classical body splits precisely along the rigid edge which is its defence against heterogeneity: its closure and purity are quite illusory and it will perpetually rediscover in itself ... the grotesque, the protean and the motley...' (110). They conclude: 'The mitigating fact of Pope's superior poetic ability could not save him from being immersed in the very process of grotesque debasement which he scorned in others' (117).

A further analysis of the significance of Pope's bodily metaphors is found in Ferguson (1990); for her, the images of parodic birth, breeding, generation and lineage, and the nightmare corporeality of books figured as bodies bespeak a set of key concerns: 'the nature of literary engendering, creativity and organic growth, sexual and linguistic conjunctions, and also the genealogy and behaviour of offspring (which may be passively subject to defilement, mutilation and mortality, but may equally engage in wilful rebellion and deviance)' (138). Concentrating mainly on the *Epistle to Dr Arbuthnot* **[110–9]** and *The Dunciad* **[130–49]**, Ferguson argues that 'the predominant force of these metaphors is to probe the difficult issue of what is supposedly 'legitimate' and 'illegitimate' in the processes of writing and reading, and to emphasise the vulnerability of the written word and of authors themselves' (138). Finding a different kind of vulnerability from that examined by Stallybrass and White, she concludes:

> While Pope at some points links the ideas of bodily integrity and 'legitimate' breeding with the integrity of the author and that of the work as his undisputed offspring, by his elaboration of such themes as spontaneous generation, prostitution, illegitimacy, plagiarism and the dissemination of printed texts, he effectively shows that the purity and immortality of the written work cannot be guaranteed. Indeed, it can scarcely be hoped for.
>
> (Ferguson 1990: 149)

Dulness and her Dunces are at once *logos* and *anti-logos*, 'the enemies of writing and, in other guises, the embodiments of writing or writers themselves, expressing all the anxieties attendant on authorship' (149).

(d) POPE IN PRINT AND MANUSCRIPT

'Books and the man'

Pope is the pre-eminent case of a poet who speaks through writing: never to occupy any public position which required oratory, Pope preferred to advise and cajole those of his acquaintance who had money and power through the form of 'Epistles' which constructed dialogues for public consumption. Self-dramatizing and self-implicating rather than unmediatedly self-revealing, his work is designed (the word is the exact one) to present a controlled textual self. Pope regulated the passage of his work into the public domain as no poet had done before him and as few could aspire to do after him, ceaselessly devising and revising, adjusting format, page layout, typography and fount, capitalisation, italicisation, even the kind of paper and the blackness of the ink. In this sense he was a creature of the age of print. He also had, however, a strong atavistic sense of manuscript culture, his own calligraphic manuscripts sometimes forming the basis for the circulation of poems amongst a select circle, or a resource to return to for later printed editions. In this sense he was antagonistic to the print age and its venal manipulations of private creativity. His relations with the book trade, satirically presented in *The Dunciad* and the *Epistle to Dr Arbuthnot*, have formed a lively subject for exploration amongst critics and theorists over the last half-century.

In *Grub Street: Studies in a Subculture* (1972; later abridged as *Hacks and Dunces*, 1980), Pat Rogers unpicks the mythology, etymology and topology of the phrase 'Grub Street', loosely used to indicate worthless writing, to establish a kind of geographical and sociological validity to the Scriblerian analysis of Duncehood. By analysing the life stories of several of those writers metaphorically pilloried in *The Dunciad* **[130–49]** and by insisting on the historical content of Grub Street and its environs, Rogers locates in the Scriblerian mythology a core of literal truth. The proximity of the actual Grub Street to Bedlam (a sort of prison for the insane), the location of the journalistic centre of Fleet Street close by the Fleet Ditch, an appalling open sewer that ran into the Thames, and the key position of Newgate prison between both these writerly locales, enables Rogers to flesh out Pope's mythology of Dulness with some lively details about the Dunces. The 'Cloacina' episode from Book II of *The Dunciad*, for example, is not mere mischief but a highlighting of the local connection between journalism and the sewer which was visible to every Londoner. The prevailing metaphors and images of *The Dunciad* – disease, fire, plague, poverty, prostitution, riot, madness, mud, excrement – are shown to derive their power and resonance from actual historical circumstances in a fairly narrow area of London: 'the region was uniquely suited to the symbolic role cast for it by the satirists' (20–1). This involves, in effect, validating Pope's point of view and his cultural stance: the Dunces *did* see themselves as members of a sort of professional association, they *were* prone to legal sanction (imprisonment for debt or 'seditious libel', that is, anything regarded as suspect by the government), they were involved in shambolic festivity, they wrote for money and did not succeed in anything like Pope's way.

In contrast, Rogers (1978) offers a sociological analysis of a somewhat different kind by setting the subscription ventures in which Pope was involved (the two Homer translations **[17–18, 35]**, and Tonson's *Shakespeare* **[26–8]**) alongside similar projects of the period. Contesting earlier judgments in which Pope was thought to have received something like a commission from on high to produce an English Homer, Rogers shows that the project which gave Pope his financial and literary independence was in essence a risky, anxious business, requiring almost as much energy in the business details as in the translation itself. So far from knowing his audience in advance, Pope's contact with his public had been 'vague, fitful and slight' (14). It was a somewhat vexed opportunity to assess his own career to date: 'to estimate how far he had arrived, to sort out varying reactions in his audience, to get a line on his own ambiguous situation in politics and religion' (12). Pope had to work hard, and get his friends to work hard, in lobbying the aristocracy, parliament, the universities and the clergy to subscribe; in the end he succeeded well with the former two constituencies, and rather less well with the latter. He scored some notable successes: Newton, Wren and Marlbrough subscribed to the *Iliad*, and somehow he managed to obtain the patronage of the King and the Prince and Princess of Wales for the *Odyssey*, as well as obtaining, presumably with Walpole's approval, a £200 grant from the Civil List to encourage the work. The Shakespeare subscription, which was not for Pope's benefit, was a relative failure. Rogers concludes that the 'easy "commission" is a myth: there was only the struggle to find, and to keep, an audience interested enough to subscribe' (35).

David Foxon approaches Pope's work from a strictly bibliographic standpoint, and for most general readers his 1991 study of Pope and the book trade will be too specialised; nonetheless it should be mentioned not only as an authoritative guide to the factual details of Pope's dealings with members of the book trade but also as a sympathetic analysis of Pope's attempts to 'design' his books for a varying audience. Foxon finds Pope more or less a favoured author from his first publications, with good printers and fine paper put at his disposal by his booksellers; Pope was already aiming for a clear, classic page design, against cumbersome folio formats or close printing. From the start he was contemplating the place individual poems would have in a self-edited *Works*. Foxon re-evaluates the Homer translations **[17–18, 35]** from the point of view of page design (amply illustrated), analysing Pope's careful choice of ornament and illustration, the innovative choice of a spacious but easy-to-handle quarto format, which he went on to use for his Shakespeare and his collected works (63). This aspiration to classic status was also accorded extraordinary financial reward: Foxon recalculates the Homer contracts, estimating that Pope probably made about £5000 from each translation, bearing out Lady Mary Wortley Montagu's assertion that Pope had 'outwitted Lintot in his very trade' (63).

Foxon goes on to detail Pope's move towards independent dealings with the book trade; he set up his own printer, and more than one bookseller, in business. This brought its own problems, not least because as an independent author Pope had less 'muscle' in dealing with copyright infringements than the large players in the trade, and was forced to resort to adversarial lawsuits more than befitted his pose of rural aloofness and moderation. He had a closer knowledge of copyright law than any author of the time; the concept of authorial property (as opposed to bookseller's property) was enshrined in the 'Act for the encouragement of learning' which became law in 1710, a year after Pope's first publication, though the word 'copyright' itself is later (it is possible that the word is first recorded in Pope's own usage: 237). For *The Dunciad*, he felt compelled to arrange for aristocratic 'ownership' and circulation as a defence against piracy and libel (111). Some accused Pope of turning bookseller on his own account, and practising 'the lowest Craft of the Trade, such as different Editions in various Forms, with perpetual Additions and improvements, so as to render all but the *last* worth nothing; and, by that Means, fooling many People into buying them several times over' (144), though Foxon acquits Pope of any charge of avarice, stressing instead his concern for design excellence. It was true, however, that an economic sense of audience did stimulate particular kinds of creativity at particular times, that Pope was aware of the need to fulfil contracts with particular kinds of material, and that he was aware of the different audiences who collected his work in aristocratic quarto or the cheaper octavo formats, and laid out the page, and details of punctuation, capitalisation and italicisation accordingly.

The quartos have a clearer, more modern appearance, with less typographic emphasis, while the octavos tend to retain an older style in which argument and antitheses are pointed up by typographic means (196). This kind of artistic system can be found in a number of texts: Rideout (1992) analyses Pope's printing styles in editions of *The Essay on Man* and finds that Pope's typographic system of hierarchical orders of emphasis mirrors the philosophical system it presents.

Brean Hammond studies Pope's estimation of the book trade from the theoretical perspective of cultural materialism. For Hammond, while *The Dunciad* **[130–49]** attempts to police the boundary between 'high' and 'low' culture, it necessarily feeds on demotic culture in a way which it cannot articulate. Theobald is offensive for openly crossing between Shakespeare and pantomime, the classics and the stage; but Hammond argues that Pope's pose of artistic independence and his association of dirty materialism with professional authorship conceals the engagement with a bourgeois economy of literature which funded that moral high ground (Hammond 1990). Hammond (1997) replies more fully to the cultural position from which Rogers (1972a) endorses Pope's analysis of the book trade. Taking a line in which the professionalisation of literature is less mired in disrepute, Hammond discusses the context of literary property disputes and the empirical evidence for changes in the ways authors made a living from their works. Non-canonical authors, especially women authors, get a look in here which is not limited to the role assigned them by Pope and his allies. *The Dunciad* is a kind of negative canon, a baneful labelling of those writers who appeared to transgress against social strata or mix literary forms, an attempt to scrutinise and police cultural spaces. Again, the self-presentation of the Scriblerians tends to render opaque a 'massive paradox' (292) in their mode of operation, in that they were all hugely successful in the professional market their work deplored, and all derived considerable energy (parodic and subversive, but still delightedly engaged) from the lunatic physicality and generic hybridisation they discerned in the Dunces. Pope, whose mastery of book production remains one of the most astonishing feats of literary self-fashioning in history, would be the villain of the piece, as 'the oppressor of other writers, the Canute trying to send back the waves of professional progress, the satirist who attempted to preserve the property of literary appreciation in the hands of his own and his adopted class-fraction'; yet Hammond in the end discovers in Pope's covert self-celebrations some genuinely self-deprecating subversiveness, a layer of nuance which happily 'keeps us there, reading' (302).

Swift described the piecemeal nature of Pope's habits of writing in a poem on the composition of *The Dunciad*:

> Now Backs of Letters, though design'd
>   For those who more will need 'em,
> Are fill'd with Hints, and interlin'd,
>   Himself can hardly read 'em.
> Each Atom by some other struck,
>   All Turns and Motion tries;
> Till in a Lump together stuck,
>   Behold a *Poem* rise!
>
>   ('Dr *Sw*— to Mr *P—e*, While he was writing the
>   *Dunciad*'; Swift 1967: 321)

In a comic parody of the Dunces' own travesty of gravitational force, Pope's hasty, profuse and disparate scraps become a unified whole without any apparent agency, almost in default of Pope's 'reading'. The reality of 'composition' is of course more complex than this, and the results more fluid; Sherburn (1945) described how Pope habitually 'worked by paragraphs or passages ... his great problem was arranging the paragraphs and tying them together tactfully' (55). He also moved elements from poem to poem, recycling parts which didn't fit into wholes into other compositions, and following his own advice to delete ruthlessly in 'The last and greatest Art, the Art to blot' (*Ep. 2.i*, 281). He noted how Denham had spent a lifetime altering, revising, and excising *Cooper's Hill* (the poem which Pope drew on in *Windsor-Forest*) and approved: 'the whole read together is a very strong proof of what Mr. Waller says: Poets lose half the praise they should have got,/Could it be known what they discreetly blot' (Spence 1966: 194). The studied process which Pope admires here is something he celebrated in his own practice.

All students of this aspect of Pope's work are hugely indebted to Maynard Mack, whose bibliographic research illuminates the complex and meticulous revisal Pope undertook in each published text of his output, his often devious relation to the notion of publication itself (Mack 1982). Mack transcribes Pope's manuscript notations on other published books; his copies of Chaucer, Montaigne, and Rochester for example, survive with illuminating glosses in his hand. His library indicates a 'marked interest in exact learning' of the kind which he satirised in Theobald ('All such reading as was never read'), in a well-known strategy of exorcism; it also shows Pope's commitment to the wisdom of the past (Mack 1982: 307–21, 394–460). Mack also celebrates the rich resource of manuscript material which remains (Mack 1982: 322–47). Though Bolingbroke, to whom Pope willed his unpublished manuscripts, neglected them, Jonathan Richardson, who had been given many papers in gratitude for his work as Pope's amanuensis, treasured them. They preserve a wealth of unique details, offering insights into Pope's revisions, improvements, reversions, and transfers of material: lines originally designed for *Eloisa to Abelard*, for example, were eventually mutated into a passage in the *Elegy to the Memory of an Unfortunate Lady*, a transposition which cements the link between those two expositions of 'female' emotion.

In *The Last and Greatest Art* (1984), Mack presents facsimiles and transcripts of manuscript drafts of *Pastorals, Sapho to Phaon, Epistle to Jervas, The Dunciad, Epistle to Burlington, The First Satire of the Second Book of Horace, Essay on Man* and *Epistle to Dr Arbuthnot*. Even a look at these facsimiles can be instructive. The manuscript of the *Pastorals* is an extraordinary calligraphic feat, as close to print as handwriting can get; the papers relating to the *Essay on Man*, by contrast, are heavily blotted, interlined, deleted and rearranged, suggesting an altogether different level of labour, the careful production of diagrammatic system out of disparate inspirations. The manuscripts bear witness both to Pope's flow of creativity (or 'invention' as he would call it) and his painstaking efforts to get everything right. 'There's a happiness as well as care', he argues in the *Essay on Criticism*, suggesting that laborious adherence to rules needs supplementing by lucky inspiration; Mack uses the manuscripts to show that 'happiness is seldom distinguishable from care' (198).

Mack also contends that Pope's manuscripts give us 'an exhilarating realism about the nature of art':

> His practice reflects … a poetic in which the poem is assumed to be a process of exploration and discovery, the poet's individual sensibility acting and reacting with the common language of men and the common symbolic language of mankind to produce a structure that is responsive to all three of these centers of poetic energy, but is at the same time available and gratifying to other readers, and, though determinate in the sense of having shape, remains capable of change and growth without loss of identity. Poetry, in what seems to be Pope's conception of it, is not history, but a form of action within history that has a history: his completed poem presents itself not as a species of Scripture or Revelation, but as a configuration of elements arranged in dramatic and dynamic poise

by an entirely human wit that is ever susceptible to second (and even third) thoughts.

(Mack 1984: 16)

The 'stately processional of perceived intent coursing in a firm column down one side of the page' is always offset by 'the dance and play of new perceptions spinning off, developing their own fields of force, some wandering afield to die upon the margins or possibly to be revived in later contexts, others colliding, warring, at last fusing with the original column, altering its direction, sometimes causing it to disintegrate altogether' (17).

Indeed, there have been several studies of Pope's compositional practices which have illuminated particular poems in substantial ways. The manuscripts of *Windsor-Forest* and *Essay on Criticism* have been published by R.M. Schmitz (1952 and 1962); Wasserman (1960) presents the manuscripts of the *Epistle to Bathurst* alongside the early printed editions. Robson (1988), commenting on 'To a Young Lady, on leaving the Town after the Coronation', draws divisions between a 'licentious' version for intimate private circulation and a pointedly bowdlerised 'public' version. Phillips (1988) uses the manuscript of Pope's first Horatian imitation to uncover the hesitations and energies which went into the 'composition' of that defining voice; Ferraro (1993), considers that a reading of the variants suggests that the poem was more a critique of satire than a satiric manifesto. Vander Meulen (1991) presents a facsimile of the 1728 *Dunciad* **[28–31, 130–49]**, with annotations by Pope's friend Jonathan Richardson recording his collations of two early holograph manuscripts of the poem, to discover something of its decade-long compositional history: 'this contestant in the War of the Dunces hardly sprang fully armed from the head of Zeus' (61). It is possible to see from the drafts and early printings how Pope toned down some of the more explicit bawdy in the poem into a more calculatedly euphemistic indecorousness; how he vacillated over the explicitness of the political component of the satire; how he changed the names of Dunces in response to altered circumstances, or deliberately left names ambiguous in the printed version when he had made clear decisions about identities in the drafts (59–62). Ferraro (1996) uses the manuscripts and early printings of the *Epistle to Burlington* to indicate how Pope's expressed praise of Burlington became more ambivalent in later versions.

'Composition' means not only the creative act but the created artefact; literally 'placing together', it also refers to the setting of type in the printer's shop, a process in which Pope was conspicuously interested. Critics such as Leavis have defended Pope by celebrating the 'poetry' against the bibliographic and contingent husk in which it appears, but recently textual scholarship itself has come to see print and format as not so much 'accidental' as a constitutive part of a literary work's meaning. McLaverty (1984) mounts an impressive instance of this argument in relation to *The Dunciad* **[130–49]**, the text which Leavis had particularly in mind (Leavis 1976). Objecting both to Leavis's contention that *The Dunciad* is a poem to which notes are a distraction, and to the bibliographic theory that literary works of art exist as a series of utterances in the author's mind, of which printed texts are merely inferior copies, McLaverty shows that *The Dunciad Variorum* makes its impact by manipulating the appearance of the printed book. In theme, the poem charts in ironic epic the degradation of culture through uncontrolled printing into crass materialism. In appearance, it manipulates the status of print itself: it mimics the editorial intrusiveness of editors and critics like Richard Bentley, whose heavily-emended edition of Horace (second edition, 1713), ventured to put the notes on the page, and Lewis Theobald, *The Dunciad*'s early hero who modelled his edition of Shakespeare on Bentley's Horace. 'Variorum' editing was actually associated less with Bentley, whose notorious arrogance did not allow for the tedious labour of collating what everyone else had already said, than with Dutch scholars, but to align Bentley with the 'lumber' of 'all such reading as was never read' was a useful short-cut for Pope in his mission to exemplify culture's ways of reducing literature to material. In addition, however, Pope was celebrating his poem as a true modern epic – 'the pomp of the presentation is genuinely appropriate to the poem's importance; the ancillary material makes it clear that we have here the work of a major author, an important sociological document, and a witty and learned poem' – and one which did actually require notes for his wider purpose of mapping the London literary scene (101). As Pope put it, even while mocking the 'Trade' in 'English classicks with huge Commentaries', 'What a Glory will it be to the Dunciad, that it was the First Modern Work publish'd in this manner?' (101). The pleasures of *The Dunciad* are complex but at least partially visual ones: the joke about the notes only works if you can see them the way Pope intended. That this commitment to a multi-vocal set of textual presences demands 'considerable powers of discrimination' is itself of course part of the point of a poem which resists the easy commodification of culture: 'These pressures are, of course, the subject of Pope's poem and he manipulates the materials of production in order to evade them' (104–5).

McLaverty places *The Dunciad* at a key node in literary history where awareness of 'audience' marks the division between an oral culture, in which the text is a 'score' for performance, and print culture, where multiple copies are distributed for private reading, severing the close bond between author and listener (95). Pope is the first author to manipulate the culture of print to say something about that culture and its problems. McLaverty's article sets itself within a wider aesthetic debate about the status of literary works of art in comparison with 'unique' physical presences such as the Leonardo's *Mona Lisa* or Michelangelo's *David*. This debate is relevant to Pope in other ways, for his habits of composition and revision were such that the notion of a final 'essence' to any of his poems is (at the least) problematic. Not only did he revise and correct continually, he reverted to earlier versions, suppressed passages in some editions but not in others, reserved particularly dangerous passages for second or third editions (when they were less noticed) and 'customised' some editions for particular purposes. The process of revisal was ended only by death – or by Warburton, his collaborating editor, who persuaded Pope to revise his work along particular lines of moral consistency and whose own revisions to the text may or may not have authorial sanction.

Mack (1984: 16–17) states:

> Throughout his career, the typical Pope poem is a work-in-progress. States of provisional wholeness and balance occur along the way, some more inclusive than others but each conceivable as an end stage; and the one at which the poet finally rests, though in most cases recognisably superior, never declares itself to be definitive in any absolute sense.

Ferraro (1998) asks similar questions of the 'essence' of particular poems. Questioning the established editorial principle associated with the scholarly tradition of W. W. Greg and Fredson Bowers, whereby all states of composition lead to a 'final' or 'best' authorial text, usually of an ideal nature, underlying all actual textual manifestations, and subjugating all textual variants to that final state, Ferraro contends that Pope's 'textual field' is much wider than the theory of final intention can allow for. Though Pope's attention to manuscript detail, and the minutiae of print (paper, typography, ink, ornament) gives his page a monumental appearance, his perennial revision and reversion to earlier drafts makes his text rather more fluid. Pope often returned to earlier thoughts from his manuscripts: revision was sometimes return, as well as second thought. He was interested in his own textual variants and rejected manuscript versions to the extent of getting Jonathan Richardson to collate them; he published a selection of them as footnotes to his self-edited *Works*, and chose his moment to supplant 'printed' lines with 'manuscript' ones. Thus Pope retains a kind of flexible, private 'manuscript' control even in the public arena of print; but the question of what then constitutes 'the poem' remains. The matter of organisation is also sometimes problematic, the title *Epistles to Several Persons* **[93–110]** being applied on different occasions to groups of seven, eleven, or four poems (the last being the conventional, Warburtonian position). One's reading of these poems may be affected by the position in which they are read: putting the four epistles alongside the four of *Essay on Man* **[82–93]** emphasises their abstract moral reasoning; looking at them individually in their chronological order, and as they underwent revision, suggests more localised disputations, greater play of ambiguous suggestion.

The 'zigzag' nature of Pope's textual process (Vander Meulen 1991: 54) naturally causes problems for modern editors of Pope. The standard scholarly text, the *Twickenham Edition* (1939–69), quoted throughout this book, ignored manuscript evidence (except in volume VI, *Minor Poems*) and often followed the punctuation, capitalisation and italicisation of first edition copy-texts, a decision argued by Foxon 1991 to be erroneous in the light of Pope's peculiar practices. On the other hand, 'last' authorised editions do not solve the problem, for Pope did not revise all his work into a consistent typography, and those 'deathbed' editions he did complete have probably been unduly affected by Warburton and the printer. Herbert Davis, in the Oxford Standard Authors edition (Davis 1966), relied on the 'death-bed' quartos and Warburton's 1751 edition, purged of Warburton's interference with the punctuation. While not without its own problems, this edition 'has a consistency of accidentals which is preferable to the *Twickenham* text' (Foxon 1991: 233). It also has the great merit of allowing students to see the four-book *Dunciad*, notes, prose and all, in something close to the form in which Pope finally issued it; the poem can also be found in this form, but with succinct and reliable modern commentary appended, in Rumbold (1999). Davis also includes an early three-book *Dunciad* and *The Rape of the Lock* is present in two-canto and five-canto versions. In his Oxford Authors edition Pat Rogers (1993a) abandons the late ordering of the poems established under Warburton's influence and prints the epistles and imitations of Horace chronologically, in the order they first appeared, though his actual text is based on later revisions. Elsewhere (Rogers 1993b, xiii–xiv) he cautions against the tendency to push the unstable aspects of Pope's text too far; the variants are, for the most part, authorial, to be treated as an unusually rich archive rather than a chaotic undermining of textual authority, and Rogers sees a fairly orderly progression towards 'final' texts in most cases. A wholly new edition of Pope's poems is now planned, under the editorship of Julian Ferraro. Presenting in chronological order the complete run of Pope's poetry, in unmodernised texts from first printed editions but taking account of manuscript versions, with full annotation, this undertaking will offer a new sense of the corpus of Pope's work.

Further Reading

The purpose of Part III of this book has been to offer a guide to some of the main developments in the criticism of Pope, with special emphasis on interpretations from the last fifty years. Contemporary reception of Pope (often hostile, though not necessarily for strictly literary reasons) can be studied in Guerinot (1969) and Barnard (1973); Bateson and Joukovsky (1971) offers a handy collection of short responses to Pope's work from the beginnings to 1968. Helpful general introductions to the main developments in literary theory of the last half century, which bear particularly on subsections **b**, **c**, and **d** of this section, are Eagleton (1985) and Selden (1993); Rylance (1987) is a useful anthology of relevant primary documents in literary theory. For the political history of Pope's day and its relation to literature, see Speck (1998). Moi (1985) is a very lucid and instructive introduction to feminist literary theory. For the history of printed books, Steinberg (1961) is an excellent place to start; Johns (1998) gives an advanced view of the significance of print culture.

CHRONOLOGY

1688   Alexander Pope (AP) born in London (21 May); James II flees to France.

1689   William and Mary offered English crown; war declared on France.

1692   AP's family move to Hammersmith.

1694   Death of Queen Mary.

1696   AP taught by priest, then at clandestine Catholic school at Twyford, then at Marylebone.

1698   AP's father takes over house at Binfield, Windsor Forest.

1700   Death of John Dryden.

1701   Act of Settlement ensures Protestant succession.

1702   Death of King William; accession of Queen Anne.

1705   AP's first surviving letters, to Wycherley, discuss *Pastorals*; AP becomes friendly with William Walsh and William Trumbull.

1706   AP begins revising Wycherley's work for him.

1707   AP becomes friendly with Henry Cromwell. AP begins to circulate portions of *Essay on Criticism* and *Windsor-Forest*.

1709   *Pastorals* published.

1711   *Spectator* begins publication; AP's *Essay on Criticism* published; Dennis's attack on the poem published.

1712   Two-canto *Rape of the Locke* published; AP contributes to *Spectator*.

1713   AP studies painting with Charles Jervas; *Windsor-Forest* published; AP contributes to *Guardian*. Treaty of Utrecht ends war. Addison's *Cato* performed with prologue by AP. AP issues proposals for translating the *Iliad*.

1714   Five-canto *Rape of the Lock* published; Scriblerus Club active. Death of Queen Anne; accession of George I; Whigs assume power; Swift returns to Ireland; Scriblerus Club terminated..

1715   *Temple of Fame* published. Bolingbroke flees to France. Volume I of the *Iliad* translation. Jacobite rising put down.

1716   AP's family sell Binfield and move to Chiswick. Volume II of *Iliad* published. First skirmish with Edmund Curll. AP attacked as Jacobite. Lady Mary Wortley Montagu leaves England for Constantinople.

1717   AP publishes first collected *Works* alongside Volume III of *Iliad*. Death of AP's father.

1718   Volume IV of the *Iliad*. Lady Mary returns from abroad. Death of Parnell.
1719   AP leases villa at Twickenham overlooking the Thames.
1720   South Sea Bubble. Volumes V and VI complete *Iliad* translation.
1721   AP edits Parnell's poems.
1722   AP editing Shakespeare and translating *Odyssey*; Atterbury arrested on suspicion of treason.
1723   AP publishes *Works* of John Sheffield; edition seized on suspicion of treasonable material; Atterbury tried and exiled; Bolingbroke returns.
1725   AP publishes 6-volume edition of Shakespeare. Bolingbroke settles at Dawley Farm. First three volumes of *Odyssey* translation published.
1726   Theobald attacks AP in *Shakespeare Restored*. Volumes IV-V of *Odyssey* published. Swift visits; Swift's *Gulliver's Travels* published.
1727   Death of George I; accession of George II. AP and Swift publish two volumes of *Miscellanies*.
1728   Gay's *Beggar's Opera* begins huge run. AP and Swift publish third volume of *Miscellanies*, including *Peri Bathous*. First version of *The Dunciad* published, to controversial reception.
1729   *Dunciad Variorum* published; advance copy presented by Walpole to King and Queen.
1730   Cibber appointed Poet Laureate.
1731   First version of *Epistle to Burlington* published.
1732   AP and Swift publish fourth volume of *Miscellanies*. Death of Atterbury; death of Gay.
1733   *Epistle to Bathurst* published. *Imitations of Horace* series begins with *The First Satire of the Second Book of Horace*. Montagu/ Hervey *Verses* attacking Pope. *Essay on Man*, Epistles I-III. Death of AP's mother.
1734   *Epistle to Cobham* published. *Essay on Man*, Epistle IV. *Second Satire of the Second Book of Horace, Sober Advice from Horace* published.
1735   *Epistle to Dr Arbuthnot* published. *Epistle to a Lady* published. Death of Arbuthnot. Second volume of AP's *Works* published. Curll publishes edition of AP's *Letters*.
1736   AP gives Prince of Wales a puppy.
1737   *Second Epistle...* and *First Epistle of the Second Book of Horace* published. Authorized edition of AP's *Letters*. *Essay on Man* attacked by Crousaz.

1738   *Sixth Epistle...* and *First Epistle of the Second Book of Horace* published. *Epilogue to the Satires* published. Warburton begins defence of *Essay on Man*.

1739   AP befriends Warburton. Various editions of AP's *Works*.

1740   AP undergoes surgery; health worsening. *Apology for the Life of Colley Cibber* published.

1741   AP begins to edit his works with Warburton; successful Chancery suit against Curll.

1742   Walpole resigns. *The New Dunciad* published; Cibber's *Letter ... to Pope*.

1743   *The Dunciad in Four Books*, with Cibber as hero; AP writes will.

1744   AP undergoing medical treatment; editing *Works*; 'death-bed' edition of *Epistles to Several Persons*. AP dies (30 May).

BIBLIOGRAPHY

Aden, John M. (1972): 'Pope and Politics: "The Farce of State"', in Dixon (1972), 172–99

Aden, John M. (1978): *Pope's Once and Future Kings: Satire and Politics in the Early Career* (Knoxville, TN: University of Tennessee Press)

Atkins, G. Douglas (1986): *Quests of Difference: Reading Pope's Poems* (Lexington: Kentucky State University Press)

Ault, Norman (1949): *New Light on Pope: With some Additions to his Poetry Hitherto Unknown* (London: Methuen and Co.)

Ayres, Philip (1990): 'Pope's *Epistle to Burlington*: The Vitruvian Analogies', *Studies in English Literature, 1500–1900*, 30: 429–44

Barnard, John, ed. (1973): *Pope: The Critical Heritage* (London and Boston: Routledge and Kegan Paul)

Barrell, John and Guest, Harriet, 'On the Use of Contradiction: Economics and Morality in the Eighteenth-Century Long Poem', in Nussbaum and Brown (1987), 121–43

Bateson, F.W. and Joukovsky, N.A., eds, (1971): *Alexander Pope: A Critical Anthology* (Harmondsworth: Penguin Books)

Beer, Gillian, (1982): '"Our unnatural No-voice": The Heroic Epistle, Pope, and Women's Gothic', *Yearbook of English Studies*, 12: 125–51

Benjamin, Walter (1969): 'The Storyteller', in *Illuminations*, translated by Harry Zohn (New York: Schocken Books), 83–110

Berry, Reginald (1988): *A Pope Chronology* (Basingstoke: Macmillan Press)

Bloom, Harold, ed. (1988): *Modern Critical Interpretations: The Rape of the Lock* (New York: Chelsea House)

Bogel, Fredric V. (1982), 'Dulness Unbound: Rhetoric and Pope's *Dunciad*', *PMLA* 97: 844–55

Brooks, Cleanth (1949): 'The Case of Miss Arabella Fermor', in *The Well-Wrought Urn: Studies in the Structure of Poetry* (London: Dennis Dobson), 74–95

Brooks-Davies, Douglas (1983): *The Mercurian Monarch: Magical Politics from Spenser to Pope* (Manchester: Manchester University Press)

Brooks-Davies, Douglas (1985): *Pope's Dunciad and the Queen of the Night: A Study in Emotional Jacobitism* (Manchester: Manchester University Press)

Brooks-Davies, Douglas (1988): '"Thoughts of Gods": Messianic Alchemy in *Windsor-Forest*', *Yearbook of English Studies*, 18: 125–42

Brower, Reuben (1959): *Alexander Pope: The Poetry of Allusion* (Oxford: Clarendon Press)

Brown, Laura (1985): *Alexander Pope* (Oxford: Basil Blackwell)

Brown, Norman O. (1959): 'The Excremental Vision', in *Life Against Death* (Middletown, CT: Wesleyan University Press)

Bygrave, Stephen (1990): 'Missing parts: Voice and Spectacle in *Eloisa to Abelard*', in Fairer (1990), 121–136

Caretta, Vincent (1981): 'Anne and Elizabeth: The Poet as Historian in *Windsor-Forest*', *Studies in English Literature* 21: 425–37

Chapin, Chester (1986): 'Pope and the Jacobites', *Eighteenth-Century Life*, 10: 59–73

Claridge, Laura (1988): 'Pope's Rape of Excess', in Day and Bloom (1988), 129–43; reprinted in Hammond (1996), 88–100

Clark, Steve (1990): '"Let Blood and Body bear the fault": Pope and misogyny', in Fairer (1990), 81–102

Clifford, J.L. and Landa, L., eds (1949): *Pope and his Contemporaries* (Oxford: Clarendon Press)

Copley, Stephen and Fairer, David (1990): '*An Essay on Man* and the polite reader', in Fairer (1990), 205–24

Crehan, Stewart (1997): '*The Rape of the Lock* and the Economy of "Trivial Things"', *Eighteenth-Century Studies*, 31: 45–68

Damrosch, Leopold (1987): *The Imaginative World of Alexander Pope* (Berkeley and London: University of California Press)

Davis, Herbert ed. (1966): *Pope: Poetical Works* (Oxford: Oxford University Press)

Day, Gary and Bloom, Clive, eds (1988): *Perspectives on Pornography: Sexuality in Film and Literature* (Basingstoke: Macmillan Press)

Dennis, Rodney G, ed. (1992): *The Marks in the Fields* (Cambridge, MA: Houghton Library)

Deutsch, Helen (1996): *Resemblance and Disgrace: Alexander Pope and the Deformation of Culture* (Cambridge, MA: Harvard University Press)

Dickinson, H. T. (1988): 'The Politics of Pope', in Nicholson (1988), 1–21

Dixon, Peter (1968): *The World of Pope's Satires: An Introduction to the 'Epistles' and the Imitations of Horace* (London: Methuen & Co.)

Dixon, Peter, ed. (1972): *Alexander Pope* (London: G. Bell and Sons)

Donaldson, Ian (1988): 'Concealing and Revealing: Pope's *Epistle to Arbuthnot*', *Yearbook of English Studies* 18: 181–99

Downie, J. A. (1990): '1688: Pope and the rhetoric of Jacobitism', in Fairer (1990), 9–24

Eagleton, Terry (1985): *Literary Theory: An Introduction* (Oxford: Basil Blackwell)

Empson, William (1950): 'Wit in the *Essay on Criticism*', *Hudson Review*, 2: 559–77

Empson, William (1961): *Seven Types of Ambiguity* (Harmondsworth: Penguin Books)

Engell, James (1988): 'Wealth and Words: Pope's *Epistle to Bathurst*', *Modern Philology*, 85: 433–46

Erskine-Hill, Howard (1972a): *Pope: The Dunciad* (London: Edward Arnold)

Erskine-Hill. Howard (1972b): 'Pope and the Financial Revolution', in Dixon (1972), 200–29

Erskine-Hill, Howard (1975): *The Social Milieu of Alexander Pope* (New Haven: Yale University Press)

Erskine-Hill, Howard and Smith, Anne, eds (1979): *The Art of Alexander Pope* (London: Vision Press)

Erskine-Hill, Howard (1982): 'Alexander Pope: The Political Poet in his Time', *Eighteenth-Century Studies*, 15: 123–148

Erskine-Hill, Howard (1983): *The Augustan Idea in English Literature* (London: Edward Arnold)

Erskine-Hill, Howard (1988): 'Pope on the origins of society', in Rousseau and Rogers (1988), 79–93

Erskine-Hill, Howard and McCabe, Richard A., eds, *Presenting Poetry: Composition, Publication, Reception* (Cambridge: Cambridge University Press)

Erskine-Hill, Howard (1996): *Poetry of Opposition and Revolution: Dryden to Wordsworth* (Oxford: Clarendon Press)

Erskine-Hill, Howard, ed. (1998): *Alexander Pope: World and Word* (Oxford: Oxford University Press for The British Academy)

Fabricant, Carole (1988): 'Pope's Moral, Political and Cultural Combat', *Eighteenth-Century Theory and Interpretation* 29: 165–87; reprinted in Hammond (1996), 41–57

Fairer, David (1984): *Pope's Imagination* (Manchester: Manchester University Press)

Fairer, David, ed. (1990): *Pope: New Contexts* (Hemel Hempstead: Harvester Wheatsheaf)

Ferguson, Rebecca (1986): *The Unbalanced Mind: Pope and the Rule of Passion* (Brighton: Harvester Press)

Ferguson, Rebecca (1990): '"Intestine Wars": Body and text in *An Epistle to Dr Arbuthnot* and *The Dunciad*, in Fairer 1990, 137–52

Ferguson, Rebecca (1992): '"Quick as her Eyes, and as unfix'd as those": Objectification and Seeing in Pope's *Rape of the Lock*', *Critical Survey* 4: 140–6

Ferraro, Julian (1993): 'The Satirist, the Text and "The World Beside": Pope's *First Satire of the Second Book of Horace Imitated*', *Translation and Literature* 2: 37–63

Ferraro, Julian (1996): 'From Taste to Use: Pope's *Epistle to Burlington*', *British Journal for Eighteenth-Century Studies* 19: 141–59

Ferraro, Julian (1998): 'From Text to Work: The Presentation and Representation of *Epistles to Several Persons*', in Erskine-Hill (1998), 111–34

Fowler, Alastair (1988): 'The Paradoxical Machinery of *The Rape of the Lock*', in Nicholson (1988), 151–170

Foxon, David (1991): *Pope and the Early Eighteenth-Century Book Trade*, revised and edited by James McLaverty (Oxford: Clarendon Press)

Francus, Marilyn (1994), 'The monstrous mother: reproductive anxiety in Swift and Pope', *ELH* 61, 829–51.

Fuchs, Jacob (1989): *Reading Pope's Imitations of Horace* (Lewisburg: Bucknell University Press)

Gerrard, Christine (1990), 'Pope and the Patriots', in Fairer (1990), 25–44

Gerrard, Christine (1994): *The Patriot Opposition to Walpole: Politics, party, and national Myth, 1725–1742* (Oxford: Clarendon Press).

Goldgar, Bertrand (1976): *Walpole and the Wits: The Relation of Politics to Literature, 1722–1742* (Lincoln: University of Nebraska Press)

Griffin, Dustin (1978): *Alexander Pope: The Poet in the Poems* (Princeton, NJ: Princeton University Press)

Griffin, Robert J. (1995): *Wordsworth's Pope: A Study in Literary Historiography* (Cambridge: Cambridge University Press)

Guerinot, J. V. (1969): *Pamphlet Attacks on Alexander Pope 1771–1714: A Descriptive Bibliography* (London: Methuen & Co.)

Halsband, Robert (1980) *The Rape of the Lock and its Illustrations, 1714–1896* (Oxford: Clarendon Press)

Hammond, Brean (1984): *Pope and Bolingbroke: A Study of Friendship and Influence* (Columbia: University of Missouri Press)

Hammond, Brean (1986): *Pope* (Brighton: Harvester Press)

Hammond, Brean (1990): '"Guard the sure barrier', Pope and the partitioning of culture', in Fairer (1990), 225–40

Hammond, Brean, editor (1996): *Pope* (Harlow: Longman)

Hammond, Brean (1997): *Professional Imaginative Writing in England, 1670–1740: 'Hackney for Bread'* (Oxford: Clarendon Press)

Hotch, Ripley (1974): 'The Dilemma of an Obedient Son': Pope's *Epistle to Dr Arbuthnot'*, *Essays in Literature* 1: 37–45; reprinted in Mack and Winn (1980), 428–43

Hunt, John Dixon, ed. (1968): *Pope: The Rape of the Lock, A Casebook* (London: Macmillan and Co.)

Ingrassia, Catherine (1991): 'Women writing/writing women: Pope, Dulness, and "feminization" in the *Dunciad'*, *Eighteenth-Century Life* 14: 40–58

Jack, R. D. S. (1988): 'Pope's Mediaeval Heroine: *Eloisa to Abelard'*, in Nicholson (1988), 206–21

Jackson, Wallace (1983), *Vision and Re-Vision in Alexander Pope* (Detroit: Wayne State University Press)

Johns, Adrian (1998): *The Notion of the Book: Print and Knowledge in the Making* (Chicago: University of Chicago Press)

Johnson, Samuel (1905): 'Pope', in *Lives of the English Poets*, edited by George Birkbeck Hill, 3 vols (Oxford: Clarendon Press), iii: 82–276

Jones, Emrys (1968): 'Pope and Dulness', *Proceedings of the British Academy* 54: 231–63; reprinted in Mack and Winn (1980), 612–51

Kallich, Martin (1967): *Heav'n's First Law: Rhetoric and Order in Pope's Essay on Man* (De Kalb: Northern Illinois University Press)

Kalmey, Robert P. (1968): 'Pope's *Eloisa to Abelard* and "Those Celebrated Letters"', *Philological Quarterly* 47: 164–78; reprinted in Mack and Winn (1980), 247–65

Keener, Frederick M. (1973): *An Essay on Pope* (New York: Columbia University Press)

Kinsley, William, ed. (1979): *The Rape of the Lock* (Hamden, CT: Archon Books)

Knellwolf, Christa (1998): *A Contradiction Still: Representations of the Feminine in the Poetry of Alexander Pope* (Manchester: Manchester University Press)

Knight, G. Wilson (1955): *Laureate of Peace: On the Genius of Alexander Pope* (London: Routledge and Kegan Paul)

Kramnick, Isaac (1968): *Bolingbroke and his Circle: The Politics of Nostalgia in the Age of Walpole* (Cambridge, MA: University of Massachusetts Press)

Landa, Louis A. (1971): 'Pope's Belinda, The General Emporie of the World, and the Wondrous Worm', *South Atlantic Quarterly* 70, 215–35, reprinted in Mack and Winn (1980), 177–200

Leavis, F.R. (1972): *Revaluation* (Harmondsworth: Penguin Books)

Leavis, F.R. (1976): 'The Dunciad', in *The Common Pursuit* (Harmondsworth: Penguin Books)

Lerenbaum, Miriam (1977): *Alexander Pope's 'Opus Magnum', 1729–1744* (Oxford: Clarendon Press)

Mack, Maynard (1949): '"Wit and Poetry and Pope": Some Observations on His Imagery', from Clifford and Landa (1949), 20–40, reprinted in Mack (1982), 37–54

Mack, Maynard (1969): *The Garden and the City: Retirement and Politics in the Later Poetry of Pope 1731–1743* (Toronto: University of Toronto Press)

Mack, Maynard (1978): 'Pope: The Shape of the Man in his Work', *Yale Review* 67: 493–516; reprinted in Mack (1982), 372–92

Mack, Maynard and Winn, James A., eds (1980), *Pope: Recent Essays by Several Hands* (Brighton: Harvester Press)

Mack, Maynard (1982): *Collected in Himself: Essays Critical, Biographical, and Bibliographical on Pope and Some of His Contemporaries* (Newark: University of Delaware Press)

Mack, Maynard (1984): *The Last and Greatest Art: Some Unpublished Poetical Manuscripts of Alexander Pope* (Newark: University of Delaware Press)

Mack, Maynard (1985): *Alexander Pope: A Life* (New Haven and London: Yale University Press)

McLaverty, James (1984): 'The Mode of Existence of Literary Works of Art: The Case of the *Dunciad* Variorum, *Studies in Bibliography*, 37: 82–105; reprinted in Hammond (1996), 220–232

Manning, Susan (1993): 'Eloisa's Abandonment', *Cambridge Quarterly* 22: 231–40

Martindale, Charles (1983): 'Sense and Sensibility: The Child and the Man in *The Rape of the Lock*', *Modern Language Review*, 78: 273–84

Mason, H.A. (1985): *To Homer Through Pope: An Introduction to Homer's Iliad and Pope's Translation* (Bristol: Bristol Classical Press)

Matthews, Susan (1990): '"Matter too soft": Pope and the women's novel', in Fairer (1990), 103–20

Meyers, Kate Beaird (1988): 'Feminist Hermeneutics and Reader Response: The Role of Gender in Reading *The Rape of the Lock*', *New Orleans Review* 15: 43–50

Moi, Toril (1985): *Sexual/Textual Politics: Feminist Literary Theory* (London: Routledge)

Morris, David B. (1984): *Alexander Pope: The Genius of Sense* (Cambridge, MA: Harvard University Press)

Nicholson, Colin (1979): 'A World of Artefacts: *The Rape of the Lock* as social history', *Literature and History* 5: 183–93

Nicholson, Colin, ed. (1988): *Alexander Pope: Essays for the Tercentenary* (Aberdeen: Aberdeen University Press)

Nicholson, Colin (1994): *Writing and the Rise of Finance: Capital Satires of the Early Eighteenth Century* (Cambridge: Cambridge University Press)

Nicolson, Marjorie H. and Rousseau, G.S. (1968): *This Long Disease, My Life: Alexander Pope and the Sciences* (Princeton: Princeton University Press)

Nussbaum, Felicity (1984): *The Brink of All we Hate: English Satires on Women, 1660–1750* (Lexington: University Press of Kentucky)

Nussbaum, Felicity and Brown, Laura (eds) (1987): *The New Eighteenth Century* (New York and London: Routledge)

Nuttall, A.D. (1984): *Pope's 'Essay on Man'* (London: George Allen and Unwin)

Parker, G.F. (1990): 'Pope and Alceste', *Cambridge Quarterly* 19: 336–59

Parkin, Rebecca P. (1955): *The Poetic Workmanship of Alexander Pope* (Minneapolis: University of Minnesota Press)

Perry, Ruth (1981): 'Anality and Ethics in Pope's Late Satires', *British Journal for Eighteenth-Century Studies* 4: 139–54; reprinted in Hammond (1996), 170–84

Phillips, Michael (1988): 'The Composition of Pope's *Imitation of Horace, Satire II, i*', in Nicholson (1988), 171–94

Plowden, G. F. C. (1983): *Pope on Classic Ground* (Athens, OH: Ohio University Press)

Pollak, Ellen (1985): *The Poetics of Sexual Myth: Gender and Ideology in the Verse of Swift and Pope* (Chicago: University of Chicago Press)

Quintero, Reuben (1992): *Literate Culture: Pope's Rhetorical Art* (Newark: University of Delaware Press)

Rideout, Tania (1992): 'The Reasoning Eye: Alexander Pope's Typographic Vision in the *Essay on Man*', *Journal of the Warburg and Courtauld Institutes* 55: 249–62

Robson, W.W. (1988): 'Text and Context: Pope's "Coronation Epistle"', in Nicholson (1988), 195-205

Rogers, Pat (1972a): *Grub Street: Studies in a Subculture* (London: Methuen & Co.); abridged (1980) as *Hacks and Dunces: Pope, Swift and Grub Street* (London: Methuen & Co.)

Rogers, Pat (1972b): 'Pope and the Social Scene', in Dixon (1972), 101–42

Rogers, Pat (1973a): '"The Enamelled Ground": The Language of Heraldry and Natural Description in *Windsor-Forest*', *Studia Neophilologica* 45: 356-371

Rogers, Pat (1973b): 'A drama of mixed feelings: the *Epistle to Arbuthnot*', *The Use of English* 142–6; reprinted in Rogers (1993b), 93–7

Rogers, Pat (1974a): 'Faery Lore and *The Rape of the Lock*', *Review of English Studies* 25: 25-38; reprinted in Rogers (1993b), 70-84

Rogers, Pat (1974b): 'The Name and Nature of Dulness: proper nouns in *The Dunciad*', *Anglia* 92: 79–112; reprinted in Rogers (1993b), 98–128

Rogers, Pat (1978): 'Pope and his Subscribers', *Publishing History*, 3: 7–36

Rogers, Pat (1979): 'Time and Space in *Windsor-Forest*', in Erskine-Hill and Smith (1979), 40–51

Rogers, Pat (1985): 'Ermine, Gold and Lawn: *The Dunciad* and the Coronation of George II', in *Literature and Popular Culture in Eighteenth-Century England* (Brighton: Harvester Press), 120–50

Rogers, Pat (1993a): *Alexander Pope* (Oxford: Oxford University Press)

Rogers, Pat (1993b): *Essays on Pope* (Cambridge: Cambridge University Press)

Rogers, Pat (1995): 'Sequences of Reading: Pope's *Moral Essays* and *Imitations of Horace*', in Erskine-Hill and McCabe (1995), 75–94

Rogers, Robert W. (1955): *The Major Satires of Alexander Pope* (Urbana: University of Illinois Press)

Rosslyn, Felicity (1986): '"The Dear Ideas": Pope on Passion', *Cambridge Quarterly*, 15: 216–28

Rosslyn, Felicity (1988): '"Dipt in the Rainbow": Pope on Women', in Rousseau and Rogers (1988), 51–62

Rosslyn, Felicity (1990): *Alexander Pope: a Literary Life* (Basingstoke: Macmillan Press)

Rousseau, G.S., and Rogers, Pat, eds (1988): *The Enduring Legacy: Alexander Pope Tercentenary Essays* (Cambridge: Cambridge University Press)

Rumbold, Valerie (1989): *Women's Place in Pope's World* (Cambridge: Cambridge University Press)

Rumbold, Valerie, ed. (1999): *Alexander Pope: The Dunciad In Four Books* (Harlow: Pearson Education)

Russo, John Paul (1972): *Alexander Pope: Tradition and Identity* (Cambridge, MA: Harvard University Press)

Rylance, Rick ed. (1987): *Debating Texts: A Reader in Twentieth-Century Literary Theory and Method* (Milton Keynes: Open University Press)

Savage, Roger (1988) 'Antiquity as Nature: Pope's Fable of "Young Maro"', in *An Essay on Criticism*, in Nicholson (1988), 83–116

Schmitz, R.M. (1952): *Pope's Windsor Forest 1712: A Study of the Washington University Holograph* (St Louis: Washington University Press)

Schmitz, R. M. (1962): *Pope's Essay on Criticism 1709: A Study of the Bodleian MS Text, with Facsimiles, Transcripts and Variants* (St Louis: Washington University Press)

Selden, Raman (1993): *A Reader's Guide to Contemporary Literary Theory*, third edition (New York: Harvester Wheatsheaf)

Shankman, Steven (1983): *Pope's "Iliad": Homer in the Age of Passion* (Princeton: Princeton University Press)

Sherburn, George (1934): *The Early Career of Alexander Pope* (Oxford: Clarendon Press)

Sherburn, George (1945): 'Pope at Work', *Essays on the Eighteenth Century Presented to David Nichol Smith* (Oxford: Clarendon Press)

Sitter, John E. (1971): *The Poetry of Pope's Dunciad* (Minneapolis: University of Minnesota Press)

Sitwell, Edith (1930): *Alexander Pope* (London: Faber and Faber)

Solomon, Harry M. (1993): *The Rape of the Text: Reading and Misreading Pope's Essay on Man* (Tuscaloosa: University of Alabama Press)

Spacks, Patricia Meyer (1971): *An Argument of Images* (Cambridge, MA: Harvard University Press)

Speck, W.A. (1998): *Literature and Society in Eighteenth-Century England: Ideology, Politics and Culture, 1680–1820* (Harlow: Addison Wesley Longman)

Spence, Joseph (1966): *Observations, Anecdotes, and Characters of Books and Men: Collected from Conversation*, edited by James M. Osborn, 2 vols (Oxford: Clarendon Press)

Stack, Frank (1985): *Pope and Horace: Studies in Imitation* (Cambridge: Cambridge University Press)

Stallybrass, Peter, and White, Allon (1985): *The Politics and Poetics of Transgression* (London: Methuen & Co.), 80–118; reprinted in Hammond (1996), 200–19

Steinberg, S.H. (1961): *Five Hundred Years of Printing* (Harmondsworth: Penguin Books)

Straub, Kristina (1992): *Sexual Suspects: Eighteenth-Century Players and Sexual Ideology* (Princeton: Princeton University Press); reprinted in Hammond (1996), 185–99

Swift, Jonathan (1967): *Swift: Poetical Works*, ed. Herbert Davis (London: Oxford University Press)

Thomas, Claudia N. (1994): *Alexander Pope and His Eighteenth-Century Women Readers* (Carbondale and Edwardsville, Illinois: Southern Illinois University Press)

Tillotson, Geoffrey (1938): *On the Poetry of Pope* (Oxford: Clarendon Press)

Tillotson, Geoffrey (1958): *Pope and Human Nature* (Oxford: Clarendon Press)

Tracy, Clarence, ed. (1974): *The Rape Observed: An Edition of Alexander Pope's Poem "The Rape of the Lock"* (Toronto: University of Toronto Press)

Vander Meulen, David L. (1991): *Pope's Dunciad of 1728: A History and Facsimile* (Charlottesville, VA: University of Virginia Press)

Varey, Simon (1979): 'Rhetoric and *An Essay on Man*', in Erskine-Hill and Smith (1979), 132–43

Wall, Cynthia ed. (1998): *Alexander Pope, The Rape of the Lock* (Boston: Bedford Books)

Warren, Austin (1929): *Alexander Pope as Critic and Humanist* (Princeton: Princeton University Press)

Wasserman, Earl R. (1959): *The Subtler Language: Critical Readings of Neoclassic and Romantic Poems* (Baltimore: Johns Hopkins Press)

Wasserman, Earl R. (1960): *Pope's Epistle to Bathurst: A Critical Reading with An Edition of the Manuscripts* (Baltimore: Johns Hopkins Press)

Wasserman, Earl R. (1966): 'The Limits of Allusion in *The Rape of the Lock*', reprinted in Mack and Winn (1980), 224-246.

Weinbrot, Howard D. (1982): *Alexander Pope and the Traditions of Formal Verse Satire* (Princeton: Princeton University Press)

Wendorf, Richard (1992): 'Alexander Pope, *An Essay on Man*, Epistles I-III', in Dennis (1992), 47-57

White, Douglas H. (1970): *Pope and the Context of Controversy: The Manipulation of Ideas in 'An Essay on Man'* (Chicago: University of Chicago Press)

Williams, Anne (1995): 'Pope as Gothic Novelist', in *Art of Darkness: A Poetics of Gothic* (Chicago: University of Chicago Press), 49-65

Williams, Aubrey (1955): *Pope's Dunciad: A Study of its Meaning* (London: Methuen & Co.)

Williams, Carolyn (1986): 'Westphalia Revisited', *British Journal for Eighteenth-Century Studies*, 9:19-32

Williams, Carolyn (1993): *Pope, Homer, and Manliness* (London and New York: Routledge)

Wimsatt, William K. (1965): *The Portraits of Alexander Pope* (New Haven and London: Yale University Press)

Wimsatt, William K. (1973): 'Belinda Ludens: Strife and Play in *The Rape of the Lock*', *New Literary History* 4 (1973), 357-74, reprinted in Mack and Winn (1980), 201-223

Winn, J. A. (1977): *A Window in the Bosom: The Letters of Alexander Pope* (Hamden, Conn.: Archon Books)

Woodman, Thomas (1989): *Politeness and Poetry in the Age of Pope* (Rutherford, New Jersey: Fairleigh Dickinson University Press)

INDEX

Book are to be returned on or before